# iPhone 16 for Seniors and Beginners Guide

Unlock the Full Potential of That $1,000 Thing in Your Pocket. A Clear, Visual Guide to Connect, Capture Memories, and Simplify Your Life

ANDREW DANIEL TURNER

**Copyright © 2025 Andrew Daniel Turner**

**Disclaimer**

This book is intended for educational and informational purposes only. While every effort has been made to ensure accuracy, the author and publisher do not guarantee that all content is free of errors or omissions. The information provided in this book is based on personal research and publicly available data at the time of writing.

The author and publisher are not affiliated with Apple Inc., and this book is not sponsored, endorsed, or authorized by Apple Inc. iPhone, iOS, and all related trademarks are the property of Apple Inc. The content herein is meant to serve as a general guide and should not be considered official Apple documentation or technical support.

The reader assumes full responsibility for using any of the information, recommendations, or tutorials provided in this book. The author and publisher shall not be liable for any damages, losses, or issues arising from the use or misuse of the information contained in this book, including but not limited to device malfunctions, software failures, data loss, or security breaches.

Before making changes to your device settings, updating software, or attempting troubleshooting steps, it is always recommended to back up your data and refer to official Apple support resources. If you encounter technical issues beyond basic troubleshooting, consult Apple Support or a qualified professional.

By using this book, you agree that the author and publisher are not responsible for any outcomes, financial losses, personal damages, or other liabilities resulting from the application of the information provided.

# Table of Contents

**CHAPTER 15**

# Looking Ahead: Staying Updated and Excited

# CHAPTER 1

# Getting Started with Your iPhone 16

## Unboxing Your iPhone: What's Inside and How to Set Up Easily

Unboxing a brand-new iPhone 16 is an exciting moment—one filled with antici-pation and, for some, a little bit of nervousness. Whether it's your very first iPhone or an upgrade from an older model, this guide will walk you through everything you need to know about what's inside the box, what each item is for, and how to set up your device quickly and easily.

If you've ever felt overwhelmed by new technology or worried about making a mistake during setup, don't worry—you're not alone. This chapter is designed to make the process smooth, stress-free, and even enjoyable. Let's take it step by step.

### What's Inside the Box?

Apple is known for its minimalist packaging—sleek, compact, and free from un-necessary clutter. When you open the box, here's what you'll find inside:

- iPhone 16: The star of the show! Wrapped in protective film, your new iPhone sits neatly on top. Carefully lift it out and set it aside for now.
- USB-C to USB-C Cable: Unlike previous models that came with a USB-A to Lightning cable, the iPhone 16 now supports **faster charging and data transfer** with USB-C.
- SIM Ejector Tool (Only for Certain Models): If your iPhone still uses a physical SIM card (this varies by region), you'll find a small pin-like tool in the box. You'll need this to insert or remove a SIM card.
- Quick Start Guide: A small folded pamphlet with a few essential tips on setup. It's helpful, but you won't need it   you have this guide.
- Apple Stickers: Apple still includes its iconic sticker, though it's more of a nostalgic touch than a necessity.

What isn't inside the box?

Apple has stopped including power adapters and wired EarPods since the iPhone 12. If you don't already own a USB-C power adapter, you'll need to purchase one separately. The reason? Apple claims this helps reduce electronic waste—but it also means you might have to spend extra if you need a charger.

## Preparing for Setup

Before turning on your iPhone, take a moment to set up your workspace. Find a quiet, well-lit area and gather everything you need:

- Previous iPhone (if upgrading): This makes transferring your data much easier.
- A stable Wi-Fi connection: Essential for activation and updates.
- Apple ID credentials: If you already have an Apple account, having your email and password ready will speed up the setup process.
- USB-C charger (if the battery is low): iPhones typically arrive with some battery charge, but it's always best to be prepared.

If you're setting up an iPhone for the first time, don't worry about the Apple ID just yet—we'll cover that shortly.

## Turning On Your iPhone for the First Time

Now, it's time for the big moment—powering on your new iPhone 16.

1. Press and hold the **Side Button** (on the right side of the device) until the Apple logo appears.
2. After a few seconds, you'll see the **"Hello" screen**, which greets you in multiple languages.
3. Swipe up from the bottom of the screen to begin the setup process.

If your iPhone doesn't turn on, don't panic! It might need a quick charge. Plug it in using the USB-C cable and a compatible adapter, wait a few minutes, then try again.

The first few setup screens will guide you through some basic preferences:

- Language Selection: Choose the language you're most comfortable with.
- Region Selection: This determines your default settings for time, currency, and certain apps.
- Quick Start (For Upgraders): If you're transferring from an older iPhone, place your new iPhone **next to the old one**. A popup will appear on your old iPhone asking if you'd like to set up the new device using Quick Start.

### SHOULD YOU USE QUICK START?

- Yes: If you want a **fast, seamless transfer** of your apps, settings, and data from an old iPhone.
- No: If you're setting up from scratch or switching from Android.

For Quick Start:

- Scan the on-screen **animated code** with your old iPhone's camera.
- Enter your old iPhone's **passcode** on the new device.
- Follow the prompts to **transfer your data wirelessly**.

This process can take anywhere from a few minutes to an hour, depending on how much data you have. If you prefer to start fresh, tap "Set Up Manually" instead.

## Connecting to Wi-Fi and Activating Your iPhone

Your iPhone needs an internet connection to complete setup. Choose a stable Wi-Fi network (not mobile data) and enter the password if necessary. Once connected, your iPhone will automatically activate.

### IF YOU SEE AN "ACTIVATION ERROR"

1. Make sure your SIM card is inserted correctly (if applicable).
2. Try restarting your iPhone and reconnecting to Wi-Fi.
3. If activation fails repeatedly, connect your iPhone to a computer using a USB-C cable and open iTunes (Windows) or Finder (Mac).

## Setting Up Face ID and Passcode

Next, you'll be asked to set up Face ID, Apple's facial recognition security feature. Here's how:

1. Tap **"Continue"** and position your face in the center of the screen.
2. Slowly move your head in a circular motion as instructed.
3. After the first scan, tap **"Continue"** again for a second scan.
4. Done! Your iPhone is now secured with **Face ID**, allowing you to unlock your device, authorize payments, and access secure apps.

### CHOOSING A PASSCODE

If Face ID isn't for you, or you prefer extra security, you'll need to create a six-digit passcode. For better security, tap "Passcode Options" and choose a longer alphanumeric code.

## Finalizing the Setup

At this point, your iPhone will ask you to:

- Restore from iCloud, Mac/PC, or Android (if transferring data).
- Sign in with an Apple ID or create one.
- Agree to Apple's Terms & Conditions (yes, those long ones no one reads).
- Customize settings like Siri, App Analytics, and Screen Time.

Once you've completed these steps, your iPhone 16 is officially ready to use! You'll land on the Home Screen, where you can start exploring.

By now, you've successfully unboxed and set up your iPhone 16 without stress. From here, you'll start personalizing your device and learning how to make the most of its incredible features. Let's move on!

## Creating and Managing Your Apple ID for a Seamless Experience

One of the most crucial steps in setting up your iPhone 16 is creating and managing your Apple ID. This single account unlocks everything Apple has to offer—from downloading apps and using iCloud to making secure payments with Apple Pay. Without an Apple ID, you're missing out on most of what makes the iPhone so powerful.

If you're new to Apple devices, the thought of creating and managing an account may seem daunting. But don't worry—this guide will walk you through every step, ensuring that your Apple ID is set up securely and managed efficiently.

### What Is an Apple ID and Why Do You Need One?

Your Apple ID is like a master key that grants access to Apple's ecosystem:

- **App Store & iTunes**: Download and purchase apps, music, and books.
- **iCloud**: Sync your photos, contacts, notes, and more across all Apple devices.
- **FaceTime & iMessage**: Communicate with family and friends seamlessly.
- **Apple Pay**: Make secure purchases online and in stores.
- **Find My iPhone**: Locate your lost device in case of theft or misplacement.

Think of your Apple ID as your personal passport into Apple's world. It keeps everything synced, protected, and accessible wherever you go.

### How to Create an Apple ID

If you're setting up a brand-new iPhone or if this is your first Apple device, you'll need to create an Apple ID from scratch. Here's how:

1. Turn on your iPhone and proceed through the initial setup screens until you reach **"Apple ID"**.
2. Tap **"Don't have an Apple ID or forgot it?"**, then select **"Create Free Apple ID"**.
3. Enter your **first name, last name, and date of birth**. Apple uses your birthdate to provide appropriate features and security settings.

4. Choose an **email address** to use as your Apple ID. You can:

- Use an **existing email address** (such as Gmail or Yahoo).
- Create a free **@icloud.com email** during setup.

5. Create a **strong password** for security:

- Use at **least 8 characters.**
- Include a **mix of uppercase and lowercase letters, numbers, and symbols.**
- Avoid using easy-to-guess passwords like "123456" or "password."

6. Set up **security questions** (optional, but recommended).
7. Agree to **Apple's Terms & Conditions** and **Privacy Policy**.
8. Verify your email address by checking your inbox for a **confirmation email from Apple**. Enter the code when prompted.

Once completed, your Apple ID is ready to go!

## Signing in With an Existing Apple ID

If you already have an Apple ID (from a previous iPhone, iPad, or Mac), signing in is easy:

1. On the **Apple ID** screen during setup, enter your email and password.
2. If prompted, **verify your identity** with two-factor authentication (2FA):

- Apple will send a **six-digit code** to your trusted device or phone number.
- Enter the code on your new iPhone to confirm your identity.

3. Once signed in, your data—like contacts, notes, and purchased apps—will **automatically sync** if iCloud is enabled.

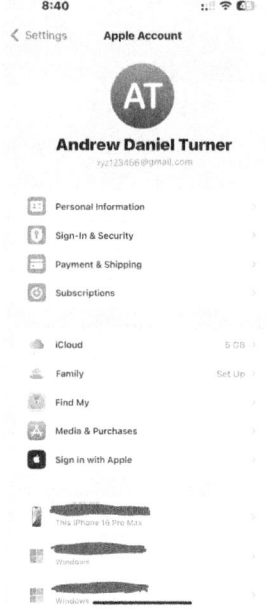

## Managing Your Apple ID on Your iPhone

Once your Apple ID is set up, managing it properly ensures security and seamless access. You can update settings anytime by following these steps:

1. Open the **Settings** app.
2. Tap your **name** at the top of the screen.
3. This will take you to your **Apple ID settings**, where you can:

- Change your pa**ssword o**r update security settings.
- Manage your **iCloud storage and backups.**
- Set up **Family Sharing f**or shared purchases.
- Update **payment and shipping information.**

## Adding a Payment Method for App Store and Subscriptions

Many iPhone features—like buying apps, subscribing to services (Apple Music, iCloud+), and making in-app purchases—require a valid payment method linked to your Apple ID. Here's how to add or update your payment details:

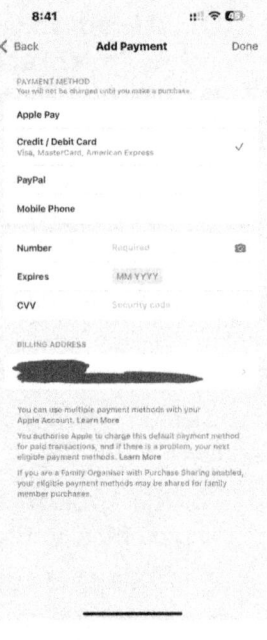

1. Go to **Settings** and tap your **Apple ID**.
2. Select **"Payment & Shipping"**.
3. Tap **"Add Payment Method"**.
4. Choose a method:

- Credit/Debit Card
- PayPal
- Apple Account Balance (if applicable)

5. Enter your payment details and billing address.

If you prefer not to use a credit card, you can buy Apple Gift Cards and add funds directly to your Apple ID.

## Securing Your Apple ID

Since your Apple ID holds sensitive personal data, it's critical to keep it secure. Here's how:

- **Enable Two-Factor Authentication (2FA)**: Adds an extra layer of security by requiring a unique code when signing in from a new device.
- **Use a Strong Password**: Avoid reusing passwords from other accounts.
- **Monitor Account Activity**: Check for any unauthorized logins in your Apple ID settings.
- **Keep Recovery Information Updated**: Ensure your phone number and backup email are current.

If you ever forget your Apple ID password, you can reset it by:

1. Going to **Settings** > **Apple ID** > **Password & Security** > **Change Password**.
2. Answering your security questions or using your recovery email.
3. Creating a new password and signing back in.

## What to Do If You Get Locked Out of Your Apple ID

If you enter the wrong password too many times, Apple temporarily locks your account to protect it. Here's what to do:

1. Go to [iforgot.apple.com] (https://iforgot.apple.com).
2. Enter your Apple ID email and follow the recovery steps.
3. If prompted, **use another trusted Apple device** to verify your identity.

If you're still unable to access your account, contact Apple Support for further assistance.

Your Apple ID is the gateway to everything your iPhone 16 has to offer. Setting it up correctly and managing it well will ensure a seamless, stress-free experience as you start exploring all the features of your device.

## Essential First Steps: Connecting to Wi-Fi, Updating iOS, and More

Now that your iPhone 16 is powered on and your Apple ID is set up, it's time to take the essential first steps that will ensure your device runs smoothly. Connecting to Wi-Fi, updating to the latest version of iOS, and configuring key settings are crucial to getting the most out of your iPhone from day one.

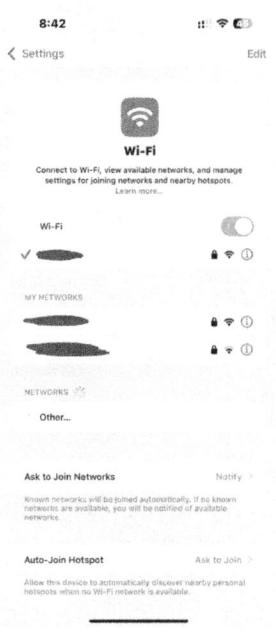

Many beginners either skip these steps or rush through them, leading to slow performance, security vulnerabilities, or difficulty accessing features later on. This section will walk you through everything you need to know—no guesswork, no frustration.

### Connecting to Wi-Fi: Your First Step to Unlocking Your iPhone's Full Potential

A stable Wi-Fi connection is required for almost every essential iPhone function: downloading apps, backing up data, sending messages, and even activating your device. Here's how to connect:

1. Open the **Settings** app.
2. Tap **Wi-Fi** at the top of the screen.
3. Ensure Wi-Fi is **turned on** (toggle should be green).
4. Select your **home Wi-Fi network** from the list.
5. Enter the **Wi-Fi password** and tap **Join**.

Once connected, you should see a Wi-Fi icon in the top-right corner of your screen. If it's missing or shows an exclamation mark (!), your connection may not be stable.

#### WHAT IF YOU CAN'T CONNECT?

- **Wrong password?** Double-check for typos, especially capital letters and special characters.
- **No networks showing?** Make sure your router is powered on and nearby.

- **Still not working?** Tap **Forget This Network**, then reconnect by entering the password again.

## Updating iOS: Why It's Critical to Do This First

The iPhone 16 ships with the latest iOS version available at the time of production, but Apple frequently releases updates to improve security, fix bugs, and introduce new features. Skipping updates can leave your phone vulnerable to security risks or cause apps to misbehave.

To check for updates and install the latest iOS version:

1. Open **Settings**.
2. Scroll down and tap **General**.
3. Tap **Software Update**.
4. If an update is available, tap **Download and Install**.
5. Enter your **passcode** (if prompted), then wait for the update to complete.

### HOW LONG DOES AN UPDATE TAKE?

- **Small updates** (under 500MB) take **5–10 minutes**.
- **Major updates** (over 1GB) may take **30–45 minutes**.
- If you see **"Preparing Update"**, don't panic! This step can take time, depending on your internet speed.

## Setting Up Auto-Updates (So You Never Have to Worry Again)

Instead of manually updating iOS, you can enable automatic updates, so your iPhone always stays up to date overnight.

1. Go to **Settings** > **General** > **Software Update**.
2. Tap **Automatic Updates**.
3. Toggle on **Download iOS Updates** and **Install iOS Updates**.

Now, your iPhone will update itself while you sleep, ensuring you always have the latest security patches and features.

## Setting Up Location Services: Making Your iPhone Smarter

Location Services allows your iPhone to determine your location, which is useful for apps like Maps, Weather, and Find My iPhone. While some worry about privacy, Apple lets you control which apps can access your location.

To enable or customize Location Services:

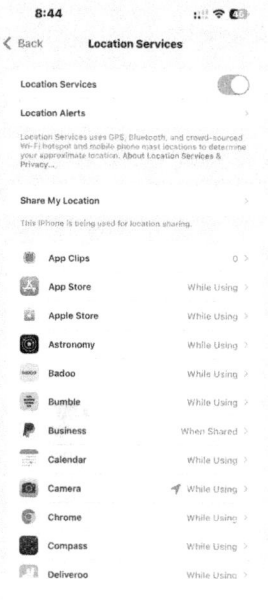

1. Open **Settings**.
2. Scroll down and tap **Privacy & Security**.
3. Tap **Location Services** and toggle it **on**.
4. Review each app's permissions and choose:

   » **"Never"** (denies access completely).
   » **"Ask Next Time"** (prompts you for approval when needed).
   » **"While Using the App"** (best for navigation apps like Google Maps).
   » **"Always"** (only recommended for apps like Find My iPhone).

SHOULD YOU ENABLE LOCATION SERVICES?

- **Yes**: If you use navigation apps, food delivery, or want to track your phone in case of theft.
- **No**: If you're concerned about battery life or privacy (though settings can be adjusted app by app).

## Setting Up Face ID (or Touch ID) for Secure Access

Your iPhone 16 comes with Face ID, Apple's advanced facial recognition technology that lets you unlock your phone, sign into apps, and authorize payments securely.

To set up Face ID:

1. Open **Settings** > **Face ID & Passcode**.
2. Tap **Set Up Face ID** and position your face in the camera frame.
3. Slowly move your head to complete the scan.
4. Tap **Continue** for a second scan, then **Done**.

If you prefer not to use Face ID, you can set up a six-digit passcode instead. For added security, choose a longer alphanumeric passcode under Passcode Options.

## Turning On Find My iPhone: Your Safety Net for Lost or Stolen Devices

Find My iPhone is one of Apple's most powerful security features—it lets you locate, lock, or erase your device if it's lost or stolen.

To enable Find My iPhone:

1.  Open **Settings**.
2.  Tap your **Apple ID name** at the top.
3.  Select **Find My** > **Find My iPhone**.
4.  Toggle on **Find My iPhone**, **Find My Network**, and **Send Last Location**.

If your phone ever goes missing, simply log into [iCloud. com](https://www.icloud.com) or use the Find My app on another Apple device to track its location.

## Enabling Siri for Hands-Free Assistance

Siri is Apple's virtual assistant, capable of setting reminders, sending messages, and even answering questions—all with just your voice.

To enable Siri:

**Say**

**"Hey Siri, get directions home."**

1.  Open **Settings** > **Siri & Search**.
2.  Toggle on **Listen for "Hey Siri"**.
3.  Follow the on-screen prompts to train Siri to recognize your voice.

Now, you can ask Siri anything—from checking the weather to setting an alarm—without touching your phone.

These essential first steps ensure that your iPhone 16 is fully optimized and secure from the start. With Wi-Fi connected, iOS updated, and key features enabled, you're ready to explore everything your device has to offer!

# Exploring the Basics: Buttons, Gestures, and Home Screen Navigation

The iPhone 16 has been designed with simplicity and ease of use in mind, yet for beginners, learning the basics can feel overwhelming. With no physical home button and an interface that relies heavily on gestures, adapting to the new way of navigating may take a little practice.

But don't worry—you're about to discover how every button and gesture works, how to move around your iPhone efficiently, and how to customize your home screen for a smoother experience. By the end of this section, you'll feel confident handling your iPhone like a pro!

## Understanding the Physical Buttons on Your iPhone

Apple keeps its devices minimalistic by reducing the number of physical buttons, but the ones that remain serve essential functions.

- **Side Button (Right Side)**:
  - » Press and hold to power **on/off t**he device.
  - » Press once to lo**ck/unlock t**he screen.
  - » Double press to activate Ap**ple Pay.**
  - » Press and hold to summon Si**ri.**

- **Volume Buttons (Left Side)**:
  - » Press up **or down t**o control volume.
  - » Hold down the volume up or down button during a call to ad**just earpiece volume.**
  - » Use the volume buttons in the Camera app to ta**ke a photo (**great for steady shots).

- **Ring/Silent Switch (Above Volume Buttons)**:
  - » Flip the switch down to si**lent mode (**the orange indicator will appear).
  - » Flip it up to turn so**und back on.**

- **Action Button (Only on iPhone 16 Pro Models)**:
  - » The new customizable Ac**tion Button a**llows you to assign quick actions, such as opening the Camera, launching an app, or turning on Do Not Disturb.

If you're coming from an older iPhone with a Home button, the transition may feel unfamiliar. But don't worry—the new gesture-based navigation makes everything faster and more intuitive.

## Mastering iPhone Gestures

Without a physical home button, gestures replace traditional button presses for most actions. Here's how to navigate with ease:

- **Return to Home Screen**:
  - » Swipe up from the bo**ttom of the screen.**
  - » Works from any app—no need for a Home button!

- **Switch Between Apps (App Switcher)**:

- » Swipe up ha**lfway f**rom the bottom and pause.
- » You'll see a ca**rousel o**f open apps—swipe left or right to switch.
- **Go Back to the Previous Screen**:
  - » In most apps, swipe fr**om the left edge o**f the screen toward the right.
- **Open Control Center** (for quick access to Wi-Fi, flashlight, and more):
  - » Swipe do**wn from the top-right corner o**f the screen.

- **Open Notification Center**:
  - » Swipe do**wn from the top-left corner o**f the screen.
- **Activate Siri**:
  - » Press and hold the Si**de Button o**r say, "H**ey Siri".**

These gestures eliminate extra steps, making navigation smooth and fast. After a few tries, you'll never miss the Home button again!

## Customizing Your Home Screen

The Home Screen is your personal dashboard, where your most-used apps, widgets, and settings are located.

### REARRANGING APPS

Want to move your apps around? It's easy:

1. Press and **hold** any app icon until it **wiggles**.
2. Drag it to a **new position** or onto another app to create a **folder**.
3. Tap **Done** (top right corner) or press the **Side But-ton** to save changes.

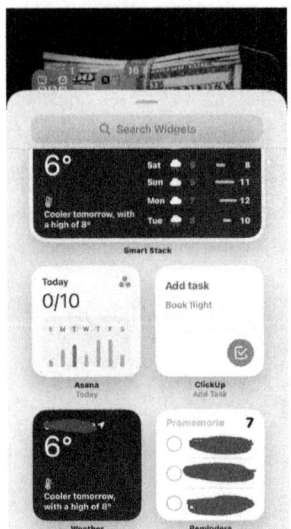

### ADDING WIDGETS

Widgets provide at-a-glance information, like weather, calendar events, or fitness stats.

1. **Press and hold** anywhere on the Home Screen until icons jiggle.
2. Tap the **"+"** in the top-left corner.
3. Select a **widget** (like Weather, Clock, or Remind-ers).
4. Choose a **size** and tap **Add Widget**.

If an app is cluttering your screen:

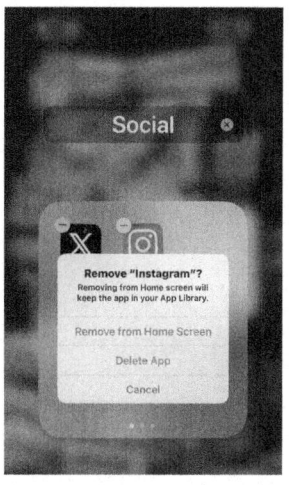

- **To remove an app**: Press and hold, tap **Remove App**, then choose **Delete** or **Move to App Library**.
- **To hide entire pages**: Press and hold anywhere on the Home Screen, tap the **dots at the bottom**, and uncheck the pages you want hidden.

## Using the Dock for Quick Access

The Dock (the row of icons at the bottom of the screen) keeps your most important apps within reach at all times.

- By default, the Dock holds **Phone, Messages, Safari, and Music**.
- To customize it, **drag any app** in or out of the Dock.

## The App Library: Finding Apps Faster

With so many apps on your phone, scrolling through pages can be tedious. Instead, use the App Library:

1. Swipe left **past the last Home Screen page** to open the **App Library**.
2. Apps are **automatically sorted into categories** (Social, Productivity, Entertainment, etc.).
3. Tap the **search bar** at the top to quickly find any app.

## Spotlight Search: Your Shortcut to Everything

Spotlight Search lets you find anything on your iPhone in seconds—apps, contacts, emails, settings, and even web results.

1. Swipe **down from the middle of the Home Screen**.
2. Type your search (e.g., "Photos" or "Wi-Fi settings").
3. Tap the result to open it instantly.

## Multitasking with Picture-in-Picture

Ever wanted to watch a video while using another app? Picture-in-Picture mode lets you do just that!

- Start a video in Safari, YouTube, or FaceTime.

- Swipe up to go Home—the video shrinks into a floating window.
- Move it around or swipe it off-screen to temporarily hide it.

### Navigating with Confidence

Understanding buttons, gestures, and Home Screen navigation is the foundation of using your iPhone efficiently. Once these basics feel natural, you'll be ready to explore more advanced features with ease. Now, let's dive deeper into how you can troubleshoot common issues if something doesn't go as expected!

# Troubleshooting First-Time Setup Challenges

Even with Apple's intuitive design, first-time setup can sometimes be frustrating. Whether it's a Wi-Fi connection issue, an Apple ID login error, or an unresponsive screen, these roadblocks can make the process feel overwhelming.

The good news? Most setup issues have quick, simple fixes. In this section, we'll cover the most common problems you might face and walk you through step-by-step solutions to get your iPhone 16 up and running smoothly.

### iPhone Won't Turn On

If you've unboxed your iPhone and nothing happens when you press the Side Button, don't panic. Try these steps:

- **Check the battery**: The iPhone may have been in storage for a while and could need a charge. Plug it into a power source using the cable and adapter that came in the box.
- **Force restart**: If the screen remains black after charging, try a force restart:

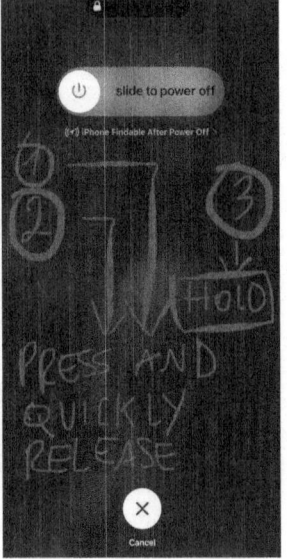

1. Press and quickly release the **Volume Up** button.
2. Press and quickly release the **Volume Down** button.
3. Press and hold the **Side Button** until the Apple logo appears.

- **Check the charging cable and adapter**: If your iPhone still won't turn on, test with another **USB-C cable** and **charger** to ensure the issue isn't with your power source.

### Can't Connect to Wi-Fi

A stable Wi-Fi connection is crucial during setup, as it allows iCloud sign-in, data transfer, and software updates. If your iPhone won't connect to Wi-Fi:

1. Open **Settings** > **Wi-Fi**.
2. Ensure **Wi-Fi is turned on** and select your network.
3. If prompted, enter the correct **Wi-Fi password** (check for typos!).

If you still can't connect:

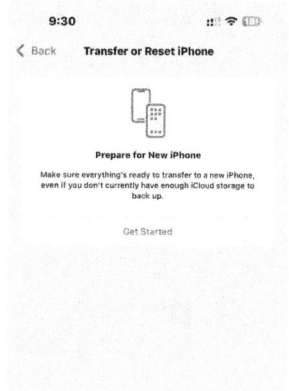

- **Restart your router**: Unplug it for 30 seconds and plug it back in.
- **Forget and reconnect to the network**: Tap the **info (i)** button next to your Wi-Fi name and select **Forget This Network**. Then try reconnecting.
- **Reset network settings**: If nothing works, go to **Settings** > **General** > **Transfer or Reset iPhone** > **Reset** > **Reset Network Settings**. This erases saved Wi-Fi passwords but can fix persistent issues.

## Apple ID Setup Problems

If you can't sign in to your Apple ID, or you're getting errors like *Verification Failed* or *Incorrect Password*, try these solutions:

- **Check your internet connection**: A weak connection can prevent authentication. Try switching to a different Wi-Fi network.
- **Reset your password**: If you forgot your Apple ID password, tap **Forgot Password?** and follow the prompts to reset it.
- **Confirm Apple's servers are online**: Visit **Apple's System Status page** ([www.apple.com/support/systemstatus](https://www.apple.com/support/systemstatus)) to see if Apple ID services are temporarily down.

If you're setting up a new Apple ID and experiencing issues:

- Make sure the **email address is valid** and hasn't been used for another Apple ID.
- Check your **email inbox** for a verification link and confirm your account.
- If you see an error saying the email is **already in use**, try signing in with that email instead of creating a new account.

## Stuck on the Activation Screen

Your iPhone might display an Activation Lock screen, which asks for the previous owner's Apple ID. This typically happens if you purchased a second-hand device and the previous owner didn't remove it from their account.

If this happens:

- **Contact the seller** and ask them to remove the iPhone from their Apple ID remotely via **iCloud.com**.

- If you're the **original owner** and still see Activation Lock, ensure you're signed in with the correct Apple ID.

## Stuck on the Hello Screen or Setup Process

If your iPhone freezes on the "Hello" screen or setup process:

- **Force restart the device** (follow the steps in the "iPhone Won't Turn On" section).
- If that doesn't work, connect the iPhone to a **computer with Finder (Mac) or iTunes (Windows)** and follow these steps:

1. Put your iPhone in **recovery mode**:
   - » Press and release Vo**lume Up.**
   - » Press and release Vo**lume Down.**
   - » Hold the Si**de Button u**ntil the recovery screen appears.
2. When prompted on your computer, choose **Update** (not Restore, unless necessary).

## Touchscreen Not Responding

If your iPhone screen isn't responding to touches:

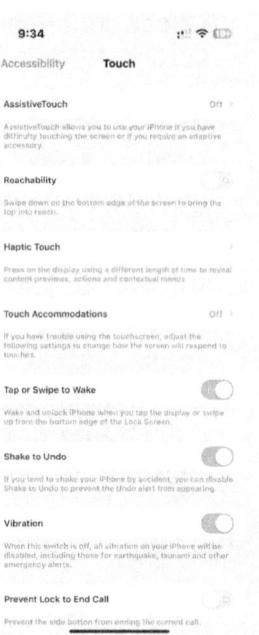

- **Remove any screen protector**: Some thick protectors may interfere with touch sensitivity.
- **Clean your screen** with a microfiber cloth to remove dirt or oil.
- **Restart your iPhone** by holding down the **Side Button** and swiping **Power Off.**

If the issue persists, go to Settings > Accessibility > Touch and ensure Touch Accommodations are turned off.

## Can't Set Up Face ID

Face ID makes unlocking your iPhone and authorizing purchases faster and more secure. If you can't set it up:

- **Make sure nothing is covering the TrueDepth camera** (like a smudged screen or case).
- **Ensure your face is fully visible**—remove sunglasses, hats, or scarves.
- **Set up Face ID in good lighting** for the best results.

If you still have trouble:

1. Go to **Settings** > **Face ID & Passcode**.
2. Tap **Reset Face ID** and try scanning your face again.

## Cellular Service Not Working

If your iPhone isn't recognizing your SIM card or says No Service:

- **Check the SIM tray**: Remove the SIM card and reinsert it.
- **Toggle Airplane Mode on and off**: Swipe down from the top-right corner, tap **Airplane Mode**, wait 10 seconds, then turn it off.
- **Go to Settings** > **Cellular** and ensure cellular data is on.

If you still have issues, contact your carrier to check for activation problems.

## When to Contact Apple Support

If none of these troubleshooting steps work, it may be time to reach out to Apple Support. You can:

- Visit **[support.apple.com](https://support.apple.com)** for troubleshooting guides.
- Chat with Apple Support through the **Apple Support app**.
- Schedule an appointment at an **Apple Store** or an **Authorized Service Provider**.

By following these troubleshooting steps, you'll be able to solve 99% of common setup issues without frustration. Now that your iPhone 16 is set up and running smoothly, let's move on to exploring its powerful features!

# CHAPTER 2

# Personalizing Your iPhone for Comfort and Joy

## Customizing Accessibility Features for Better Visibility and Ease of Use

Apple has made accessibility a priority with the iPhone 16, ensuring that everyone, regardless of vision, hearing, or dexterity challenges, can comfortably use their device. Whether you need larger text, higher contrast, voice control, or custom touch settings, your iPhone can be tailored to fit your needs.

In this section, we'll explore the most useful accessibility features that will help you see, hear, and interact with your iPhone effortlessly—turning it into a truly personalized device that works for you.

### Adjusting Display Settings for Better Visibility

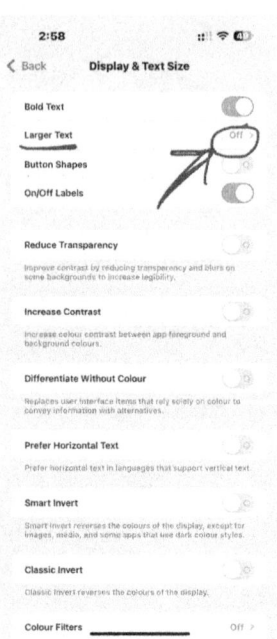

Many users find small text and dim screens frustrating—but with a few quick adjustments, your iPhone's screen can become easier to read and navigate.

To access Display & Text settings:

1.  Open **Settings** > **Accessibility** > **Display & Text Size**.
2.  Adjust the following settings to improve readability:

*   **Bold Text**: Makes text easier to read by increasing its thickness.
*   **Larger Text**: Adjust the font size using the slider. If you need even larger text, enable **Larger Accessibility Sizes** for additional options.
*   **Increase Contrast**: Enhances text visibility by darkening text against light backgrounds.

- **Reduce Transparency**: Improves clarity by reducing background blurring effects.

## Enabling Dark Mode and Color Filters

For those who find bright screens uncomfortable, enabling Dark Mode can reduce eye strain.

To turn on Dark Mode:

1. Open **Settings** > **Display & Brightness**.
2. Select **Dark** under Appearance.
3. You can also set it to **Automatic** so it adjusts based on time of day.

For users with color blindness or difficulty distinguishing colors, Apple offers Color Filters:

1. Go to **Settings** > **Accessibility** > **Display & Text Size** > **Color Filters**.
2. Enable **Color Filters**, then choose from options like **Grayscale, Red/Green Filter, or Blue/Yellow Filter**.

## Customizing Touch and Interaction for Ease of Use

If tapping small icons or swiping feels difficult, you can modify how your iPhone responds to touch.

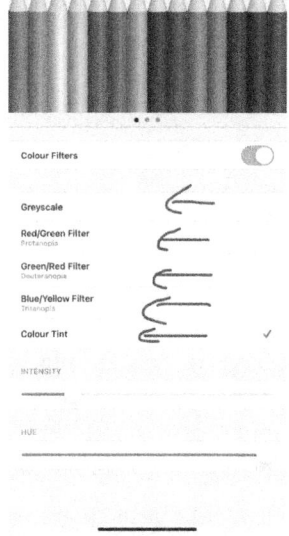

1. Open **Settings** > **Accessibility** > **Touch**.
2. Adjust the following settings:

- **AssistiveTouch**: Adds an on-screen menu for common actions (great for users who have trouble pressing buttons).
- **Touch Accommodations**: Adjusts how your iPhone recognizes taps—helpful if you tend to press too lightly or too long.
- **Haptic Touch**: Allows you to set how fast the iPhone responds to long presses.

For one-handed use, Reachability can make the top of the screen easier to access:

- Open **Settings** > **Accessibility** > **Touch** > **Enable Reachability**.
- Swipe **down** on the bottom edge of the screen to bring the top of the display within reach.

## Using Voice Control and Spoken Content

If you prefer voice commands over touch, or if reading small text is a challenge, your iPhone can assist with Voice Control and Spoken Content.

### VOICE CONTROL

- Open **Settings** > **Accessibility** > **Voice Control**.
- Enable **Voice Control**, and you'll see a blue microphone icon in the status bar.
- Now you can say commands like:
  - » *"Go home"* to return to the Home Screen.
  - » *"Tap Messages"* to open the Messages app.
  - » *"Swipe left"* to navigate pages.

### SPOKEN CONTENT

If you'd like your iPhone to read text out loud, enable Speak Screen:

1. Open **Settings** > **Accessibility** > **Spoken Content**.
2. Enable **Speak Screen**.
3. Swipe down with **two fingers** from the top of the screen to have the iPhone read content aloud.

## Creating a Fully Personalized iPhone Experience

The iPhone 16 isn't just another smartphone—it's a device that adapts to you. Whether you need bigger text, custom touch settings, or hands-free commands, these accessibility tools ensure that your iPhone works for your unique needs, making daily interactions smoother and more enjoyable.

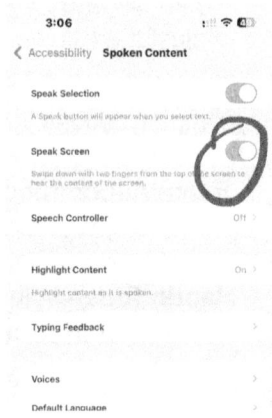

Now that your device is customized for ease of use, let's explore how to make it even more personal with ringtones, notifications, and wallpapers!

# Setting Up Custom Ringtones, Notifications, and Wallpapers

Your iPhone should feel like your iPhone, not just another factory-default device. One of the best ways to make it truly personal and enjoyable is by customizing your ringtones, notifications, and wallpapers. These small changes can make everyday interactions with your device more fun, engaging, and even more practical—ensuring that you recognize important calls and messages at a glance or a sound.

In this section, we'll walk you through how to set up and customize your ringtones, notifications, and wallpapers so your iPhone 16 feels like an extension of your personality.

## Customizing Ringtones: Assigning Personalized Sounds

Ever missed an important call because your iPhone blended in with all the others in a crowded room? Or wished you could instantly know who's calling just by the sound? Setting custom ringtones solves this problem.

### HOW TO SET A CUSTOM RINGTONE FOR ALL CALLS

1. Open **Settings** > **Sounds & Haptics**.
2. Tap **Ringtone** under **Sounds and Vibration Patterns**.
3. Scroll through the list and tap on a ringtone to preview it.
4. Select the one you want to use as your default ringtone.

### ASSIGNING A CUSTOM RINGTONE TO A SPECIFIC CONTACT

If you want to instantly recognize a caller without looking at your screen, you can assign unique ringtones to different contacts:

1. Open the **Contacts** app and select the contact you want to customize.
2. Tap **Edit** in the top-right corner.
3. Scroll down and tap **Ringtone**.
4. Choose a unique ringtone for that person and tap **Done**.

Want even more personalization? You can buy or create custom ringtones using iTunes or GarageBand.

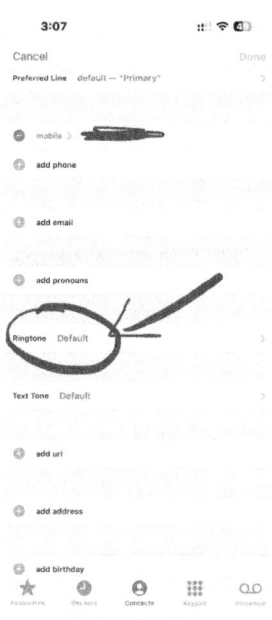

## Customizing Notifications: Never Miss an Important Alert

iPhone notifications are more than just sounds—they can include vibrations and even flash alerts to ensure you never miss something important.

### CHANGING NOTIFICATION SOUNDS FOR MESSAGES AND EMAILS

1. Go to **Settings** > **Sounds & Haptics**.
2. Scroll to **Text Tone** or **Mail** and tap it.
3. Choose a sound from the list or tap **Vibration** to select a unique pattern.

### SETTING FLASH ALERTS FOR IMPORTANT NOTIFICATIONS

If you have difficulty hearing notifications or just want a visual cue, you can enable LED Flash Alerts:

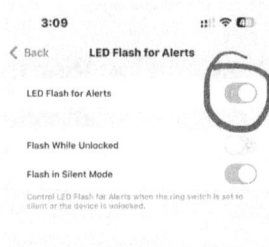

1. Open **Settings** > **Accessibility** > **Audio/Visual**.
2. Tap **LED Flash for Alerts** and turn it **on**.

Now, when you receive a call or an alert, your iPhone's camera flash will blink—perfect for noisy environments or when your phone is on silent mode.

## Customizing Wallpapers: Make Your iPhone Feel Like Home

The wallpaper on your iPhone is the first thing you see every time you pick it up—so why settle for something boring?

Your iPhone 16 lets you set separate wallpapers for the Lock Screen and Home Screen and even create dynamic wallpapers that change based on the time of day.

### HOW TO CHANGE YOUR WALLPAPER

1. Open **Settings** > **Wallpaper** > **Add New Wallpaper**.
2. Choose from:
   - » **Apple's Stock Wallpapers:** High-quality images provided by Apple.
   - » **Live Photos:** Moving wallpapers that animate when you press the screen.
   - » **Your Photos:** Use any picture from your Photos app.
3. Tap **Set as Wallpaper Pair** or **Customize Home Screen** if you want a different look for your Home Screen.

Want a wallpaper that automatically changes every time you pick up your phone? The Photo Shuffle feature lets you display multiple favorite pictures on your Lock Screen.

1. Open **Settings** > **Wallpaper** > **Add New Wallpaper**.
2. Select **Photo Shuffle** and pick a collection of images.
3. Choose how often you want the image to change (**on tap, hourly, daily, or on wake**).
4. Tap **Set as Wallpaper Pair**.

This feature is great for keeping your home screen fresh and engaging, letting you relive favorite moments throughout the day.

## Fine-Tuning Your Customization for the Perfect Experience

Now that you've set your custom ringtones, notifications, and wallpapers, your iPhone 16 will truly feel like your device. Whether it's instantly recognizing who's calling, never missing a notification, or enjoying a dynamic wallpaper that reflects your mood, these settings enhance your overall experience and make using your phone more enjoyable.

In the next section, we'll explore how to optimize your iPhone's sound settings, including hearing aid support and voice clarity features.

# Adapting the iPhone for Hearing Aids and Voice Clarity

Apple has long been committed to making its devices inclusive and accessible for users with hearing impairments. The iPhone 16 offers built-in hearing aid support, enhanced sound clarity, and live captions, ensuring that you don't miss a single conversation, phone call, or important alert.

Whether you use Made for iPhone (MFi) hearing aids, Bluetooth hearing devices, or simply want to fine-tune your iPhone's sound settings for better clarity, this guide will walk you through every essential adjustment.

## Connecting Hearing Aids to Your iPhone

One of the most powerful accessibility features Apple offers is its Made for iPhone (MFi) hearing aids. These are specially designed hearing aids that seamlessly connect to your iPhone, delivering clear, customized audio without interference.

PAIRING MFI HEARING AIDS WITH YOUR IPHONE

1. Open **Settings** > **Accessibility** > **Hearing Devices**.
2. Ensure your hearing aids are **turned on and in pairing mode**.

3. Your iPhone will search for available hearing aids—tap on your device when it appears.
4. Follow the on-screen instructions to **pair** and **connect** your hearing aids.

Once paired, your hearing aids will automatically connect when turned on. You can even check battery levels directly from your iPhone's Control Center.

## Adjusting Hearing Aid Settings for the Best Sound

Your iPhone allows you to fine-tune how sound is transmitted to your hearing aids.

### How to Customize Hearing Aid Sound Settings

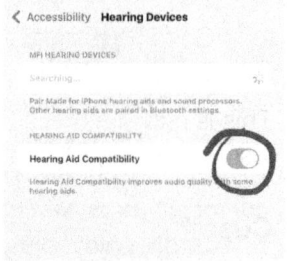

1. Open **Settings** > **Accessibility** > **Hearing Devices**.
2. Tap on your connected hearing aid.
3. Adjust **Microphone Directionality**, **Background Noise Reduction**, and **Volume Balance** to improve speech clarity.

Apple also lets you set up an audio preset for different environments—whether you're in a noisy restaurant or a quiet home, you can switch modes for the best listening experience.

## Enhancing Phone Calls and Media Audio

If you struggle to hear clearly during phone calls, FaceTime, or while listening to music, iPhone 16 has built-in features to amplify sound and improve clarity.

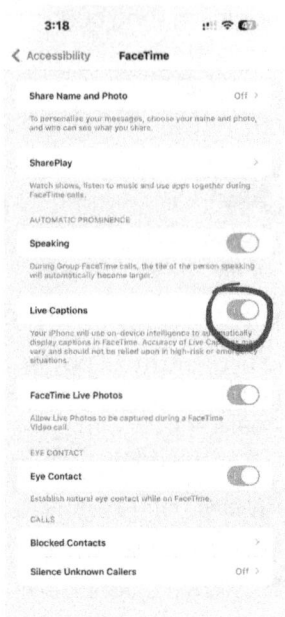

### Turning on Phone Noise Cancellation

This setting reduces background noise during phone calls so voices sound clearer.

1. Go to **Settings** > **Accessibility** > **Audio/Visual**.
2. Toggle **Phone Noise Cancellation** to on.

### Using Live Captions for Real-Time Speech Transcription

For moments when audio clarity isn't enough, Live Captions provide real-time subtitles for phone calls, FaceTime, and media.

1. Open **Settings** > **Accessibility** > **Live Captions**.
2. Toggle **Live Captions** on to enable automatic subtitles.

This feature is especially useful for video calls, lectures, and social media videos, ensuring you never miss a word.

## Optimizing Audio for Bluetooth Hearing Devices

Even if you don't have MFi hearing aids, Bluetooth hearing devices like cochlear implants and wireless headphones can still be optimized for clearer, crisper sound.

### ENABLING MONO AUDIO FOR BETTER SPEECH UNDERSTANDING

Many people struggle with stereo audio, where different sounds are played in separate ears. Mono Audio ensures both ears hear the same thing for better clarity.

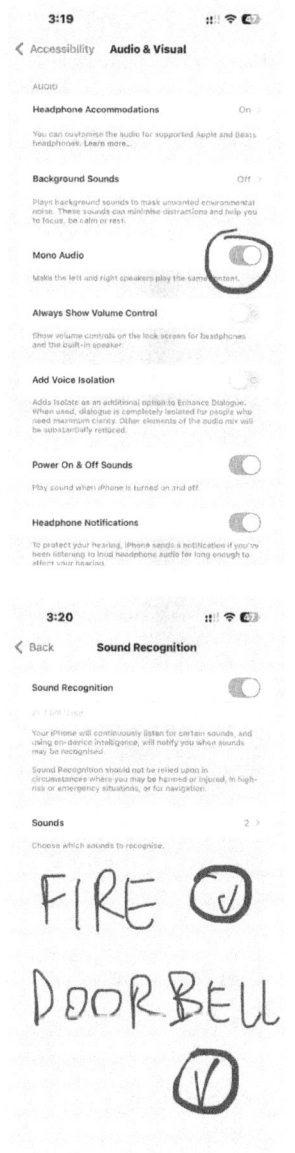

1.  Go to **Settings** > **Accessibility** > **Audio/Visual**.
2.  Toggle **Mono Audio** to **on**.

This is especially helpful for those who have hearing loss in one ear or prefer more balanced audio input.

## Customizing Sound Recognition Alerts

For those who may not always hear important alerts, Apple's Sound Recognition feature detects and notifies you of important environmental sounds—like a doorbell, a baby crying, or a fire alarm.

### HOW TO TURN ON SOUND RECOGNITION

1.  Open **Settings** > **Accessibility** > **Sound Recognition**.
2.  Toggle it **on**, then tap **Sounds** to choose which alerts you want to be notified about.

Your iPhone will vibrate and display a notification when it detects the selected sounds, providing an extra layer of security and awareness.

## Maximizing Your iPhone for Better Hearing

With Made for iPhone hearing aids, voice clarity settings, real-time captions, and customizable alerts, the iPhone 16 is one of the most hearing-accessible smartphones available.

By setting up these features, you can ensure a seamless,

frustration-free experience while using your iPhone for calls, music, and daily activities.

In the next section, we'll explore how to organize your apps and widgets for a smoother, more efficient iPhone experience.

# Organizing Apps and Widgets to Fit Your Daily Routine

Your iPhone is more than just a phone—it's your digital command center for communication, productivity, entertainment, and daily life. But if your home screen is cluttered with dozens of apps or if you struggle to find what you need quickly, your iPhone can feel overwhelming instead of convenient.

The good news? A little organization goes a long way. With a few tweaks, you can customize your home screen, group apps for efficiency, and use widgets to get real-time information at a glance. Whether you want a streamlined layout for easier navigation or a screen optimized for daily productivity, this section will guide you through it step by step.

## Customizing Your Home Screen Layout

Your home screen should be designed to support your habits and routines. Instead of letting apps be arranged randomly, strategically position them based on how often you use them.

### How to Move and Rearrange Apps

1. **Press and hold any app** until the icons start jiggling.
2. Drag the app to a new position on the screen or into the dock at the bottom for quick access.
3. Tap **Done** in the top-right corner when you're finished arranging.

To minimize clutter, consider placing less frequently used apps into folders or hiding them from the main screen.

## Creating and Managing App Folders

If you have multiple apps for similar purposes, grouping them into folders can reduce visual clutter and make navigation easier.

### How to Create a Folder

1. Press and hold an app, then drag it on top of another similar app.
2. A folder will be automatically created with a suggested name (which you can change).
3. Drag additional apps into the folder if needed.
4. Tap the **folder name** to rename it based on its function, like "Social Media," "Finance," or "Health."

You can also move entire folders to different pages or to the dock for easier access.

## Using the App Library for Quick Access

Did you know your iPhone has a built-in way to organize apps automatically? The App Library (introduced in iOS 14) automatically sorts your apps into categories like Social, Productivity, and Entertainment.

### How to Access the App Library

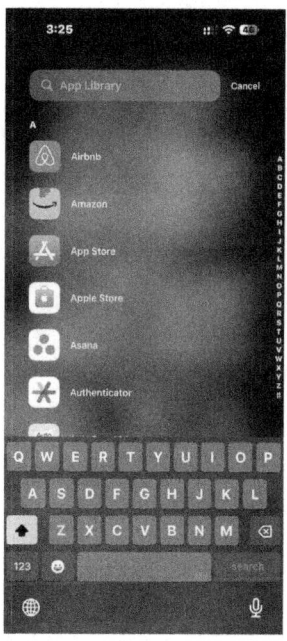

- Swipe left past your last home screen page to enter the **App Library**.
- Use the **search bar** at the top to quickly locate an app.
- Tap a **category folder** to expand it and see all related apps.

The App Library is especially useful for reducing home screen clutter. If you don't need an app on your home screen but still want quick access, remove it and rely on the App Library instead.

## Adding and Customizing Widgets for Instant Information

Widgets are one of the best ways to see important information at a glance without even opening an app. You can use widgets for:

- **Weather updates** without opening the weather app.
- **Upcoming calendar events** for quick scheduling.
- **Reminders and to-do lists** that stay visible.
- **Battery percentage** for your iPhone and connected devices.

## How to Add a Widget to Your Home Screen

1. Press and hold an empty space on your home screen until the apps start jiggling.
2. Tap the **+ icon** in the top-left corner.
3. Scroll or search for the **widget** you want to add.
4. Select the widget size and tap **Add Widget**.
5. Drag the widget to your preferred position, then tap **Done**.

You can stack widgets on top of each other to save space and swipe between them as needed.

## Using Smart Stacks for a Dynamic Home Screen

Smart Stacks are interactive widgets that change throughout the day based on your habits. For example, in the morning, you might see weather and news updates, while in the evening, your iPhone might show your bedtime routine.

### How to Create a Smart Stack

1. **Add a widget** to your home screen as described above.
2. **Drag another widget of the same size** on top of it to create a stack.
3. Your iPhone will **automatically rotate** the widgets based on your usage.

If you prefer more control, you can manually swipe through the widgets in the stack.

## Keeping Your Most-Used Apps in the Dock

The dock at the bottom of your screen holds up to four apps and remains visible across all home screen pages. Place your most frequently used apps here for quick access.

Recommended apps for the dock might include:

- **Phone** (for quick calls)
- **Messages** (for texting and FaceTime)
- **Safari** (for web browsing)
- **Email or Calendar** (for staying organized)

To move apps into the dock:

1. Press and hold the app icon.
2. Drag it to the dock and release.
3. If the dock is full, remove an app first by dragging it out.

## Optimizing Your Home Screen for Your Daily Routine

By organizing your apps, widgets, and dock strategically, you can tailor your iPhone to fit your lifestyle. Whether you're prioritizing productivity, keeping in touch with family, or managing your schedule, a well-organized home screen will save you time and frustration.

In the next section, we'll explore how to make Siri your personal assistant for even more hands-free convenience.

# Making Siri Your Personal Assistant: Hands-Free Convenience

Your iPhone is more than just a device—it's your personal assistant, ready to help you navigate daily life effortlessly. Siri, Apple's voice-activated assistant, can send messages, set reminders, play music, control smart home devices, and even answer random questions. But the real magic happens when you customize Siri to fit your needs, making it a truly hands-free companion.

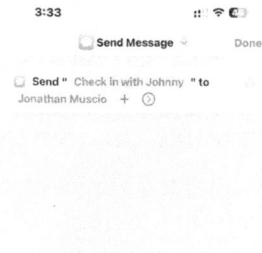

Many people don't take full advantage of Siri, often because they don't realize how powerful and intuitive it can be. Whether you want to send a text without typing, set up daily routines, or get real-time updates, this guide will show you how to make Siri an essential part of your life.

## Setting Up Siri for Hands-Free Use

Before you can start using Siri effectively, you need to make sure it's properly set up.

### How to Enable Siri on Your iPhone

1. Open the **Settings** app.
2. Scroll down and tap **Siri & Search**.
3. Toggle on **Listen for "Hey Siri"** to activate voice control.
4. Enable **Press Side Button for Siri** if you want to use the button instead.
5. Turn on **Allow Siri When Locked** for access even when your screen is off.

Once enabled, you can activate Siri simply by saying "Hey Siri", or by pressing and holding the Side Button (or the Home Button on older iPhones).

## Using Siri for Everyday Tasks

Siri can handle hundreds of commands, but to truly unlock its potential, you should integrate it into your daily routine. Here are some practical ways Siri can assist you:

1. Communicating Without Touching Your Phone

- **"Hey Siri, call John on speaker."** (Great for hands-free calls)
- **"Hey Siri, send a message to Sarah saying 'I'll be there at 6 PM'."**
- **"Hey Siri, read my last message."** (Perfect when you're busy or driving)

2. Managing Your Schedule

- **"Hey Siri, set a reminder to take my medication at 8 AM every day."**
- **"Hey Siri, what's on my calendar for today?"**
- **"Hey Siri, wake me up at 7 AM."**

3. Getting Instant Information

- **"Hey Siri, what's the weather like today?"**
- **"Hey Siri, how do I convert 10 ounces to grams?"**
- **"Hey Siri, what time is it in London?"**

4. Entertainment & Music

- **"Hey Siri, play some relaxing jazz music."**
- **"Hey Siri, skip this song."**
- **"Hey Siri, turn the volume to 50%."**

## Creating Custom Siri Shortcuts for Faster Commands

Siri Shortcuts let you combine multiple tasks into a single command, saving you time and effort. You can set up shortcuts for common routines, such as sending a daily text, adjusting settings, or launching multiple apps with a single voice command.

### How to Create a Siri Shortcut

1. Open the **Shortcuts** app.
2. Tap **Create Shortcut**.
3. Choose the action you want Siri to perform (e.g., **"Send a message to Mom"**).
4. Tap **Add to Siri** and **record a phrase** to trigger it (e.g., **"Check in with Mom"**).

Now, whenever you say "Hey Siri, check in with Mom," Siri will automatically send her a pre-written message!

## Hands-Free Control of Smart Home Devices

If you have smart home gadgets like lights, thermostats, or security cameras, Siri can help you control them effortlessly.

### Examples of Smart Home Commands

- **"Hey Siri, turn off the kitchen lights."**
- **"Hey Siri, set the thermostat to 72 degrees."**
- **"Hey Siri, lock the front door."**

These commands work instantly, giving you full control of your home without lifting a finger.

## Using Siri When Driving for a Safer Experience

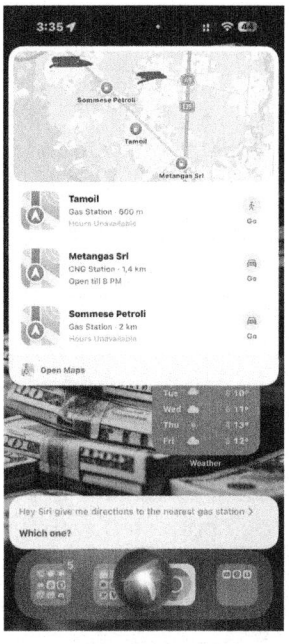

One of the best places to use Siri is in the car, allowing you to stay focused on the road. With CarPlay or Bluetooth-enabled vehicles, you can make calls, send messages, get directions, and play music hands-free.

SAFE DRIVING COMMANDS

- **"Hey Siri, give me directions to the nearest gas station."**
- **"Hey Siri, play my road trip playlist."**
- **"Hey Siri, read my latest text message."**

## Getting the Most Out of Siri's Learning Capabilities

Siri adapts to your habits over time, learning which apps you use most, who you contact frequently, and what information you request often. You can improve Siri's accuracy by:

- Making sure Siri Suggestions are enabled in **Settings > Siri & Search**.
- Correcting Siri when it mispronounces names (**"Hey Siri, that's not how you say my name"**).
- Using Siri regularly for tasks—**the more you use it, the better it gets!**

By integrating Siri into your daily life, you'll save time, reduce distractions, and make your iPhone work harder for you.

# CHAPTER 3

# Staying Connected: Messages, FaceTime, and Beyond

## Mastering Messages: Sending Texts, Photos, and Videos with Ease

Your iPhone isn't just a phone—it's a powerful communication tool that keeps you connected with family, friends, and colleagues, no matter where they are. Whether you want to send a quick text, share a funny photo, or record a heartfelt video message, the Messages app makes it easy and intuitive.

For many, texting is second nature, but did you know your iPhone's Messages app is packed with features that go beyond simple texting? From voice messages to Live Photos and even screen effects, mastering Messages means unlocking an entirely new way of staying in touch.

### Getting Started with Messages

Before diving into advanced features, let's go over the basics of sending and receiving messages.

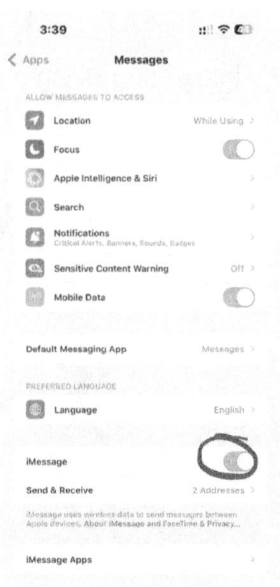

#### OPENING AND SETTING UP THE MESSAGES APP

1. Locate the **Messages** app on your iPhone's home screen and tap to open it.
2. If you haven't already, sign in with your **Apple ID** to enable **iMessage**, Apple's messaging service.
3. You can send texts via:

- iM**essage (**blue bubbles) to other Apple devices using Wi-Fi or cellular data.
- SM**S/MMS (**green bubbles) to non-Apple users via your cellular network.

To ensure iMessage is activated, go to Settings > Messages and toggle iMessage ON.

## Sending a Text Message

Once the Messages app is open, follow these steps:

1. Tap the **compose button** (a pencil inside a square) in the top-right corner.
2. In the **To:** field, type the recipient's name or phone number. If they're in your contacts, their name will appear automatically.
3. Tap inside the text field at the bottom and type your message.
4. Press the **blue send arrow** to send an iMessage or the **green arrow** for an SMS.

### REPLYING TO A MESSAGE

- Simply tap on an existing conversation and type your response.
- Swipe right on a message to **reply in a thread**, making conversations easier to follow.

## Sending Photos and Videos

Text messages are great, but sometimes a picture or video says it best. Here's how to add media to your messages.

### ATTACHING A PHOTO FROM YOUR CAMERA ROLL

1. Open a conversation and tap the **Photos icon** (a small picture) next to the text field.
2. Select a photo from your library and tap **Send**.

### TAKING AND SENDING A NEW PHOTO OR VIDEO

1. Open a conversation and tap the **Camera icon**.
2. Choose **Photo** or **Video**, then take your shot.
3. Tap **Send** to share instantly.

Tip: Press and hold the camera shutter button to record a quick video instead of taking a still photo.

## Sending Voice Messages

When texting isn't enough, you can record a voice mes-sage:

1. Open a conversation and tap the **microphone icon** next to the text field.
2. Hold the button and speak your message.
3. Release the button to send, or swipe left to cancel.

Why use voice messages? They're great for capturing emotion, tone, and details that text can't convey.

## Using Tapbacks and Reactions

Want to acknowledge a message quickly without typing a reply? Try Tapbacks—Apple's built-in emoji-style reactions.

### How to Use Tapbacks

1. Press and hold on a message bubble.
2. Select an **emoji reaction** (thumbs up, heart, exclamation, etc.).
3. The reaction appears in the corner of the message bubble.

This feature is great for group chats, helping reduce clutter when everyone wants to respond without overwhelming the conversation.

## Enhancing Messages with Effects

Apple Messages lets you send texts with fun animations like confetti, fireworks, and more.

### How to Send a Message with Effects

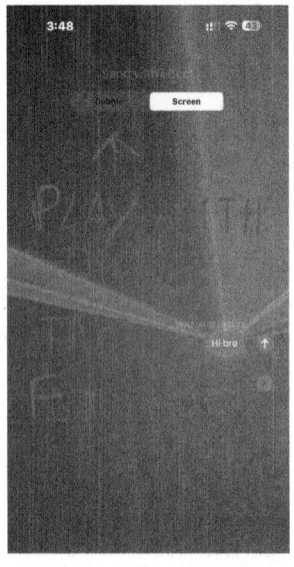

1. Type your message but **don't send it yet**.
2. Press and hold the **Send button**.
3. Choose **Bubble Effects** (e.g., Slam, Gentle) or **Screen Effects** (e.g., Balloons, Confetti).
4. Tap **Send** to deliver with style!

Use this for:

- **Birthday wishes** 🎉 (send with "Balloons")
- **Celebrations** 🍾 (send with "Confetti")
- **Exciting news** 🎆 (send with "Fireworks")

## Managing Conversations Like a Pro

As your conversations pile up, keeping them organized can be a challenge. Here's how to stay in control:

### Pin Important Conversations

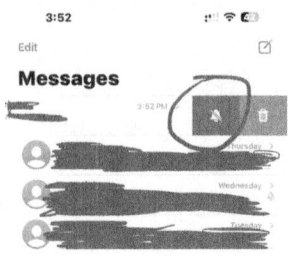

1. In the Messages app, press and hold a conversation.
2. Tap **Pin** to move it to the top of your messages list.

Why? Your most important chats—like family and best friends—will always be easily accessible.

- To mute notifications from a conversation, swipe left and tap **Hide Alerts**.
- For **group chats**, tap the group name and select **Leave this Conversation**.

## Keeping Messages Safe with Backups

Losing important messages can be frustrating, but backing them up ensures you never lose a precious conversation.

### ENABLE ICLOUD BACKUP FOR MESSAGES

1. Go to **Settings > [Your Name] > iCloud**.
2. Toggle **Messages** ON to sync across devices.

With iCloud backup enabled, your messages stay safe and accessible even if you switch iPhones.

Mastering the Messages app is about more than just texting—it's about staying connected in the most engaging and expressive way possible. Whether you're sending a quick text, sharing a memory, or reacting with a Tapback, Apple's messaging tools make every conversation effortless and fun.

# Group Chats Made Simple: Staying Connected with Family and Friends

Texting is great, but group chats take communication to the next level, making it easy to keep family, friends, and even work teams connected in one place. With the Messages app, you can create group chats that bring everyone together, whether it's for planning events, sharing updates, or just keeping in touch.

If you've ever struggled with juggling multiple conversations or felt overwhelmed by notifications, don't worry—this guide will help you set up, manage, and enjoy group chats effortlessly.

## Creating a Group Chat

Starting a group chat is as simple as sending a regular message, but with more people included.

### HOW TO START A GROUP CHAT

1. Open the **Messages app**.
2. Tap the **compose button** (a square with a pencil) in the top-right corner.
3. In the **To:** field, type the names or phone numbers of the people you want to include. You can also tap the **+ icon** to select contacts.

4. Type your first message and tap **Send**.

Congratulations! You've just started a group chat. Now let's customize and optimize it for better communication.

## Naming Your Group Chat

Once your group chat is created, you can give it a name to make it easier to find in your message list. This is especially useful if you have multiple group chats with different people.

### How to Name a Group Chat

1. Open the group conversation.
2. Tap the **group name or contact icons** at the top.
3. Select **Change Name and Photo**.
4. Enter a new name and tap **Done**.

Example: If you're planning a family vacation, you could name the chat "Hawaii 2024 Trip".

## Managing Notifications and Alerts

Group chats can be lively and engaging, but constant notifications can become distracting. Fortunately, you can mute notifications or leave a group chat if needed.

### Muting a Group Chat

1. Swipe left on the conversation in the Messages list.
2. Tap **Hide Alerts** (a bell with a line through it).
3. A small **moon icon** will appear next to the chat, indicating it's muted.

You'll still receive messages, but your phone won't alert you every time someone sends one.

## Sending Photos, Videos, and Links

Group chats aren't just for text—sharing photos, videos, and links makes conversations more engaging.

### How to Share Media in a Group Chat

- **Photos & Videos**: Tap the **Photos icon** next to the text field and select an image or video.
- **Live Photos**: Send motion-enhanced images captured with the iPhone camera.
- **Links**: Copy a URL and paste it into the chat—Messages will generate a preview of the website.

Tip: Tap on a shared link to open it, or press and hold to preview before opening.

## Reacting and Replying in Group Chats

Group conversations can get fast-paced, making it easy to lose track of important messages. Apple's Tapback reactions and threaded replies help you keep discussions organized.

### USING TAPBACK REACTIONS

- Press and hold on a message bubble.
- Choose from 👍 👎 ❤️ ● ❗ ! to react quickly.

### REPLYING IN A THREAD

1. Press and hold on a message.
2. Tap **Reply** and type your response.
3. Your reply appears **nested** under the original message, keeping the conversation organized.

## Adding or Removing People

Need to add someone new to the conversation? No problem! As long as all members are using iMessage (blue bubbles), you can add or remove participants.

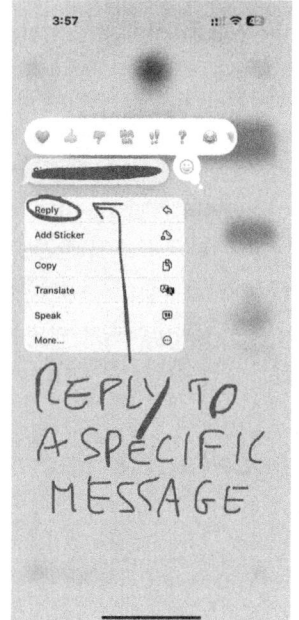

REPLY TO A SPECIFIC MESSAGE

### ADDING SOMEONE TO A GROUP CHAT

1. Open the group conversation.
2. Tap the **group name** at the top.
3. Scroll down and tap **Add Contact**.
4. Select the new participant and tap **Done**.

### REMOVING SOMEONE (IMESSAGE ONLY)

1. Open the group chat.
2. Tap the **group name**.
3. Find the person's name, swipe left, and tap **Remove**.

## Leaving a Group Chat

If a conversation is no longer relevant, you can leave without deleting the chat history.

### HOW TO LEAVE A GROUP CHAT

1. Open the group chat.
2. Tap the **group name** at the top.
3. Scroll down and tap **Leave this Conversation**.

Note: You can only leave if everyone in the chat is using iMessage. If the group includes SMS users (green bubbles), you'll need to mute the chat instead.

## Keeping Group Chats Organized

Managing multiple group chats can feel overwhelming. Here are some pro tips to stay organized:

- **Pin important chats**: Swipe right on a conversation and tap **Pin** to keep it at the top.
- **Use search**: Swipe down in Messages and type a keyword to find old messages.
- **Archive old chats**: While you can't officially archive chats in Messages, **deleting older conversations** can keep your app clean.

Group chats make staying connected fun, fast, and easy. Whether you're planning a trip, organizing a family event, or just sharing daily moments, the Messages app ensures everyone stays in the loop.

# FaceTime Basics: Video Calling Across Devices

FaceTime has revolutionized the way we connect with family and friends, making video calls as simple as placing a phone call. Whether you want to see your grandkids grow up in real-time, stay in touch with friends across the country, or even attend a virtual meeting, FaceTime ensures you can stay connected no matter where you are.

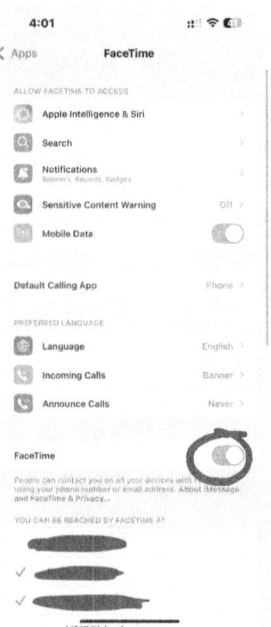

If you're new to FaceTime, don't worry—this guide will walk you through everything, from setting up your first call to using advanced features like SharePlay and effects.

## Getting Started with FaceTime

Before making your first FaceTime call, you'll need to make sure it's set up correctly.

### How to Enable FaceTime on Your iPhone

1. Open the **Settings app**.
2. Scroll down and tap **FaceTime**.
3. Toggle the **FaceTime switch** to turn it on.

4. Under **You Can Be Reached By FaceTime At**, ensure your **phone number and email address** are checked.
5. Under **Caller ID**, select the phone number or email you want to use for outgoing FaceTime calls.

That's it! Your FaceTime is now active and ready to use.

## Making a FaceTime Call

FaceTime is available on iPhones, iPads, Macs, and even Windows and Android via a web link, so you can reach almost anyone.

### HOW TO MAKE A FACETIME CALL

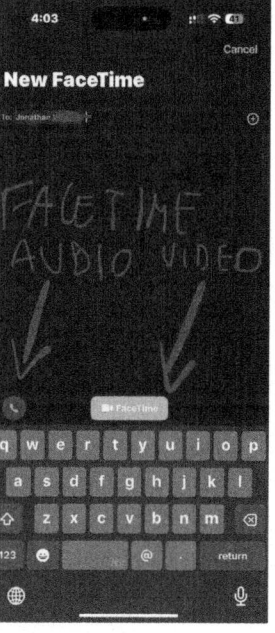

1. Open the **FaceTime app** on your iPhone.
2. Tap the **New FaceTime** button.
3. Enter the person's **name, phone number, or email** (they must have FaceTime enabled).
4. Tap the **FaceTime Video** button to start a video call or **FaceTime Audio** for a voice-only call.

Your call will begin, and when the other person picks up, you'll see them on your screen.

Tip: You can also make FaceTime calls directly from the Contacts app—just tap the FaceTime icon next to their name.

## Receiving a FaceTime Call

When someone calls you via FaceTime, you'll see an incoming call screen with their name, profile picture (if available), and options to accept or decline.

- **To Answer**: Tap the **green video button**.
- **To Decline**: Tap the **red decline button** or press the side button on your iPhone.

If you miss a FaceTime call, don't worry—you can call back by opening FaceTime and selecting the missed call from the recent calls list.

## Switching Between FaceTime Video and Audio

Sometimes, you might want to switch from a video call to an audio-only call, especially if your internet connection is weak or you need to save battery.

### How to Switch from Video to Audio Mid-Call

1. During a FaceTime video call, swipe up on the screen.
2. Tap **Camera Off**—this will disable your video but keep the call running as audio-only.

To turn the camera back on, simply tap Camera On in the FaceTime call menu.

## Using FaceTime Across Multiple Devices

If you own multiple Apple devices, FaceTime syncs across all of them, so you can answer a call on whichever is most convenient.

### FaceTime on Different Devices

- **On Mac**: Open the **FaceTime app** and sign in with the same Apple ID as your iPhone.
- **On iPad**: Open FaceTime and use it just like on an iPhone.
- **On Windows/Android**: Someone with an iPhone can send you a FaceTime **link** to join via a web browser.

Tip: If you answer a FaceTime call on your Mac but want to switch to your iPhone, simply pick up your iPhone and tap the FaceTime banner at the top.

## Group FaceTime: Chat with Multiple People

FaceTime isn't just for one-on-one conversations—you can have group calls with up to 32 people at once!

### Starting a Group FaceTime Call

1. Open the **FaceTime app**.
2. Tap **New FaceTime** and add multiple contacts.
3. Tap **FaceTime Video** to start the call.

Tip: If you're already in a one-on-one FaceTime call, you can add more people mid-call by tapping the + button in the menu.

## Fun Features: Filters, Effects, and SharePlay

FaceTime offers some fun features that make calls more engaging.

### Using Filters and Effects

1. During a FaceTime call, tap your screen to open the controls.
2. Tap the **Effects** button (star icon).
3. Choose from **filters, Memoji, and stickers** to personalize your video.

SharePlay allows you to watch movies, listen to music, or browse apps together during a FaceTime call.

1. Start a FaceTime call.
2. Open a supported app (e.g., Apple TV, Spotify).
3. Tap **SharePlay** and select the content to share.

Tip: Everyone in the call can control playback, so you can pause, rewind, or fast-for-ward together.

## FaceTime Troubleshooting

If FaceTime isn't working as expected, try these quick fixes:

- **FaceTime Not Connecting?** Ensure you have a **strong Wi-Fi or cellular signal**.
- **Can't Hear the Other Person?** Make sure your **volume is up** and **mute is off**.
- **FaceTime Button Missing?** Go to **Settings > FaceTime** and ensure it's enabled.

FaceTime makes staying connected effortless and fun. Whether you're catching up with family, coordinating with friends, or watching movies together, mastering FaceTime will keep you closer to those who matter most.

# Using Emojis, Stickers, and Effects to Add Fun to Your Conversations

Texting doesn't have to be just words on a screen—with iMessage, you can express yourself in fun and creative ways using emojis, stickers, and special effects. Whether you're sending a playful message to your grandkids, reacting to a funny story, or making a conversation more lively, these features add a personal touch that makes digital communication feel more engaging and expressive.

This guide will help you master emojis, stickers, and effects so you can make your messages more vibrant and entertaining.

## Emojis: The Universal Language of Expression

Sometimes, words aren't enough to express emotions. That's where emojis come in. These small icons add personality and clarity to your messages, helping you convey humor, excitement, sarcasm, or even frustration without needing long explanations.

## How to Use Emojis in Messages

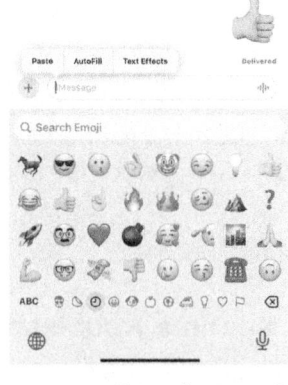

1. Open the **Messages app** and tap on a conversation.
2. Tap the **emoji button** (the smiley face) on the keyboard.
3. Scroll through or **search for an emoji** using the search bar.
4. Tap an emoji to insert it into your message.
5. Send the message by tapping the **blue arrow button**.

Tip: Your iPhone suggests emojis as you type. For example, if you type "happy," the ● emoji may appear as a suggestion—just tap it to replace the word.

## Emoji Reactions (Tapbacks): Quick and Easy Responses

If you don't feel like typing, you can react to a message with a quick emoji Tapback. This is perfect for acknowledging a message without needing to send a full reply.

### How to React with a Tapback

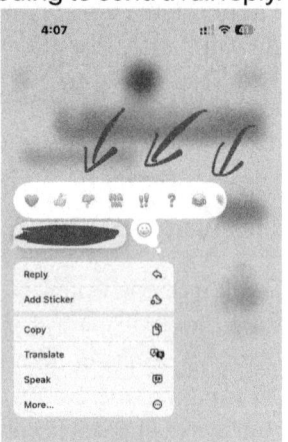

1. Press and hold a message bubble.
2. A pop-up menu will appear with six emoji reactions:
   » **Thumbs up** 👍: Approval or agreement.
   » **Thumbs down** 👎: Disapproval.
   » **Heart** ❤: Love or appreciation.
   » **Ha ha** 😂: Laughter.
   » **Exclamation marks** ‼️: Emphasis or surprise.
   » **Question mark ?** : Confusion or curiosity.
3. Tap an emoji to apply it to the message.

The reaction will appear in the top corner of the message bubble for both you and the recipient to see.

## Stickers: Fun and Personalized Messaging

Stickers are a great way to add personality to your texts. They function like large emojis but are often animated and customizable. You can use pre-made sticker packs or even create your own stickers from photos.

1. Open a conversation in the **Messages app**.
2. Tap the **App Store icon** next to the text box.
3. Select **Stickers** from the menu.
4. Browse and tap a sticker to insert it into the chat.
5. You can **drag stickers onto messages** to place them anywhere in the conversation.

Tip: You can download additional sticker packs from the iMessage App Store to expand your collection.

## Creating Custom Stickers from Your Photos

Did you know you can turn your own pictures into stickers? If you want to make a funny sticker of your pet, a grandkid's face, or a favorite vacation moment, iOS allows you to create Live Stickers from any photo.

### How to Make a Custom Sticker

1. Open the **Photos app** and select a picture.
2. Press and hold the subject (e.g., a person or pet) until a glowing outline appears.
3. Tap **Add Sticker** from the pop-up menu.
4. Your sticker is now saved in the **Stickers menu** within iMessage.

## Message Effects: Adding Flair to Your Conversations

If you want to make a message stand out, try using iMessage effects. These effects animate your messages with bubble and full-screen effects that make texting feel more dynamic.

### Bubble Effects: Animating Your Text Messages

Bubble effects change how your message appears inside the chat.

1. Type your message but **don't send it yet**.
2. Press and hold the **blue send arrow**.
3. Choose from four effects:

   » **Slam:** Makes the message th**ud onto the screen.**
   » **Loud:** Enlarges the message for **emphasis.**
   » **Gentle:** Shrinks the message for **a softer tone.**
   » **Invisible Ink:** Hides the message un**til the recipient swipes over it.**

4.  Tap the blue **send arrow** to apply the effect.

## Full-Screen Effects: Celebrate with Style

Full-screen effects animate the entire conversation background. These effects work great for birthdays, celebrations, and special occasions.

### How to Send a Full-Screen Effect

1.  Type your message but **don't send it yet**.
2.  Press and hold the **blue send arrow**.
3.  Tap the **Screen** tab.
4.  Swipe to choose an effect:

    » **Echo:** Duplicates the message across the screen.
    » **Spotlight:** Highlights the message.
    » **Balloons:** Floating balloons appear.
    » **Confetti:** Colorful confetti rains down.
    » **Fireworks:** A firework display lights up the screen.
    » **Lasers:** A colorful laser show.
    » **Celebration:** Golden sparkles burst onto the screen.

5.  Tap the **blue send arrow** to apply.

Tip: If you type "Happy Birthday" or "Congratulations," your iPhone automatically suggests appropriate effects!

## Live Photos and Digital Touch: More Ways to Express Yourself

### Live Photos in iMessage

You can send Live Photos that capture motion and sound rather than just a still image.

1.  Open **Messages** and select a conversation.
2.  Tap the **camera icon** and switch to **Live Photo mode**.
3.  Snap a picture and send it—your recipient can **press and hold** to see it move!

### Digital Touch: Draw and Animate Your Messages

With Digital Touch, you can draw doodles, send animated hearts, or tap patterns to express emotions.

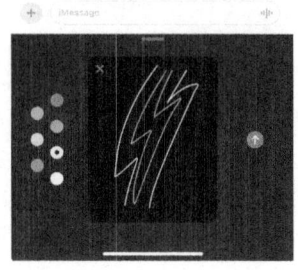

1. Open a conversation and tap the **heart icon** in the app drawer.
2. Use your finger to **draw a shape, scribble, or tap patterns**.
3. Send it to your recipient!

Enhance Your Conversations with Fun Features

Adding emojis, stickers, and effects makes texting more exciting and expressive. Whether you're sending a quick thumbs-up, creating a custom sticker, or celebrating a big moment with fireworks, these features help make your digital conversations feel more personal and lively.

# Troubleshooting Common Communication Issues

Even with the most advanced technology, communication issues still happen. Maybe your messages won't send, FaceTime keeps disconnecting, or notifications aren't appearing. It can be frustrating, especially when you're trying to stay in touch with family and friends.

Luckily, most issues can be fixed easily with a few quick adjustments. This guide will help you diagnose and resolve common problems in Messages, FaceTime, and notifications so you can get back to chatting without interruptions.

## Messages Not Sending or Receiving

Nothing is more annoying than seeing a "Not Delivered" message or realizing you haven't received a text someone sent hours ago. There are a few reasons why this might happen.

### CHECK YOUR INTERNET CONNECTION

Messages sent between Apple devices (iMessage) require Wi-Fi or cellular data, while regular SMS texts use your carrier's network. If your iPhone isn't connected properly, messages won't go through.

- Open **Safari** and try loading a website. If it doesn't load, you have an internet issue.
- Go to **Settings > Wi-Fi** and make sure you're connected. If using **cellular data**, check **Settings > Cellular** and ensure **Mobile Data** is turned on.

### VERIFY IMESSAGE SETTINGS

If you're sending an iMessage (blue bubble) but it's failing, your iMessage settings may not be enabled.

1. Go to **Settings > Messages**.
2. Make sure **iMessage** is turned ON.

3. Tap **Send & Receive** and confirm the correct phone number and Apple ID are listed.

## FaceTime Calls Keep Dropping or Won't Connect

FaceTime is great when it works smoothly, but dropped calls, frozen video, or no audio can quickly ruin the experience.

### CHECK YOUR INTERNET CONNECTION

FaceTime requires a strong internet connection to work properly. If you experience lagging or disconnections:

- **Move closer to your Wi-Fi router** or switch to a stronger network.
- Try turning Wi-Fi **OFF and ON** in **Settings > Wi-Fi**.
- If using cellular data, go to **Settings > Cellular** and ensure **FaceTime** is enabled.

### RESTART FACETIME

If FaceTime isn't working, try turning it OFF and ON:

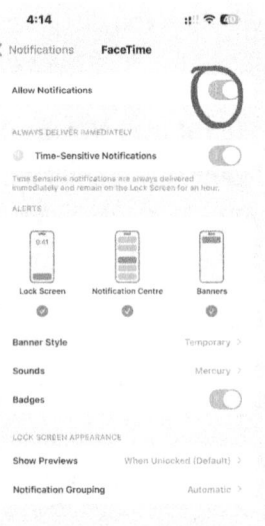

1. Go to **Settings > FaceTime**.
2. Toggle **FaceTime OFF**, wait a few seconds, then turn it **ON again**.

## Delayed or Missing Notifications

If you're missing important messages or FaceTime calls, notifications may not be working correctly.

### ENABLE NOTIFICATIONS FOR MESSAGES AND FACETIME

1. Go to **Settings > Notifications**.
2. Tap **Messages** or **FaceTime**.
3. Ensure **Allow Notifications** is turned ON.
4. Choose how you want alerts to appear (**Lock Screen, Notification Center, and Banners**).

### DISABLE FOCUS OR DO NOT DISTURB

Focus mode (formerly Do Not Disturb) silences no-tifications, which may explain why you're not seeing messages or calls.

- Swipe **down from the top-right corner** of your screen to open **Control Center**.
- If **Focus** (moon icon) is highlighted, tap it to turn it **OFF**.
- Or go to **Settings > Focus** and check if any focus modes are enabled.

## Why Can't I See Read Receipts or Typing Indicators?

If you don't see "Delivered" or "Read" under an iMessage, or the typing bubble is missing, one of the following may be the issue:

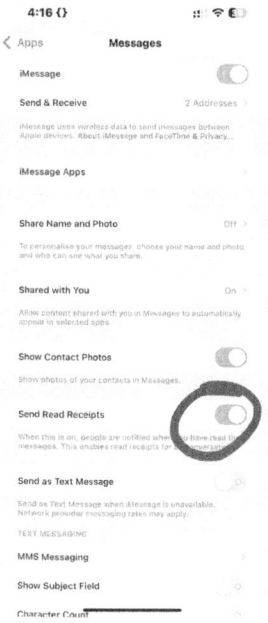

- **Read Receipts are disabled**: Go to **Settings > Messages** and turn ON **Send Read Receipts**.
- **The recipient has turned off iMessage or is on Android**: Read receipts only work between Apple devices.
- **Network connection issues**: If either you or the recipient **lose internet access**, iMessage features won't update.

## What If My Messages Are Green Instead of Blue?

Blue messages mean iMessage, while green messages mean SMS (regular text message). If your messages are suddenly green:

- The recipient may be using an **Android phone**.
- Their **iPhone may be turned off** or **out of internet range**.
- Your iMessage may be **disabled** (Check **Settings > Messages** to turn it back on).

## Troubleshooting When Nothing Else Works

If you've tried everything and your messaging apps are still acting up, here are three last resort fixes:

1. Restart Your iPhone

Sometimes, a simple restart resolves connectivity and messaging issues.

1. Press and hold the **Side button + Volume Up button** until you see **"Slide to Power Off"**.
2. Swipe to turn off your iPhone.
3. Wait **10 seconds**, then turn it back on by pressing and holding the **Side button**.
2. Update iOS

Apple frequently releases updates to fix bugs and improve communication features.

1.  Go to **Settings > General > Software Update**.
2.  If an update is available, tap **Download and Install**.
3.  Reset Network Settings

If nothing else works, resetting your network settings can clear out any connection issues.

1.  Go to **Settings > General > Transfer or Reset iPhone**.
2.  Tap **Reset > Reset Network Settings**.
3.  Your iPhone will **restart** and reset Wi-Fi, Bluetooth, and cellular settings.

Warning: This will erase saved Wi-Fi passwords, so make sure you have them written down.

By following these troubleshooting steps, you can quickly fix common communication issues and ensure that Messages, FaceTime, and notifications work smoothly every time.

# Taking and Sharing Photos Like a Pro

## Exploring the Camera Interface and Settings for Stunning Shots

The iPhone 16 camera is one of the most advanced smartphone cameras available, packed with features that make capturing stunning photos effortless. Whether you're snapping a family portrait, a beautiful sunset, or a quick candid moment, understanding the camera interface and settings will help you get the best possible shots every time.

This section will walk you through the camera app's layout, essential settings, and how to adjust them for different shooting scenarios.

### Navigating the Camera Interface

When you open the Camera app, you'll see a clean, intuitive interface designed for quick access to essential features. Let's break it down:

1.  The Viewfinder

The large preview window in the center of your screen is called the viewfinder. This is where you frame your shot before taking a photo.

*   **Tap anywhere on the screen** to focus on a subject manually.
*   **Pinch in and out** to zoom in on an object.
*   **Swipe left or right** to switch between different shooting modes (Photo, Video, Portrait, etc.).

2.  The Camera Modes

At the bottom of the screen, you'll see different camera modes. Swiping left or right lets you choose:

- **Photo**: Standard still image mode.
- **Portrait**: Blurs the background for professional-style photos.
- **Night Mode**: Enhances low-light shots automatically.
- **Cinematic**: For high-quality, depth-effect videos.
- **Slo-Mo & Time-Lapse**: Creative video features for speed adjustments.
- **Pano**: For capturing wide panoramic shots.

3. The Camera Controls

At the top of the screen, you'll see several useful camera settings:

- **Flash ( ? )⚡**Tap to turn on/off or set to auto.
- **Live Photos ( ⧖ )**: Captures a few seconds of motion before and after your shot.
- **Timer ( ⧖ )**: Set a countdown for hands-free photography.
- **Filters (🎨)**: Apply color filters before snapping a photo.

## Adjusting Camera Settings for Best Results

To truly master your iPhone's camera, you'll want to understand how to optimize its settings for different scenarios.

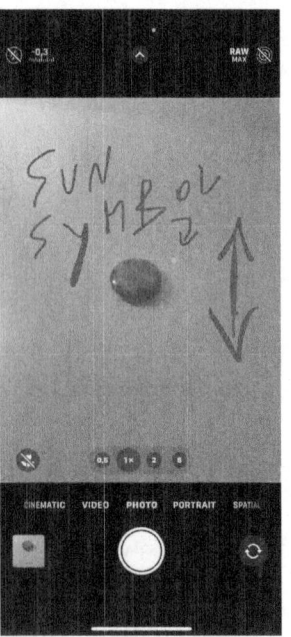

1. Focusing and Exposure Control

By default, the iPhone camera automatically adjusts focus and exposure, but you can manually control these settings for better results:

- **Tap on your subject** in the viewfinder to focus manually.
- **Hold your finger down** to lock focus (AE/AF Lock).
- **Swipe up or down on the sun icon** 🎨☀ adjust brightness (exposure).

2. Adjusting Resolution and Formats

For high-quality shots, you can adjust the resolution in Settings > Camera > Formats:

- Choose **High Efficiency (HEIF/HEVC)** for smaller file sizes without losing quality.
- Select **Most Compatible (JPEG)** if you need easier compatibility with older devices.

For videos, adjust Settings > Camera > Record Video:

- **4K at 60fps** for ultra-clear videos.
- **1080p at 30fps** for smooth, space-saving recording.

## Using Camera Features for Better Photography

Now that you're familiar with the basics, let's look at a few pro tips to make your iPhone photos stand out.

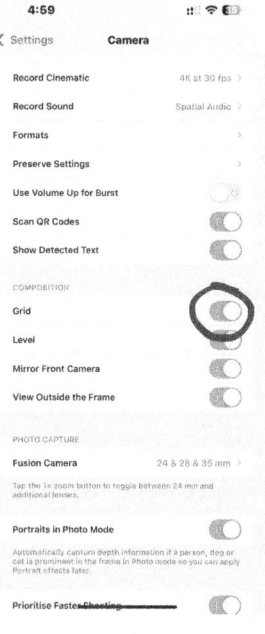

1.  Grid and Composition Tools

Turning on the grid lines helps you follow the rule of thirds, a fundamental photography technique for better composition.

To enable:

1.  Go to **Settings > Camera**.
2.  Toggle on **Grid**.
2.  HDR Mode for Balanced Lighting

HDR (High Dynamic Range) helps balance bright and dark areas in a photo, preventing overexposed highlights and underexposed shadows.

*   If you're photographing a **sunset**, a **landscape**, or a scene with **both light and dark areas, turn HDR on** for the best results.
*   You can enable Auto HDR in **Settings > Camera > Smart HDR**.

3.  Burst Mode for Action Shots

If you're trying to capture a fast-moving subject, such as kids playing or a pet running, use Burst Mode:

*   **Hold down the shutter button** to take multiple shots rapidly.
*   Later, you can **select the best frame** and delete the rest to save space.

## Quick Tips for Stunning iPhone Photos

*   **Use Natural Light**: Your photos will look more vibrant if you shoot in **natural light** instead of artificial lighting.
*   **Experiment with Angles**: Try shooting from **different perspectives** for a more dynamic composition.
*   **Avoid Using Digital Zoom**: Instead of pinching to zoom, **move closer** to your subject to avoid losing quality.
*   **Keep Your Lens Clean**: A **smudged camera lens** can result in blurry images. Wipe it with a soft cloth before shooting.
*   **Use the Volume Button**: For steadier shots, press the **Volume Up or Down** button to take photos instead of tapping the screen.

By mastering the camera interface and settings, you'll be able to take incredible, high-quality photos with your iPhone, whether you're a beginner or a seasoned photographer.

# Mastering Portrait, Night Mode, and Zoom Features

The iPhone 16 camera is packed with cutting-edge technology that allows you to take stunning photos in any environment. Whether you're capturing a beautifully blurred background in Portrait mode, illuminating details in Night mode, or zooming in without losing quality, these features ensure that every shot looks professional.

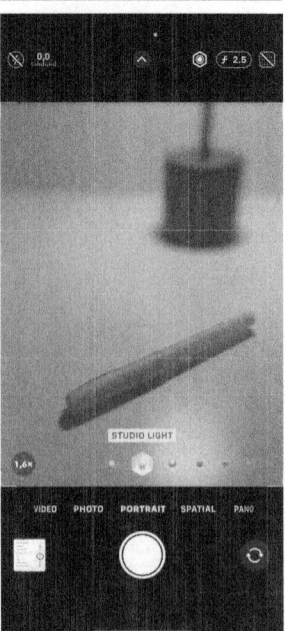

Let's break down how to use these powerful tools effectively, when to apply them, and some pro tips for getting the best results.

## Using Portrait Mode for Professional-Looking Shots

Portrait mode is one of the most popular iPhone camera features, allowing you to create a natural depth effect (also called "bokeh"), where your subject stands out crisply against a softly blurred background.

### How to Enable Portrait Mode

1. Open the **Camera app**.
2. Swipe to **Portrait mode**.
3. Position your subject **within the frame** (the camera will prompt you to move closer or farther).
4. Once the **depth effect is active**, tap the shutter button.

### Customizing Portrait Lighting

iPhone's Portrait mode includes built-in lighting effects to create studio-like images. To adjust:

- Tap the **Portrait Lighting icon** at the top of the screen.
- Select from options like **Natural Light, Studio Light, Contour Light**, or **Stage Light** for dramatic effects.

### Pro Tips for the Best Portraits

- **Use Good Lighting**: Portrait mode works best in **natural light** or well-lit indoor settings.
- **Avoid Cluttered Backgrounds**: The bokeh effect looks best when your subject is against a **simple backdrop**.
- **Tap to Focus**: If your subject isn't sharp, **tap on their face** to fine-tune the focus.

- **Experiment with Depth Control**: After taking the shot, open the **Photos app > Edit > f-stop slider** to adjust the level of background blur.

## Capturing Stunning Low-Light Shots with Night Mode

Night mode is an essential tool for capturing clear, well-lit images in dark environments. Unlike standard shots, Night mode automatically extends the exposure time, allowing more light into the camera sensor.

### How to Use Night Mode

1. Open the **Camera app** and switch to **Photo mode**.
2. If the scene is **dimly lit**, a **crescent moon icon** (🌙) appears in the top left.
3. The camera **automatically selects the exposure time** (you can adjust it manually by tapping the Night mode icon).
4. Hold the phone **steady** and tap the shutter button.

### Pro Tips for Sharp Night Shots

- **Keep Your iPhone Steady**: Since Night mode uses longer exposure, **any movement can cause blur**. Use a **tripod** or rest your phone on a stable surface.
- **Adjust the Exposure Time**: For very dark environments, increase exposure **(tap the moon icon and use the slider)** for a brighter shot.
- **Look for Light Sources**: Even a small amount of light (like a streetlamp or neon sign) can dramatically improve composition.
- **Use the Ultra-Wide Camera Sparingly**: The main camera performs best in Night mode, whereas **ultra-wide shots can sometimes look noisier**.

## Mastering Zoom for Close-Ups Without Losing Detail

With the iPhone 16 Pro's advanced zoom capabilities, you can get closer to your subject without losing quality. The latest model offers:

- **Optical Zoom (3x or more)**: Maintains image clarity while zooming.
- **Digital Zoom (Up to 15x or 30x)**: Uses software to enlarge an image, which may reduce sharpness.

### How to Use Zoom on iPhone 16

1. Open the **Camera app**.

2. **Tap the zoom buttons** (1x, 3x, etc.), or **pinch the screen** to adjust manually.

3. For **long-distance shots**, hold your phone steady to avoid blur.

### Which Zoom Setting Should You Use?

- **1x (Standard Lens)**: Best for general photography.
- **2x-3x (Telephoto Lens)**: Ideal for portraits and distant subjects.
- **10x+ (Digital Zoom)**: Use cautiously, as quality decreases at higher zoom levels.

### Pro Tips for Perfect Zoomed-In Shots

- **Use Optical Zoom Whenever Possible**: It provides **sharper images than digital zoom**.
- **Stabilize Your Hand**: A slight shake is more noticeable at **higher zoom levels**.
- **Try Portrait Mode at 3x Zoom**: This creates an even **stronger background blur effect**.

## Bringing It All Together: Combining Features for the Best Shots

Now that you know how to use Portrait mode, Night mode, and Zoom, you can start combining them for incredible results.

- **Portraits at Night**: Use **Night mode + Portrait mode** for sharp, well-lit images in dark settings.
- **Zoomed Portraits**: Try **Portrait mode at 3x zoom** for a more professional look.
- **Long-Exposure Night Shots**: Experiment with **longer Night mode exposures** for light trails and dramatic cityscapes.

Mastering these features unlocks the full potential of your iPhone's camera, helping you take photos that look like they were shot with a professional DSLR!

# Editing Photos Directly on Your iPhone: Filters, Crops, and Adjustments

Once you've captured a great photo, the next step is editing it to enhance its look. The iPhone 16 offers a powerful built-in editing suite that allows you to fine-tune your images, apply filters for creative effects, crop for better composition, and adjust brightness, contrast, and color balance—all within the Photos app.

Let's dive into how you can transform your photos directly on your iPhone, step by step.

## Accessing the Editing Tools in the Photos App

1. Open the **Photos app**.
2. Select the image you want to edit.
3. Tap **Edit** in the top-right corner.
4. You'll see a range of tools for **adjustments, cropping, and filters**.

Each editing tool serves a different purpose, and using them correctly can elevate an ordinary snapshot into a stunning image.

## Applying Filters for Instant Enhancement

Filters are pre-set adjustments that instantly change the tone and feel of your photo. The iPhone provides a variety of subtle and artistic filters to enhance different styles.

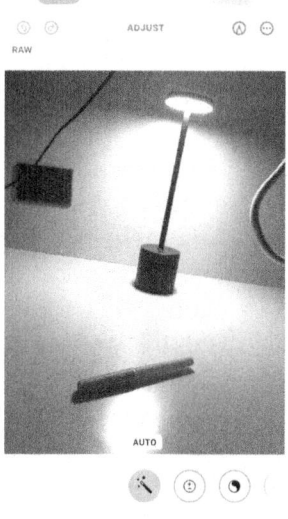

### HOW TO APPLY A FILTER

1. In the **Edit mode**, tap the **Filters icon** (it looks like three overlapping circles).
2. Swipe through the available options:

    » **Vivid:** Boosts colors for a brighter look.
    » **Dramatic:** Adds contrast for a bold effect.
    » **Mono:** Creates a **black-and-white aesthetic.**

3. Adjust the **intensity of the filter** using the slider.
4. Tap **Done** to save your changes.

### PRO TIPS FOR USING FILTERS

- **Use filters sparingly**: Subtle tweaks often look more natural than heavy filters.
- **Experiment with combinations**: Apply a filter, then fine-tune it using manual adjustments.
- **Try different styles for different moods**: A warm filter like **Warm or Vivid** works well for **sunsets**, while **Dramatic Cool** enhances **cityscapes**.

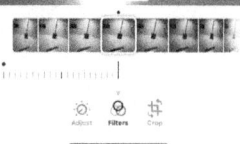

## Cropping and Straightening for Better Composition

Cropping is essential for removing unwanted elements and improving framing and balance in your photos.

### How to Crop and Straighten

1. In **Edit mode**, tap the **Crop icon** (a square with arrows).
2. **Adjust the frame** by dragging the corners inward.
3. Tap the **rotation dial** to straighten an image if it's tilted.
4. Use the **preset aspect ratios** (such as 1:1 for Instagram or 16:9 for widescreen).
5. Tap **Done** to save.

### Pro Tips for Cropping

- **Follow the Rule of Thirds**: Align key elements along the **grid lines** for a **visually balanced shot**.
- **Keep the Subject in Focus**: Crop out distractions to bring attention to the most important part of the image.
- **Experiment with Different Ratios**: A square (1:1) is great for social media, while 16:9 works well for landscapes.

## Making Manual Adjustments for a Professional Touch

For full creative control, you can adjust the brightness, contrast, shadows, highlights, and more.

### How to Adjust Brightness, Contrast, and Color

1. In **Edit mode**, tap the **Adjustments icon** (dial with small dots).
2. Scroll through the available tools, including:

   » **Exposure:** Controls the overall lightness or darkness.
   » **Brilliance:** Enhances shadows and highlights for a richer look.
   » **Contrast:** Increases the difference between light and dark tones.
   » **Saturation:** Boosts or mutes colors.

3. Use the **slider** to increase or decrease the effect.
4. Tap **Done** when satisfied.

PRO TIPS FOR ADJUSTMENTS

- **Use Brilliance instead of Brightness**: It balances highlights and shadows for a **more natural look**.
- **Lower Contrast for a Softer Look**: Too much contrast can make an image look harsh.
- **Boost Saturation Slightly**: Over-saturation can make colors look unnatural.

## Undoing Edits and Reverting to the Original Photo

If you're not happy with an edit, don't worry—you can always undo or revert to the original photo.

HOW TO UNDO EDITS

- While editing, tap **Revert** to go back to the previous step.
- To reset the photo completely, tap **Revert to Original**.

## Bringing It All Together: Editing Like a Pro

By using these tools strategically, you can enhance your photos effortlessly—whether it's a quick filter for a polished look or manual adjustments for professional-quality images.

With the iPhone's intuitive editing features, you don't need expensive software—your best shots are just a few taps away!

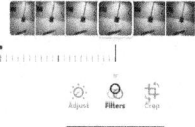

# Organizing Photos with Albums, Favorites, and Shared Folders

Taking photos is just the beginning—organizing them effectively ensures that your best shots are easy to find, share, and enjoy. The iPhone's Photos app offers a range of powerful tools to keep your pictures neatly arranged, from Albums and Favorites to Shared Folders that let you collaborate with family and friends.

Let's explore how you can streamline your photo library and maximize your iPhone's organization features.

## Using Albums to Categorize Your Photos

Albums are the best way to keep your photos grouped by theme, event, or person. Instead of scrolling through thousands of pictures in your camera roll, you can create custom albums for vacations, birthdays, pets, or even specific photography projects.

### HOW TO CREATE A CUSTOM ALBUM

1. Open the **Photos app**.
2. Tap **Albums** at the bottom.
3. Tap the **+** button in the top-left corner and select **New Album**.
4. Name your album (e.g., "Hawaii Vacation 2024").
5. Select the photos you want to include.
6. Tap **Done** to save.

### PRO TIPS FOR MANAGING ALBUMS

- **Use albums for specific themes**: Create albums like "Family Moments," "Landscapes," or "Best Shots of the Year."
- **Sort by date or location**: Albums automatically organize photos **chronologically** and can also be grouped by **places**.
- **Edit albums anytime**: Add or remove photos from an album whenever needed without deleting them from your library.

## Marking Favorites for Quick Access

Not every photo needs to be in an album, but some deserve easy access—this is where the Favorites feature comes in handy.

### HOW TO MARK A PHOTO AS A FAVORITE

1. Open a photo in the **Photos app**.
2. Tap the **heart icon** (♥) at the bottom of the screen.
3. The photo is now added to the **Favorites album**, accessible from the Albums tab.

### WHY FAVORITES ARE USEFUL

- **Easily retrieve your best photos**: No need to search through your entire camera roll.
- **Works across devices**: If you use iCloud Photos, your Favorites sync across all your Apple devices.
- **Great for short-term saves**: If you're working on

a project or sharing a specific set of images frequently, marking them as Favorites makes them **instantly accessible**.

## Smart Albums: Let iPhone Organize for You

Apple's Photos app automatically creates Smart Albums to organize certain types of content.

### PRE-BUILT SMART ALBUMS INCLUDE

- **Selfies**: Every front-camera shot is automatically grouped.
- **Screenshots**: Easily locate your saved screenshots.
- **Live Photos**: View all your Live Photos in one place.
- **Videos**: Quickly browse only your recorded videos.
- **People & Pets**: Thanks to facial and object recognition, your iPhone can create albums for individual people or pets.

### HOW TO EDIT A SMART ALBUM

1. Open a Smart Album (e.g., **People & Pets**).
2. Tap **Select** and choose multiple images.
3. Move or remove photos from the album as needed.

## Creating Shared Albums for Easy Collaboration

Want to share vacation photos without spamming a group chat? With Shared Albums, you can create collaborative folders where multiple people can view, add, and comment on photos.

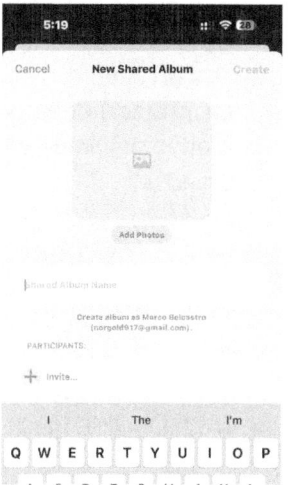

### HOW TO CREATE A SHARED ALBUM

1. Open the **Photos app** and go to **Albums**.
2. Tap **+** and choose **New Shared Album**.
3. Give your album a name.
4. Select **contacts** to invite via iMessage or email.
5. Tap **Create** and start adding photos.

### WHY USE SHARED ALBUMS?

- **Perfect for family events**: Everyone can contribute their photos from weddings, birthdays, or holidays.
- **Saves space**: Unlike AirDrop or sending photos through messaging apps, **Shared Albums do not count against iCloud storage**.
- **Interactive features**: Users can **like and comment** on shared photos, making it feel like a private photo-sharing app.

### Managing Shared Albums

- **Add or remove members anytime**: Only the album creator can **manage participants**.
- **Control who can add photos**: Enable or disable the option for contributors to add images.
- **Stop sharing when needed**: You can **delete a Shared Album** without affecting the original photos on anyone's device.

## Using iCloud Photos for Seamless Access Across Devices

If you use multiple Apple devices, iCloud Photos ensures your entire photo library is accessible from your iPhone, iPad, and Mac.

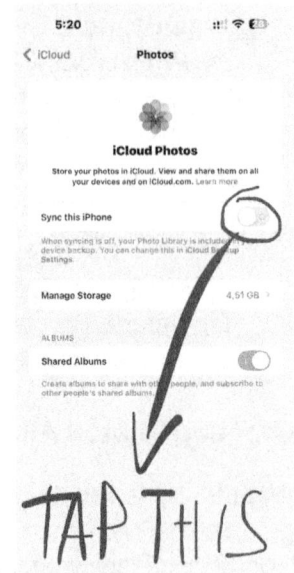

### How to Enable iCloud Photos

1. Open **Settings**.
2. Tap **Your Name > iCloud > Photos**.
3. Toggle **iCloud Photos** on.

### Benefits of iCloud Photos

- **Automatic syncing**: Any photo you take is instantly available on all devices.
- **Safe backups**: If you lose your phone, your photos remain secure.
- **Optimized storage**: Your iPhone keeps low-resolution previews, while full-size images stay in the cloud.

## Cleaning Up Your Library: Deleting and Recovering Photos

Over time, photos pile up, and storage fills up. Regular cleanup keeps your library manageable.

### How to Delete Photos

1. Open the **Photos app** and tap **Albums**.
2. Select the **photos you no longer need**.
3. Tap the **Trash icon**.

### Recovering Accidentally Deleted Photos

- Deleted photos go to the **Recently Deleted album**, where they stay for **30 days**.

- To restore a photo, go to **Recently Deleted**, select the image, and tap **Recover**.

## Bringing It All Together: A Well-Organized Photo Library

By using albums, favorites, shared folders, and smart organization features, you can effortlessly manage thousands of photos. Whether you're sorting vacation memories, collaborating on family albums, or keeping your favorite shots at your fingertips, the iPhone's built-in tools make it easy and enjoyable.

A few simple steps now will save you hours of scrolling later—so start organizing today!

# Creating Digital Photo Albums for Memorable Keepsakes

In today's digital world, capturing memories is easier than ever—but keeping them organized and accessible can be a challenge. That's where digital photo albums come in. With the iPhone's built-in Photos app, you can curate stunning digital albums that serve as cherished keepsakes for special moments—whether it's a family vacation, a milestone birthday, or a year-in-review.

In this section, we'll explore how to create digital photo albums, add meaningful details, and even share them with loved ones.

## Why Create Digital Photo Albums?

Physical photo albums are beautiful, but they come with limitations: they can be lost, damaged, or take up space. Digital albums, on the other hand, offer flexibility, security, and easy sharing.

Some key benefits of digital albums include:

- **Convenience**: Access your memories anytime, anywhere from your iPhone, iPad, or Mac.
- **Customization**: Organize photos by event, people, or themes, making it easier to relive moments.
- **Collaboration**: Easily share albums with family and friends, allowing them to contribute their own photos.
- **Backup & Security**: Store albums safely on iCloud to prevent loss.

## How to Create a Digital Photo Album on iPhone

Creating a custom digital album is quick and intuitive.

### STEPS TO CREATE A NEW ALBUM

1. Open the **Photos app**.
2. Tap **Albums** at the bottom of the screen.

3. Tap the **+** button in the top-left corner and select **New Album**.
4. Enter a **name** for the album (e.g., "2024 Family Trip" or "Emma's First Year").
5. Select the **photos you want to add**, then tap **Done**.

Your album is now saved under My Albums in the Photos app! You can always add more pictures, edit the order, or remove photos later.

## Organizing and Customizing Your Albums

Once your album is created, customizing it makes the experience more enjoyable.

### ADDING TITLES, CAPTIONS, AND LOCATIONS

To give context to your photos, add titles and descriptions:

1. Open a photo and swipe up.
2. Tap **Add a Caption** and type a short description (e.g., "Sunset in Santorini").
3. If the photo lacks location data, tap **Add Location** and search for the correct place.

This helps keep track of when and where each memory happened, making albums more meaningful.

## Adding Videos, Live Photos, and Other Media

A great album isn't just about still images. The iPhone allows you to include videos, Live Photos, and even scanned documents for a rich storytelling experience.

To add variety:

- **Include video clips** to relive special moments in motion.
- **Use Live Photos** to see the short movement before and after a picture was taken.
- **Add scanned mementos** (like handwritten notes, tickets, or event programs) using the **Notes app's scanner**.

This way, your album feels more like a time capsule rather than just a collection of images.

## Creating Smart Albums for Auto-Organization

If you take lots of photos, you may find it tedious to manually organize everything. This is where Smart Albums come in—they automatically categorize photos based on dates, locations, people, or even content types (e.g., selfies, screenshots).

### HOW TO CREATE A SMART ALBUM

1. Open **Photos** and go to **Albums**.
2. Scroll down to **People & Places** or **Categories** (e.g., Pets, Travel, Food).

3. Tap an album to view its automatically sorted content.

For example, iOS can recognize faces and group photos of your loved ones to-gether—perfect for making memory books without manual sorting.

## Sharing Albums with Friends and Family

Want to relive a family reunion or wedding with others? With Shared Albums, multiple people can view, add, and comment on a collective digital album.

### HOW TO CREATE A SHARED ALBUM

1. Open **Photos** and go to **Albums**.
2. Tap **+** and choose **New Shared Album**.
3. Give it a name (e.g., "Grandpa's 80th Birthday").
4. Select **people to invite** via iMessage or email.
5. Tap **Create** and start adding photos!

### WHY USE SHARED ALBUMS?

- **Family collaboration**: Everyone can contribute their own pictures from an event.
- **Space-saving**: Unlike AirDrop, Shared Albums don't count toward iCloud storage.
- **Interactive engagement**: Users can **like and comment** on shared photos.

## Transforming Albums into Digital Slideshows

A well-organized album can also become an instant slideshow—ideal for sharing on TV screens or during gatherings.

### HOW TO PLAY A SLIDESHOW FROM AN ALBUM

1. Open a **photo album**.
2. Tap the **three-dot menu** in the top-right.
3. Select **Slideshow**.
4. Choose a **theme and music** (optional).

Your iPhone will automatically cycle through images, making it a perfect way to share moments at family events!

## Printing Digital Albums into Physical Books

Sometimes, digital is not enough—you may want a tangible keepsake. With Apple's third-party printing services, you can turn your albums into photo books, calendars, or framed prints.

### How to Order a Printed Photo Album

1. Open an album and tap **Share**.
2. Select **Print with Shutterfly or another printing service**.
3. Choose a layout and review your book.
4. Place your order and receive a **professionally printed album** in the mail!

This way, you get the best of both worlds—digital convenience and a lasting physical keepsake.

## Final Thoughts on Digital Photo Albums

By using Albums, Smart Albums, Shared Albums, and even printed books, you can curate and preserve your most treasured moments in a way that's both practical and emotionally meaningful.

Whether you want to organize your yearly highlights, share a collection of baby photos, or document a once-in-a-lifetime trip, the iPhone's built-in tools make the process effortless and enjoyable.

Now it's time to get started—choose your favorite moments and create your first digital keepsake today!

# CHAPTER 5

# Exploring Entertainment and Media

## Streaming Movies, TV Shows, and Music: Your Entertainment Hub

Your iPhone is more than just a communication tool—it's a powerful entertainment hub that brings your favorite movies, TV shows, and music directly to your fingertips. Whether you're relaxing at home, commuting, or traveling, your iPhone can provide seamless access to streaming services, allowing you to enjoy content anytime, anywhere.

This section will guide you through the best streaming apps, tips for optimizing your viewing and listening experience, and how to manage your subscriptions effectively.

### Popular Streaming Services for Movies and TV Shows

Your iPhone supports a variety of streaming services, each offering a unique selection of movies and TV shows. Here are some of the most popular options:

- **Netflix**: The go-to platform for **binge-worthy TV series, original movies, and documentaries**.
- **Apple TV+**: Home to **high-quality Apple Originals**, including drama series, comedies, and exclusive films.
- **Disney+**: Perfect for fans of **Marvel, Star Wars, Pixar, and Disney classics**.
- **Amazon Prime Video**: Features a mix of **original content, popular movies, and rental options**.
- **HBO Max** (or **Max**, depending on your region): Offers **premium dramas, blockbusters, and Warner Bros. films**.
- **Hulu**: A solid choice for **next-day streaming of network TV shows** along with a strong original content lineup.

### How to Access and Subscribe to a Streaming Service

1. Open the **App Store** and search for your preferred streaming app.
2. Download and install the app on your iPhone.
3. Open the app and **sign in or create an account**.
4. Choose a **subscription plan** (some offer free trials).
5. Start browsing and **add movies or shows to your watchlist**.

## Enhancing Your Viewing Experience

To get the best picture and audio quality, adjust these settings:

### Adjusting Streaming Quality

- Go to **Settings > TV > iTunes Videos**.
- Under **Playback Quality**, select **Best Available** for high-definition viewing.

### Enabling Subtitles and Closed Captions

Many streaming services offer customizable subtitles:

- While watching a show, tap the **speech bubble icon**.
- Choose **Subtitles (CC)** and select your preferred language.
- Adjust **text size and background color** for better readability in **Settings > Accessibility > Subtitles & Captioning**.

## Offline Viewing: Download Movies and Shows

Don't always have Wi-Fi or cellular data? Downloading content for offline viewing is a game-changer, especially for long flights or commutes.

### How to Download Movies and TV Shows

1. Open the streaming app and find a movie or TV episode.
2. Look for the **download icon** (usually a downward arrow).
3. Tap to start downloading.
4. Access your downloaded content in the **Downloads** section.

Most services, like Netflix and Disney+, allow you to set a storage limit and automatically delete watched downloads to free up space.

## Music Streaming Services on iPhone

If you love music, podcasts, or audiobooks, your iPhone supports multiple streaming platforms.

### TOP MUSIC STREAMING APPS

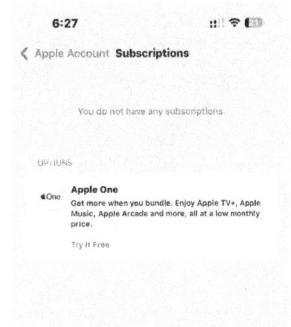

- **Apple Music**: A **vast library of over 100 million songs**, curated playlists, and exclusive releases.
- **Spotify**: A favorite for **personalized playlists and podcasts**, available in both free (ad-supported) and premium versions.
- **Amazon Music**: Offers a mix of **free, Prime, and Unlimited subscription tiers**.
- **YouTube Music**: A great option for **music videos and personalized recommendations**.
- **Tidal**: Known for **hi-fi audio quality** and exclusive artist content.

### HOW TO STREAM AND DOWNLOAD MUSIC ON APPLE MUSIC

1. Open **Apple Music** and browse or search for a song.
2. Tap **Play** to stream instantly.
3. Tap the **+ Add** button to save to your library.
4. To download for offline listening, tap the **download icon** next to the song or album.

## Managing Streaming Subscriptions

With multiple services, it's easy to lose track of subscriptions and accidentally pay for services you no longer use.

### HOW TO MANAGE SUBSCRIPTIONS ON IPHONE

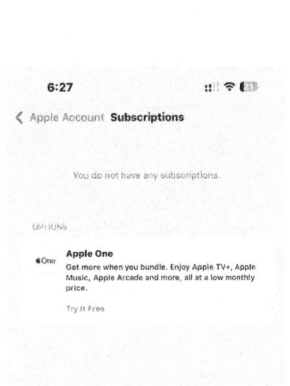

1. Open **Settings**.
2. Tap your **Apple ID (your name at the top)**.
3. Select **Subscriptions**.
4. View active subscriptions, change plans, or **cancel any you no longer need**.

To save money, consider family plans or bundled services like Apple One, which includes Apple Music, Apple TV+, Apple Arcade, and iCloud storage at a lower price than individual subscriptions.

## Streaming Content to a Bigger Screen

If you want to watch movies or shows on a bigger screen, you can connect your iPhone to a TV or external display using AirPlay or an HDMI adapter.

### USING AIRPLAY TO STREAM CONTENT

1. Ensure your **iPhone and Apple TV (or AirPlay-compatible smart TV)** are on the same Wi-Fi network.
2. Open a streaming app and start playing a movie or TV show.
3. Tap the **AirPlay icon** (a rectangle with an arrow).
4. Select your **Apple TV or Smart TV** from the list.

This allows you to mirror your iPhone's screen or stream media directly without cables.

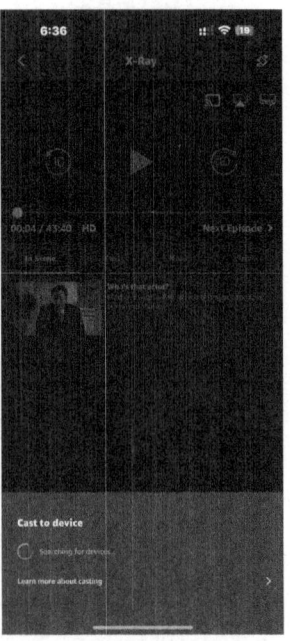

## Using Siri for Hands-Free Control

Siri makes navigating entertainment even easier. You can:

- Say **"Hey Siri, play Stranger Things on Netflix"** to start a show without touching your iPhone.
- Ask **"What song is playing?"** when listening to music to identify tracks with **Shazam integration**.
- Say **"Skip forward 10 minutes"** or **"Turn on subtitles"** for seamless control while watching.

Try different voice commands to make your entertainment experience truly hands-free.

## Maximizing Your iPhone as an Entertainment Hub

By combining the right streaming services, downloading content for offline use, optimizing settings, and using features like AirPlay and Siri, your iPhone transforms into a powerful media hub.

Whether you're catching up on TV shows, discovering new music, or watching blockbuster movies, these tools ensure a smooth and enjoyable experience anytime, anywhere.

# Using Podcasts and Audiobooks to Learn and Relax

Your iPhone is more than just a communication and entertainment device—it's also a powerful learning and relaxation tool. Whether you're interested in expanding your knowledge, finding motivation, or simply unwinding with a good story, podcasts and audiobooks offer a hands-free, immersive way to engage with content.

This section will guide you through the best apps for podcasts and audiobooks, how to find and organize content, and useful tips for optimizing your listening experience.

## Why Podcasts and Audiobooks Are Game-Changers

Podcasts and audiobooks have become essential companions for people looking to make the most of their time. Whether you're commuting, exercising, cooking, or just relaxing, you can listen and learn without needing to stare at a screen.

For our buyer persona, Susan Carter, podcasts and audiobooks are an ideal way to stay informed and entertained without feeling overwhelmed by technology. She can listen to personal development podcasts, educational history series, or even fiction audiobooks while going about her day.

### BENEFITS OF PODCASTS AND AUDIOBOOKS

- **Multitasking-friendly**: Listen while **driving, working out, or doing chores**.
- **Educational and inspiring**: Learn **new skills, stay updated on news, or gain inspiration** from thought leaders.
- **Relaxing and stress-relieving**: A good audiobook or meditation podcast can help you **unwind and sleep better**.
- **Screen-free entertainment**: Perfect for **reducing screen time** while still engaging with interesting content.

## Finding the Best Podcast Apps

There are multiple podcast platforms available on iPhone, each offering unique features. Here are some of the most popular:

- **Apple Podcasts** – The default app on iPhone, featuring a massive library and seamless **Siri integration**.
- **Spotify** – Ideal if you **already use Spotify for music**, with exclusive podcasts and curated playlists.
- **Audible** – Primarily for audiobooks but also offers a selection of **original podcasts**.
- **Pocket Casts** – A great choice for **power users** who want advanced playback controls and organization features.

- **Overcast** – A clean, user-friendly podcast app with **smart speed adjustments** and **voice boosting**.

## How to Subscribe and Listen to Podcasts

1. Open the **Apple Podcasts** app.
2. Tap the **Search** tab and enter the name of a podcast.
3. Select a show and tap **Follow** to get automatic updates for new episodes.
4. Browse available episodes and tap **Play** to start listening.
5. Adjust playback speed and **skip silences** for a better listening experience.

## Discovering and Listening to Audiobooks

If you love reading but struggle to find time for it, audiobooks are a fantastic alternative. With a good narrator, a book can come to life in a way that makes it even more engaging than reading text.

## Top Audiobook Apps for iPhone

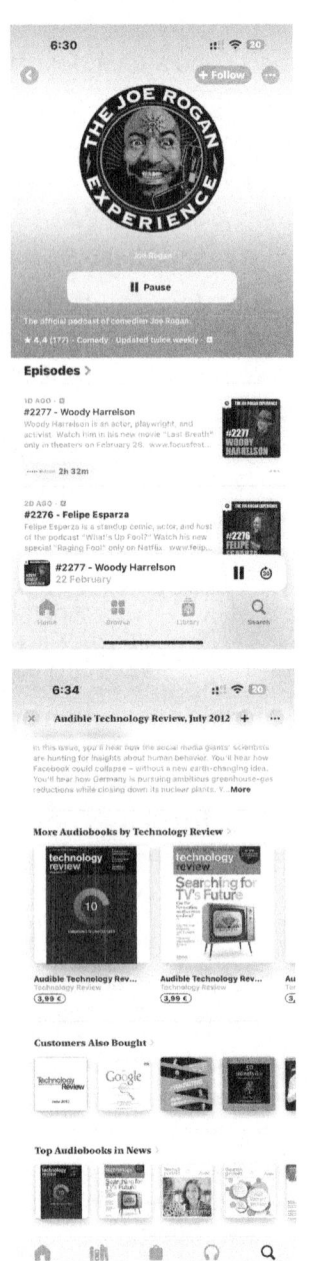

- **Apple Books** – Offers a curated selection of audiobooks that you can buy directly from the **Apple Books app**.
- **Audible (by Amazon)** – The largest audiobook platform, with a subscription-based model offering **one credit per month for any audiobook**.
- **Libby (by OverDrive)** – Lets you **borrow audiobooks for free** from your local public library.
- **Scribd** – A subscription service that provides access to **unlimited audiobooks, eBooks, and magazines**.

## How to Purchase and Listen to an Audiobook on Apple Books

1. Open the **Apple Books** app.
2. Tap **Audiobooks** in the bottom menu.
3. Browse or search for a book and tap the price to purchase.
4. Once purchased, tap **Listen** to start playing.

5. Adjust **narration speed** and **set a sleep timer** for bedtime listening.

## Organizing Your Podcasts and Audiobooks

To keep your library organized and easy to navigate, try these tips:

### MANAGING PODCASTS IN APPLE PODCASTS

- **Create a custom station**: Group multiple podcasts into a single playlist.
- **Mark episodes as played**: Helps you track what you've already listened to.
- **Enable automatic downloads**: Keep your favorite shows available offline.

### ORGANIZING AUDIOBOOKS IN APPLE BOOKS

- Use **Collections** to categorize books (e.g., Fiction, Business, Self-Help).
- Tap **"Finished"** after completing an audiobook to track progress.
- Adjust **bookmark settings** to save important moments in a book.

## Customizing Your Listening Experience

Your iPhone has several features that enhance the way you listen to podcasts and audiobooks:

### PLAYBACK SPEED AND SKIP SETTINGS

- In **Apple Podcasts or Apple Books**, you can **adjust the playback speed** (e.g., 1.25x for a slightly faster pace).
- Some podcast apps allow you to **skip silent pauses**, saving time on longer episodes.

### USING SIRI FOR HANDS-FREE CONTROL

Siri can start, pause, or skip episodes and books using simple voice commands:

- *"Hey Siri, play my latest podcast."*
- *"Hey Siri, skip forward 30 seconds."*
- *"Hey Siri, play my audiobook from Apple Books."*

## Listening Offline: Downloading Podcasts and Audiobooks

For those times when you don't have internet access, downloading content for offline listening is a must.

### DOWNLOADING PODCASTS FOR OFFLINE USE

1. Open the **Podcasts** app.
2. Tap on a podcast episode.
3. Select **Download** to save it locally.

4.   Access downloaded episodes in the **Library > Downloaded** section.

### DOWNLOADING AUDIOBOOKS IN APPLE BOOKS

1.   Open **Apple Books** and go to **Audiobooks**.
2.   Tap the **download icon** next to your purchased book.
3.   Find your downloaded books in **Library > Downloaded**.

## Using Podcasts and Audiobooks for Relaxation

Podcasts and audiobooks aren't just for learning—they're also powerful relaxation tools.

### BEST PODCAST CATEGORIES FOR RELAXATION

- **Meditation & Sleep** – Apps like **Calm** and **Headspace** offer guided sessions.
- **True Crime & Mystery** – Great for **immersive storytelling** that keeps your mind engaged.
- **Comedy & Talk Shows** – Light-hearted shows that **help reduce stress**.

### BEST AUDIOBOOKS FOR UNWINDING

- **Classic literature**: Audiobooks like *Pride and Prejudice* or *The Great Gatsby* offer immersive storytelling.
- **Fantasy & Fiction**: Books like *Harry Potter* or *The Hobbit* are perfect for escapism.
- **Self-improvement**: Titles like *Atomic Habits* or *The Power of Now* can inspire positive change.

## Maximizing Your Listening Experience

By exploring different apps, customizing playback settings, and organizing your content, you can turn your iPhone into a personal audio library.

Whether you want to stay informed, learn new things, or simply relax, podcasts and audiobooks are a convenient and enjoyable way to enrich your daily life—all without ever needing to pick up a book or stare at a screen.

# Setting Up AirPlay to Connect Your iPhone to Other Devices

One of the most underrated but incredibly powerful features of your iPhone is AirPlay—Apple's seamless wireless streaming technology that lets you mirror your screen, share media, and play audio or video on compatible devices without needing physical cables. Whether you want to watch a movie on a bigger screen, play music on high-quality speakers, or even share a slideshow during a family gathering, AirPlay makes it simple and effortless.

This section will walk you through everything you need to know about setting up and using AirPlay, troubleshooting common issues, and making the most of this feature for both entertainment and productivity.

## What is AirPlay and Why Should You Use It?

AirPlay allows you to wirelessly stream content from your iPhone to other Apple or AirPlay-compatible devices. Think of it as an invisible HDMI cable that lets you send videos, music, and even your entire iPhone screen to another device.

### KEY BENEFITS OF AIRPLAY

- **Wire-free convenience** – No more dealing with cables or adapters.
- **High-quality streaming** – Supports **HD video, lossless audio, and smooth screen mirroring**.
- **Multi-device support** – Works with **Apple TV, smart TVs, speakers, and even Mac computers**.
- **Great for entertainment and work** – Watch movies, stream music, or mirror your screen for presentations.

For Susan Carter, our buyer persona, AirPlay is perfect for watching family videos on the big screen, listening to music throughout the house, or using it for an easy FaceTime session with her children and grandkids on a larger display.

## Devices That Support AirPlay

Before getting started, it's important to know which devices are AirPlay-compatible.

### AIRPLAY-COMPATIBLE DEVICES

- **Apple TV** (all models with tvOS)
- **Smart TVs** with built-in AirPlay (LG, Samsung, Sony, Vizio, etc.)
- **Mac computers** (MacBook, iMac, Mac Mini with macOS Monterey or later)
- **HomePod & HomePod mini**
- **AirPlay-enabled speakers** (Bose, Sonos, Bang & Olufsen, etc.)
- **Other AirPlay-compatible receivers** (AV receivers, projectors, and sound systems)

If you're unsure whether your device supports AirPlay, check the manufacturer's website or look for the AirPlay icon on your TV or speaker's settings menu.

## How to Enable AirPlay on Your iPhone

To begin using AirPlay, you need to ensure it's enabled and that your devices are on the same Wi-Fi network.

### STEP 1: CONNECT TO THE SAME WI-FI NETWORK

1. Open **Settings** on your iPhone.
2. Tap **Wi-Fi** and make sure your iPhone and the AirPlay-compatible device are connected to the **same network**.

### STEP 2: TURN ON AIRPLAY ON YOUR TV OR SPEAKER

- **Apple TV**: Go to **Settings > AirPlay & HomeKit > Turn AirPlay On**.
- **Smart TVs**: Navigate to the **Settings > AirPlay** section and enable it.
- **Speakers**: Most AirPlay-compatible speakers automatically enable AirPlay when connected to Wi-Fi.

## How to Stream Video from Your iPhone Using AirPlay

Watching a video on your iPhone is great, but sometimes you want a bigger screen. Here's how to stream movies, YouTube videos, or even a FaceTime call using AirPlay.

### METHOD 1: STREAMING DIRECTLY FROM AN APP

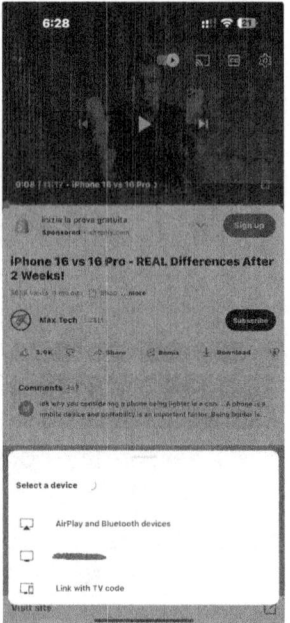

Many popular apps have built-in AirPlay support, including Apple TV, YouTube, Netflix, Hulu, and Disney+.

1. Open the **video app** (e.g., YouTube, Apple TV).
2. Start playing a video.
3. Tap the **AirPlay icon** (a rectangle with a triangle at the bottom).
4. Select your **Apple TV or Smart TV** from the list.
5. Your video will now **play on the big screen** while your iPhone acts as a remote.

### METHOD 2: MIRRORING YOUR ENTIRE IPHONE SCREEN

If an app doesn't support direct AirPlay streaming, you can use Screen Mirroring to display your entire iPhone on another screen.

1. Swipe down from the **top-right corner** of your iPhone to open **Control Center**.
2. Tap **Screen Mirroring**.
3. Select your **Apple TV or Smart TV**.

4.  Your **entire iPhone screen** will now be mirrored to the TV.

## How to Stream Music from Your iPhone Using AirPlay

If you have AirPlay-compatible speakers, you can play music wirelessly from Apple Music, Spotify, or any other audio app.

METHOD 1: USING THE AIRPLAY ICON IN MUSIC APPS

1.  Open **Apple Music** (or Spotify, Pandora, etc.).
2.  Play a song and tap the **AirPlay icon**.
3.  Choose an **AirPlay speaker** or multiple speakers for multi-room audio.

METHOD 2: USING CONTROL CENTER FOR MULTI-ROOM AUDIO

1.  Open **Control Center** on your iPhone.
2.  Tap the **Audio Playback widget**.
3.  Select **AirPlay** and choose **multiple speakers** for synchronized playback across your home.

This is a great way to fill your house with music when entertaining guests or just relaxing.

## Troubleshooting Common AirPlay Issues

If AirPlay isn't working, here are some quick fixes:

1.  Can't Find Your Device in AirPlay Menu?

- Ensure **both devices are on the same Wi-Fi network**.
- Restart your **iPhone and the AirPlay device**.
- On **Apple TV**, go to **Settings > AirPlay & HomeKit > Allow Access**, and make sure it's set to **"Everyone" or "Anyone on the Same Network"**.

2.  Video Lags or Buffers During AirPlay

- Move **closer to your Wi-Fi router**.
- Try a **wired Ethernet connection** for Apple TV or your Smart TV.
- Reduce **other Wi-Fi usage** in your home (e.g., pause downloads or streaming on other devices).

3.  No Sound When Using AirPlay?

- Ensure the **TV or speaker volume** is turned up.
- Check **iPhone volume** and mute settings.

- Restart both devices and try again.

## Creative Ways to Use AirPlay

Beyond movies and music, here are some fun and useful ways to use AirPlay:

- **Presentations** – Use AirPlay to **mirror your iPhone on a TV** for work presentations.
- **Photo slideshows** – Display family photos on your **big screen for gatherings**.
- **Gaming** – Some games support **AirPlay for a larger display experience**.
- **Workout videos** – Mirror your favorite **fitness apps to your TV** for home workouts.

With AirPlay, your iPhone becomes a wireless entertainment hub, allowing you to enjoy music, movies, and even productivity tools on bigger screens and better speakers. With just a few taps, you can elevate your entertainment experience and make your home smarter and more connected.

# Playing Games and Exploring Apple Arcade for Fun and Connection

Mobile gaming has evolved far beyond simple puzzles and time-killers. Today, the iPhone is a powerful gaming device, capable of running high-quality, console-like games while offering an extensive library of casual, family-friendly, and immersive experiences. Whether you're looking to relax with a simple puzzle game, engage in an adventure, or connect with friends and family through multiplayer gaming, your iPhone has something for everyone.

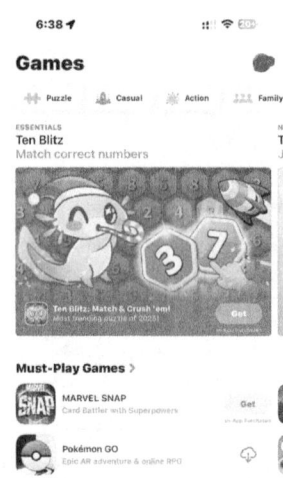

A standout feature for iPhone gamers is Apple Arcade, a subscription service offering hundreds of premium games with no ads or in-app purchases. If you're new to gaming or looking for a way to enjoy high-quality titles without the distractions of pay-to-win mechanics, Apple Arcade is worth exploring.

This section will guide you through how to find and play games on your iPhone, set up Apple Arcade, and make the most of gaming on the go.

## Discovering the World of Mobile Gaming on Your iPhone

Your iPhone's App Store is home to thousands of games across every genre imaginable, from strategy and RPGs to action-packed shooters and relaxing simulators.

### FINDING AND DOWNLOADING GAMES FROM THE APP STORE

1. Open the **App Store** on your iPhone.
2. Tap the **Games** tab at the bottom of the screen.
3. Browse through featured games, categories, or use the search bar to find specific titles.
4. Tap on a game to see its **details, ratings, screenshots, and reviews**.
5. If it's a free game, tap **Get**; if it's a paid game, tap the price and confirm with **Face ID or Touch ID**.
6. Wait for the game to download, then tap **Open** to start playing.

Once installed, games appear on your home screen or within the App Library, making it easy to launch them anytime.

## What is Apple Arcade and Why Should You Try It?

Apple Arcade is Apple's answer to premium mobile gaming without the hassle of ads, in-app purchases, or subscriptions to individual games.

### KEY FEATURES OF APPLE ARCADE

- **Access to 200+ high-quality games** – New games added regularly.
- **No ads or microtransactions** – Play without interruptions.
- **Family Sharing** – Up to **six family members** can play under one subscription.
- **Works across Apple devices** – Play on **iPhone, iPad, Mac, and Apple TV**.
- **Offline play** – Download games and play without an internet connection.

### HOW TO SUBSCRIBE TO APPLE ARCADE

1. Open the **App Store** and go to the **Arcade** tab.
2. Tap **Try It Free** (Apple offers a free trial for new subscribers).
3. Confirm the subscription using **Face ID or Touch ID**.
4. Browse the Arcade library and **tap on a game to download and play**.

Apple Arcade is perfect for casual gamers, families, and those who enjoy story-driven or immersive gameplay experiences. For Susan Carter, it's an easy way to explore

fun games without worrying about hidden costs or distractions from in-game purchases.

## Top Apple Arcade Games to Try

If you're wondering where to start, here are some must-play titles available on Apple Arcade:

- **Cozy Grove** – A relaxing, animal-filled life sim with an adorable art style.
- **Oceanhorn 2** – A Zelda-like action-adventure game with stunning graphics.
- **Mini Motorways** – A strategy game where you design city roads to keep traffic flowing.
- **Sneaky Sasquatch** – A lighthearted game where you play as a mischievous sasquatch sneaking around campsites.
- **LEGO Brawls** – A fun, multiplayer brawler featuring LEGO characters.

These games are designed to run smoothly on your iPhone and integrate seamlessly across Apple devices, allowing you to pause on one device and resume on another.

## Enhancing Your Gaming Experience on iPhone

### USING EXTERNAL CONTROLLERS FOR A CONSOLE-LIKE FEEL

While touchscreen controls work well for many games, some titles—especially action and racing games—benefit from a physical controller. Your iPhone supports PlayStation and Xbox controllers, along with Apple's own MFi (Made for iPhone) controllers.

How to Connect a Bluetooth Controller:

1. Turn on your **PlayStation or Xbox controller**.
2. Open **Settings > Bluetooth** on your iPhone.
3. Put your controller into **pairing mode** (for PS controllers, press and hold the **PS + Share** buttons; for Xbox, press and hold the **Pairing button**).
4. Select the controller from the list and **tap to pair**.

Once connected, your controller works with Apple Arcade games and many App Store titles, offering a more comfortable and precise gaming experience.

## Multiplayer and Social Gaming on iPhone

Gaming is often more fun when shared with others. Many iPhone games include multiplayer modes to connect with family and friends.

- **Game Center** – Apple's built-in gaming network lets you **track achievements, challenge friends, and join leaderboards**.
- **Multiplayer games** – Play online co-op or competitive games like **Mario Kart Tour, Among Us, or Words With Friends**.
- **Screen Sharing** – Use **AirPlay** to display your game on a TV for a **console-like gaming night**.
- **Family-Friendly Games** – Titles like **Heads Up!** or **Pictionary Air** turn game night into a fun-filled event.

For Susan Carter, multiplayer games are a great way to stay connected with her kids and grandkids, whether through word puzzles, trivia, or casual games.

## Managing Storage for Games

Games can take up a significant amount of storage space, especially large adventure or racing games. To free up space without deleting important apps, you can:

1. Go to **Settings > General > iPhone Storage**.
2. Scroll to find **games that take up the most space**.
3. Tap the game and select **Offload App** (keeps data but removes the app until reinstalled).
4. Use **iCloud to back up game data**, so you don't lose progress.

With Apple Arcade, App Store games, and multiplayer experiences, your iPhone is a full-fledged gaming device. Whether you want to relax, challenge yourself, or bond with loved ones through games, the possibilities are endless.

# Managing Your Media Library: Downloading, Storing, and Organizing

Your iPhone is more than just a communication device—it's your entertainment hub, holding your favorite movies, music, podcasts, audiobooks, and photos. But as your library grows, so does the need to effectively manage your media to avoid clutter, storage issues, and difficulty finding what you need.

This section will walk you through downloading, storing, and organizing your media library, ensuring your entertainment experience is seamless and stress-free.

# Downloading Media: How to Keep Your Favorite Content Accessible

Whether you're preparing for a long flight, heading somewhere without internet access, or simply wanting on-demand content without buffering, downloading media is a must. Your iPhone allows you to download music, movies, podcasts, and audiobooks from various platforms.

## DOWNLOADING MUSIC FROM APPLE MUSIC OR SPOTIFY

- **Apple Music**:

1. Open the **Apple Music** app.
2. Find the **song, album, or playlist** you want to download.
3. Tap the **Download icon (cloud with a downward arrow)** next to the track or album.
4. Access your downloaded music by going to **Library > Downloaded Music**.

- **Spotify (Premium Required)**:

1. Open **Spotify** and go to your **library**.
2. Select the **album, playlist, or podcast** you want to download.
3. Tap the **Download toggle** to save it offline.
4. Listen anytime via the **Downloads section**.

## DOWNLOADING MOVIES & TV SHOWS FROM APPLE TV, NETFLIX, OR PRIME VIDEO

Streaming services let you download movies and TV shows for offline viewing. Here's how:

- **Apple TV App**:

1. Open the **Apple TV** app.
2. Find a movie or show and **tap the Download button**.
3. Access it later in the **Library > Downloaded section**.

- **Netflix or Amazon Prime Video**:

1. Open the **Netflix or Prime Video** app.
2. Tap on a show or movie.
3. Look for the **Download icon** and tap it.
4. Watch offline from the **Downloads section**.

> 💡 Tip: Not all titles are downloadable due to licensing restrictions, so check availability within the app.

### Downloading Audiobooks & Podcasts

- **Apple Books & Audible (Audiobooks)**:

1. Open **Apple Books** or **Audible**.
2. Find your purchased book and tap **Download**.
3. Play from the **Library section**.

- **Apple Podcasts**:

1. Open the **Podcasts** app.
2. Browse or search for a show.
3. Tap **Download Episode** to listen offline.

Downloading content before travel or areas with poor connectivity ensures you always have entertainment at your fingertips.

## Storing Media: Managing iPhone Storage Efficiently

With so many downloads, storage space can fill up quickly. To prevent running out of space, monitor and manage your storage wisely.

### Checking Available Storage

1. Open **Settings**.
2. Tap **General > iPhone Storage**.
3. Review the breakdown of used space.
4. Delete unnecessary media to **free up storage**.

### Using iCloud for Cloud Storage

If your iPhone storage is getting tight, consider moving your media to iCloud:

1. Go to **Settings > Apple ID > iCloud**.
2. Turn on **iCloud for Photos, Music, and Books**.
3. Enable **Optimize iPhone Storage** to store only recent media locally.

> 💡 **Tip:** iCloud only offers **5GB free**—consider upgrading if you store a lot of media.

### Offloading Unused Apps and Media

For apps you rarely use but don't want to delete permanently:

1. Go to **Settings > General > iPhone Storage**.

2. Scroll down and tap an app.
3. Select **Offload App** (this removes the app but keeps its data).

For downloaded movies or music you no longer need:

- Open the **TV or Music app**.
- Go to **Downloads** and swipe left to delete content.

Regularly clearing old downloads helps keep your iPhone running smoothly.

## Organizing Media: Keeping Everything Easy to Find

A well-organized library ensures you spend less time searching and more time enjoying your media.

### CREATING PLAYLISTS FOR MUSIC & PODCASTS

- **Apple Music**:
1. Go to **Library > Playlists**.
2. Tap **New Playlist**, name it, and add songs.
3. Tap **Done** to save.

- **Spotify**:
1. Tap **Your Library > Playlists > Create Playlist**.
2. Add songs and hit **Save**.

### SORTING AUDIOBOOKS BY CATEGORIES

- In **Apple Books**, go to **Library > Collections**.
- Tap **New Collection** to organize books by **genre, author, or mood**.

### ORGANIZING MOVIES & TV SHOWS IN APPLE TV APP

- Use **Watchlist** to keep track of what you want to watch.
- Group movies into **collections** based on genre.

## Sharing Media Across Devices

Apple's ecosystem allows you to seamlessly share content across devices using:

- **AirDrop** – Quickly share music, photos, and videos with other Apple users.
- **Family Sharing** – Share purchases like **Apple Music, books, and TV shows** with family.
- **Handoff** – Start listening to a podcast on your iPhone and continue on your iPad.

Example: Susan Carter loves listening to audiobooks on her iPhone but prefers to watch movies on her iPad or Apple TV. With Handoff and iCloud, her media syncs automatically across devices.

## Maintaining a Clutter-Free Media Library

Here are some final best practices for keeping your media library clean and efficient:

- **Regularly remove old downloads** (movies, music, and podcasts).
- **Use streaming over downloading** when possible.
- **Enable iCloud storage** for photos and music.
- **Create smart playlists & folders** to keep everything organized.
- **Check storage usage monthly** to avoid slowdowns.

By following these steps, you'll always have your entertainment ready, organized, and easily accessible—without the headache of clutter or storage issues.

# CHAPTER 6

# Navigating Everyday Apps with Confidence

## Calendar and Reminders: Staying Organized Every Day

Keeping track of appointments, tasks, and daily activities can be overwhelming—especially when juggling work, personal life, and unexpected responsibilities. Thankfully, your iPhone comes equipped with two powerful built-in tools: the Calendar app and the Reminders app, designed to help you stay organized effortlessly.

With these apps, you can set alerts for important events, create to-do lists, schedule meetings, track deadlines, and even share tasks with others. This section will guide you through mastering these tools to ensure you never miss an important moment.

### Using the Calendar App to Stay on Top of Your Schedule

The Calendar app on your iPhone is more than just a digital version of a traditional planner. It integrates with email, reminders, and even third-party apps to streamline your schedule seamlessly.

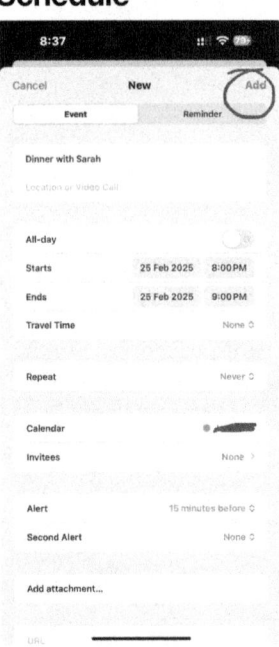

### Adding Events and Appointments

Instead of keeping mental notes about doctor's appointments, family gatherings, or work meetings, add them to your Calendar for easy reference. Here's how:

1. Open the **Calendar** app.
2. Tap the **"+" icon** in the top-right corner.
3. Enter the **event title** (e.g., "Dinner with Sarah").
4. Select the **date and time**.
5. If it's a recurring event (e.g., "Weekly Yoga Class"), tap **"Repeat"** and choose how often.
6. Set an **alert** (e.g., "15 minutes before") to get a notification.

7.  Tap **"Add"** to save the event.

> 💡 **Tip:** If you receive an email with an event invitation (e.g., a Zoom meeting), your iPhone **automatically suggests adding it to your calendar**. Simply tap **"Add to Calendar"** in the email preview.

## CREATING MULTIPLE CALENDARS FOR DIFFERENT AREAS OF YOUR LIFE

Rather than cluttering one calendar with work meetings, personal appointments, and family events, you can create separate calendars for each category.

1.  Open **Calendar > Calendars > Add Calendar**.
2.  Name it (e.g., "Work" or "Family").
3.  Assign a color to easily differentiate schedules.

Now, when adding an event, choose which calendar it belongs to—helping keep work and personal life separate but organized.

## SHARING CALENDARS WITH FAMILY AND COLLEAGUES

If you need to coordinate schedules with family members or work teams, you can share your calendar:

1.  Open **Calendar > Calendars**.
2.  Tap the "i" next to the calendar you want to share.
3.  Select **"Add Person"** and enter their email.
4.  They'll receive an invitation to view or edit the calendar.

Example: Susan Carter shares a family calendar with her husband so they both stay updated on their children's school events, doctor appointments, and vacations— eliminating the "Did you remember?" conversations.

## Using the Reminders App to Stay on Track

The Reminders app is like having a personal assistant— perfect for to-do lists, grocery shopping, medication reminders, or even work deadlines.

## CREATING A NEW REMINDER

1.  Open the **Reminders** app.
2.  Tap **"New Reminder"** and enter your task (e.g., "Pick up dry cleaning").
3.  Tap **Details** to:

- » Set a time-based alert (e.g., "Tomorrow at 3 PM").
- » Set a location-based alert (e.g., "Remind me when I arrive at the grocery store").
- » Assign a priority level to categorize urgency.

4. Tap **"Add"** to save it.

> 💡 Tip: If you say, "**Hey Siri, remind me to call Mom at 6 PM**," Siri will automatically add it to **Reminders**.

## USING SMART LISTS FOR BETTER ORGANIZATION

Your iPhone automatically sorts reminders into Smart Lists such as Today, Scheduled, and Flagged, helping you prioritize what matters most. You can also create custom lists:

1. Open the **Reminders app**.
2. Tap **"Add List"** at the bottom.
3. Name it (e.g., "Groceries" or "Work Tasks").
4. Add tasks to it for better categorization.

Example: Susan creates a "Home Tasks" list with reminders like "Change air filters" and "Water the plants."

## SETTING RECURRING REMINDERS

For tasks that repeat (like paying bills, weekly workouts, or medication reminders), set recurring alerts:

1. Create a **new reminder**.
2. Tap **Details > Repeat**.
3. Choose an option (daily, weekly, or custom).

Now, you won't have to manually enter these reminders every time!

## Syncing Calendar and Reminders Across All Devices

To ensure you never miss an event or task, sync Calendar and Reminders across all Apple devices:

1. Open **Settings > Apple ID > iCloud**.
2. Toggle **Calendar** and **Reminders** ON.

Now, any update made on your iPhone will reflect on your iPad or Mac automatically.

## Best Practices for Keeping Your Digital Life Organized

- Check your Calendar and Reminders daily—treat them as your digital planner.
- Use color-coded calendars to separate personal, work, and family events.

- Set time and location-based alerts for better reminders.
- Use Siri for hands-free organization (e.g., "Remind me to take vitamins at 9 AM").
- Sync everything with iCloud for cross-device accessibility.

With these simple strategies, your iPhone can keep your life on track effortlessly—so you can focus on what truly matters.

# Notes and To-Do Lists: Your Digital Notebook Made Simple

In a world where we are constantly juggling tasks, appointments, ideas, and reminders, having a reliable system to capture thoughts and organize tasks is essential. Thankfully, your iPhone provides two powerful built-in tools: the Notes app and the Reminders app, which work seamlessly together to keep your life on track.

Whether you're jotting down a shopping list, brainstorming ideas, keeping track of important information, or creating a structured to-do list, these apps help you stay productive and organized. This guide will walk you through how to use these tools effectively, ensuring that nothing slips through the cracks.

## Mastering the Notes App: Your Digital Notebook

The Notes app is a versatile tool that goes beyond basic text entry. It can store handwritten notes, images, checklists, scanned documents, and even audio recordings.

CREATING AND FORMATTING A NEW NOTE

1. Open the **Notes app**.
2. Tap the **compose button** (the square with a pencil icon).
3. Start typing your note.
4. Use the toolbar to:

   » **Bold, italicize, or underline i**mportant text.
   » Create bu**lleted or numbered lists.**
   » Insert ta**bles f**or structured information.
   » Add att**achments** like photos or scanned documents.

> 💡 **Tip:** Use **folders** to organize your notes. For example, create separate folders for "Work Notes," "Personal Ideas," and "Grocery Lists" to keep everything tidy.

## USING CHECKLISTS FOR TASK MANAGEMENT

Need a grocery list or a packing checklist for an upcoming trip? Convert a note into a checklist:

1. Open a note.
2. Tap the **checkmark icon** in the toolbar.
3. Start adding items—each will have a checkable box next to it.
4. Check off items as you complete them.

This feature is great for to-do lists, project planning, and tracking progress on goals.

## SCANNING DOCUMENTS AND STORING IMPORTANT INFO

Instead of keeping paper receipts, contracts, or handwritten notes, scan them directly into Notes:

1. Open a note.
2. Tap the **camera icon**.
3. Select **"Scan Documents"** and position your iPhone over the paper.
4. The document will be captured and stored in the note.

Example: Susan, our buyer persona, scans her handwritten recipes into the Notes app, so she never loses them.

## SYNCING NOTES ACROSS DEVICES

To access notes on your Mac, iPad, or even a Windows computer, enable iCloud sync:

1. Open **Settings > Apple ID > iCloud**.
2. Toggle **Notes ON**.

Now, any edits you make will sync across devices automatically.

## Using the Reminders App for To-Do Lists and Tasks

The Reminders app is the ideal tool for tracking tasks, deadlines, and errands. Unlike Notes, which are more for capturing ideas, Reminders is designed for actionable tasks with alerts and priorities.

### CREATING A NEW REMINDER

1. Open the **Reminders app**.
2. Tap **"New Reminder"** and enter your task.
3. Tap **Details** to:
   » Set a date **and time-based alert (**e.g., "Dentist appointment at 3 PM").
   » Assign a lo**cation-based reminder (**e.g., "Remind me to buy milk when I arrive at the store").

&raquo;   Add a **priority level to** mark importance.

4.   Tap **"Add"** to save.

> 💡 Tip: If you say, **"Hey Siri, remind me to call John at 7 PM,"** Siri will create the reminder for you!

## ORGANIZING REMINDERS WITH LISTS AND SMART SORTING

For better task management, create custom lists:

1.   Open the **Reminders app**.
2.   Tap **"Add List"** at the bottom.
3.   Name it (e.g., "Work Tasks" or "Home Errands").
4.   Add reminders under each list.

Your iPhone automatically categorizes reminders into Smart Lists such as:

- **Today:** Shows reminders due today.
- **Scheduled:** Displays tasks with set dates.
- **Flagged:** Prioritizes critical tasks.

Example: Susan has a "Home Tasks" list that reminds her to pay bills, call the plumber, and reorder prescriptions.

## USING LOCATION-BASED REMINDERS

Need to be reminded to pick up something when you arrive somewhere?

1.   Create a new reminder.
2.   Tap **Details > Location**.
3.   Select **"When I Arrive"** or **"When I Leave"** and enter a location (e.g., Grocery Store).
4.   Tap **Done**.

Now, as soon as you arrive at the specified location, your iPhone will alert you!

Example: Set a reminder like *"Pick up dog food when I reach the pet store"*—and let your iPhone do the rest.

## Syncing Notes and Reminders for Seamless Productivity

To ensure you never miss a note or task, sync both apps across all Apple devices:

1.   Open **Settings > Apple ID > iCloud**.
2.   Toggle **Notes** and **Reminders ON**.

Now, updates made on your iPhone will instantly reflect on your iPad or Mac.

## Best Practices for Staying Organized

- Use Notes for reference material (ideas, research, checklists).
- Use Reminders for tasks that require action (appointments, deadlines).
- Set alerts and due dates to stay on track.
- Use Siri for hands-free note-taking and reminders.
- Sync everything with iCloud for easy access from any Apple device.

With these simple strategies, your iPhone can become your ultimate digital assistant, keeping your life organized and stress-free.

# Health and Fitness Apps: Tracking Your Well-Being Effortlessly

Your iPhone can be much more than just a device for calls, texts, and social media—it can also be your personal health assistant. Whether you're trying to stay active, monitor your heart rate, track nutrition, improve sleep quality, or even manage stress levels, your iPhone comes equipped with powerful health and fitness apps to help you stay on top of your well-being.

In this guide, we'll explore how you can effortlessly track your health and fitness, integrate your iPhone with wearable devices like the Apple Watch, and use built-in and third-party apps to maintain a healthier lifestyle.

## The Health App: Your Personal Health Dashboard

The Health app, pre-installed on every iPhone, serves as your central hub for all things related to wellness. It gathers data from your iPhone, Apple Watch, and even third-party apps to provide a comprehensive overview of your health.

SETTING UP THE HEALTH APP

1. Open the **Health app**.
2. Tap **"Summary"** to see an overview of your health data.
3. Tap **your profile picture** (top right) to set up:

- Me**dical ID (**important for emergencies).
- Hea**lth details l**ike height, weight, and age.
- Ap**ps & devices t**hat sync with Health.

> 📍 Tip: The Health app automatically counts your steps, distance walked, and flights climbed—even without an Apple Watch!

## Tracking Daily Activity and Workouts

For many, staying active is a key aspect of well-being. The Activity Rings (Move, Exercise, and Stand) in the Health app and Fitness app help keep you motivated:

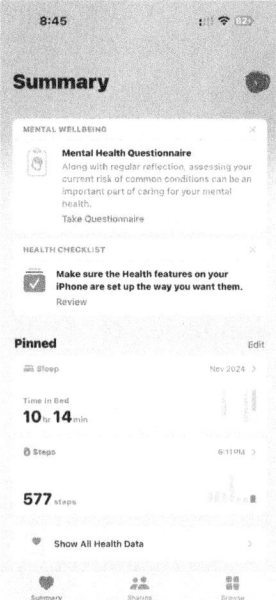

- **Move Ring**: Tracks calories burned throughout the day.
- **Exercise Ring**: Records **active exercise minutes** (e.g., brisk walking, workouts).
- **Stand Ring**: Reminds you to stand up and move at least once per hour.

If you own an Apple Watch, the Fitness app also logs heart rate, steps, and workout intensity, making it a perfect fitness tracker.

## Using Fitness Apps to Stay Active

While the Health app offers basic tracking, third-party fitness apps provide additional features to enhance your workout routine.

### Apple Fitness+: Personalized Workout Coaching

For those who prefer guided workouts, Apple Fitness+ offers:

- **On-demand workout videos** (yoga, HIIT, strength training, etc.).
- **Integration with Apple Watch** to track heart rate and calories.
- **Weekly challenges and community features** for motivation.

> 💡 **Example:** Susan, our buyer persona, uses **Fitness+** for 10-minute guided stretching routines after work.

### Third-Party Apps for Different Fitness Needs

- **Nike Training Club** – Personalized strength and cardio workouts.
- **Strava** – Ideal for runners and cyclists tracking GPS routes.
- **MyFitnessPal** – Combines **nutrition tracking** with fitness goals.

Most of these apps sync with Apple Health, so all data appears in one place!

## Tracking Sleep and Recovery

Getting enough rest is just as important as exercise. With iPhone's Sleep Tracking feature, you can monitor sleep patterns and establish better bedtime habits.

### SETTING UP SLEEP TRACKING

1. Open **Health > Sleep**.
2. Tap **Get Started** and set your bedtime schedule.
3. If you own an **Apple Watch**, wear it overnight to track sleep duration, heart rate, and respiratory rate.

For deeper insights, third-party sleep apps like AutoSleep and Pillow provide detailed sleep cycle analysis.

> 💡 Tip: Enable **Wind Down Mode** (via Sleep settings) to **reduce blue light** and help you relax before bedtime.

## Monitoring Heart Health and Stress Levels

Your iPhone can help detect irregular heart patterns and guide relaxation through mindfulness features.

### USING ECG AND HEART RATE TRACKING (APPLE WATCH REQUIRED)

1. Open **Health > Heart**.
2. Track **resting heart rate, ECG, and oxygen saturation** (Apple Watch Series 6+).
3. Set **irregular heart rhythm alerts** for early warnings.

> 💡 Tip: The Breathe app helps reduce stress by guiding you through **mindful breathing exercises**.

For stress management, apps like Calm and Headspace integrate with Apple Health to log relaxation sessions.

## Nutrition and Hydration Tracking

Staying hydrated and eating balanced meals are essential to overall health. Your iPhone can help with:

- **WaterMinder** – Logs daily **water intake** and sets reminders.
- **Lifesum** – Tracks **calories, macronutrients, and meal plans**.
- **MyFitnessPal** – Logs **food intake** and scans barcodes for easy tracking.

> 💡 Example: Susan uses **Lifesum** to track her protein intake while following a low-carb diet.

Most of these apps sync seamlessly with Health, allowing you to monitor hydration, nutrition, and exercise data in one place.

## Using Wearables and Smart Devices for Health Tracking

Your iPhone supports various smart devices that sync with Apple Health:

- **Smart Scales** (e.g., Withings) – Measures weight, BMI, and body composition.
- **Blood Pressure Monitors** (e.g., QardioArm) – Helps monitor heart health.
- **Glucose Monitors** – Tracks blood sugar for diabetes management.

> 💡 **Tip:** Check **Settings > Privacy > Health** to manage app permissions for sharing health data securely.

## Final Thoughts

With the right apps and tools, your iPhone can be a powerful health and fitness companion. Whether you're counting steps, tracking sleep, monitoring heart rate, or setting fitness goals, integrating Health, Fitness+, and third-party apps helps you stay in control of your well-being.

By syncing everything in one place, your iPhone ensures you stay on track—effortlessly.

# Weather, News, and Other Utilities for Staying Informed

Your iPhone is a powerful tool for staying informed, whether you want to check the weather before heading out, stay updated on the latest news, or access essential utilities like a calculator, translator, or voice recorder. With a combination of built-in apps and third-party options, you can ensure that you have access to accurate, real-time information whenever you need it.

Let's dive into how to use the best features and apps to stay informed effortlessly.

## The Weather App: Plan Your Day with Confidence

No one likes to be caught off guard by unexpected rain, snow, or scorching heat. The Weather app on your iPhone provides hourly, daily, and even long-term forecasts to help you prepare accordingly.

USING THE WEATHER APP

1. Open the **Weather app** to see your current location's forecast.
2. Scroll down for additional insights, including:

- » **Hourly forecast** with temperature and precipitation.
- » **10-day forecast** to help you plan ahead.
- » **Air quality index (AQI)** to check for pollution levels.
- » **Sunrise and sunset times.**
- » **Wind speed and direction** (useful for outdoor activities).

> 💡 Tip: Want to check multiple locations? Tap the **three-line menu** in the bottom right corner and add **your favorite cities**.

## Staying Updated with News and Headlines

In a world of fast-changing events, having access to trusted news sources is crucial. The Apple News app curates stories from top publishers based on your interests, ensuring you get relevant, high-quality journalism.

### USING APPLE NEWS

1. Open **Apple News** to browse the **Today feed**.
2. Customize your feed by **following topics** (e.g., technology, health, sports).
3. Save articles for later by tapping the **bookmark icon**.
4. Enable **notifications** for breaking news alerts.

> 💡 Tip: Subscribe to **Apple News+** for premium content from **The Wall Street Journal, National Geographic, and more**.

### Alternatives to Apple News

If you prefer different news formats, try:

- **Google News** – AI-powered headlines based on your interests.
- **Flipboard** – A magazine-style aggregator with customizable topics.
- **BBC News, CNN, or Reuters** – For global coverage and live updates.

> 💡 Example: Susan, our buyer persona, **uses Apple News** in the morning while drinking coffee to scan headlines about health and lifestyle trends.

## Essential Utilities: Tools That Make Life Easier

Your iPhone comes with several utility apps designed to simplify everyday tasks. Here are a few you should take full advantage of:

### CALCULATOR: MORE THAN JUST BASIC MATH

- Rotate your iPhone **sideways** to reveal the **scientific calculator**.

- Copy and paste numbers for quick calculations.
- Use **long press** on the delete button to erase digits one by one.

> 📍 Tip: Need a more advanced calculator? Download **PCalc** or **CalConvert** from the App Store.

## TRANSLATOR: BREAKING LANGUAGE BARRIERS

The Translate app on your iPhone makes it easy to communicate in different languages.

1. Open **Translate** and choose your languages.
2. Type or **speak** your phrase for an instant translation.
3. Use **Conversation Mode** for real-time bilingual dialogue.

> 📍 Tip: Download languages **offline** to use them without an internet connection—perfect for travel.

## VOICE MEMOS: CAPTURE IDEAS ON THE GO

Whether you need to record a lecture, a quick idea, or an interview, Voice Memos is a powerful yet simple tool.

- Open **Voice Memos** and tap the **red button** to start recording.
- Use **trim and edit tools** to remove unwanted parts.
- Sync recordings across devices with **iCloud**.

> 📍 Example: Susan uses **Voice Memos** to **record shopping lists** or **reminders for her kids' school activities**.

## Stock Market, Maps, and Other Useful Apps

Beyond weather and news, there are other essential apps for staying informed:

- **Stocks** – Track stock prices and market trends.
- **Maps** – Get real-time traffic updates and directions.
- **Measure** – Use augmented reality (AR) to measure objects.

> 📍 Tip: Add widgets to your **Home Screen** for quick access to **stocks, weather, and news headlines**.

## Final Thoughts

Your iPhone is a powerhouse of information, helping you stay prepared and up-to-date. From weather forecasts and breaking news to handy utilities like voice memos and translation, mastering these tools will make your everyday life smoother and more efficient.

# Finding and Using the Best Apps for Your Hobbies

Your iPhone isn't just a communication tool—it's a gateway to exploring and enhancing your hobbies. Whether you're into photography, fitness, art, gardening, music, writing, or learning a new skill, there's an app that can help you stay inspired, organized, and engaged. But with millions of apps available in the App Store, how do you find the best ones for your interests?

Let's explore how to discover the right hobby apps, evaluate their usefulness, and make the most of them.

### Exploring the App Store: Finding Apps That Match Your Interests

The App Store is packed with apps designed for every passion imaginable. But instead of endlessly scrolling, use these strategies to find quality apps:

- **Use the Search Bar Wisely**: Be specific. Instead of typing *gardening*, try *organic vegetable gardening planner* for better results.
- **Explore Curated Lists**: The **"Apps We Love"** and **"Top Charts"** sections highlight high-quality apps recommended by Apple.
- **Check User Reviews**: Look at **both positive and negative feedback** to get a realistic sense of an app's performance.
- **Look for Free Trials**: Some premium apps offer free versions or trial periods before requiring payment.
- **Check Developer Reputation**: Apps from **big-name brands** or **universities** (e.g., Duolingo for languages or Adobe for design) tend to be more reliable.

> 📍 Example: If Susan, our buyer persona, wants to **improve her photography skills**, she might search for *photo editing apps for beginners* and **find Adobe Lightroom or VSCO** with strong reviews and tutorials.

## Best Apps for Popular Hobbies

Here's a breakdown of some of the best apps for common hobbies:

### PHOTOGRAPHY & PHOTO EDITING

- **Snapseed** – A free, pro-level editing app with powerful tools.
- **VSCO** – Great for stylish filters and subtle enhancements.
- **Adobe Lightroom Mobile** – A must-have for serious photographers.
- **Halide Mark II** – A professional camera app with manual controls.

> **Tip:** If you're taking **family photos**, try an app with a **portrait enhancement feature** like Facetune.

### FITNESS & OUTDOOR ACTIVITIES

- **Nike Training Club** – Free guided workouts for all levels.
- **MyFitnessPal** – Tracks diet, exercise, and calories.
- **AllTrails** – Maps out hiking and biking trails with user reviews.
- **Strava** – Perfect for runners and cyclists to track progress.

> **Example:** Susan enjoys **weekend hiking with friends**, so she might use **AllTrails** to find scenic trails near her.

### MUSIC & CREATIVE ARTS

- **GarageBand** – Create and record your own music.
- **Yousician** – Learn to play instruments with interactive lessons.
- **Procreate Pocket** – A top-tier drawing and digital painting app.
- **Canva** – Design anything from social media posts to invitations.

> **Tip:** If you love **singing**, Smule offers **karaoke sessions** with real-time audio effects.

### GARDENING & HOME IMPROVEMENT

- **PictureThis** – Identify plants and get care tips.
- **Garden Planner** – Plan and track your garden growth.
- **iScape** – Design landscaping ideas with AR.
- **Pinterest** – Endless DIY and inspiration boards.

> **Example:** If Susan wants to **grow her own herbs**, she might use **PictureThis** to learn about different plant needs.

## LANGUAGE LEARNING & READING

- **Duolingo** – Fun, gamified language learning.
- **Rosetta Stone** – Deeper language immersion techniques.
- **Kindle** – Access thousands of books on the go.
- **Libby** – Borrow free e-books and audiobooks from local libraries.

> 💡 Tip: If you love **classic literature**, try **Serial Reader**, which delivers bite-sized portions of classic books daily.

## Maximizing the Use of Hobby Apps

Downloading an app is only the first step. Here's how to get the most out of your hobby apps:

1. Set a Routine

- If you're learning a new skill (e.g., playing the piano on **Simply Piano**), schedule **daily practice reminders**.
- For fitness, set a **goal in MyFitnessPal** or enable **Apple Health tracking**.

2. Join Communities & Challenges

- Many apps have **social features** where you can share progress and get feedback.
- Strava and Duolingo let you **compete with friends** for motivation.

3. Take Advantage of Free Content

- Many apps offer **free classes, tips, or tutorials** before requiring a subscription.
- YouTube is a great companion—if an app has a complex feature, chances are someone has uploaded a **how-to video**.

> 💡 Example: Susan, who's interested in **healthy cooking**, follows **Tasty and Yummly** to discover **easy, nutritious recipes**.

## Keeping Your Apps Organized

If you use multiple hobby apps, it helps to keep them well-organized:

- **Create Folders**: Group apps by category (e.g., "Music & Podcasts," "Photography").
- **Use Home Screen Widgets**: Add a widget for apps like Apple News or Fitness for quick updates.
- **Offload Unused Apps**: Enable **iPhone's auto-delete feature** for apps you rarely use.

> 📍 **Tip:** If you have **subscription-based apps**, set a reminder in your Calendar app to **review them before renewal**.

Your iPhone is more than just a phone—it's a personalized toolkit for exploring your passions. Whether you're a hobbyist or a serious enthusiast, the right apps can enhance your skills, connect you with communities, and make learning more enjoyable.

# iPhone Safety and Security

## Setting Up Face ID, Passcodes, and Two-Factor Authentication

Your iPhone is more than just a device—it's a personal hub filled with messages, photos, financial details, and other sensitive data. Keeping it secure is essential. With Face ID, passcodes, and two-factor authentication (2FA), Apple provides multiple layers of security to protect your information from unauthorized access. But how do you set them up effectively, and why should you? Let's break it down.

### Face ID: The Most Secure and Convenient Way to Unlock Your iPhone

Face ID uses facial recognition technology to unlock your iPhone securely while making the process effortless. It's fast, reliable, and more secure than a password—plus, it works in a variety of lighting conditions and even adapts to changes in your appearance over time.

How to Set Up Face ID on Your iPhone

Before setting up Face ID, ensure:

- You have an **iPhone with Face ID support** (iPhone X or later).
- Your screen is **clean and free from obstructions** (no dirt or smudges on the front camera).
- You're in a **well-lit environment** for better scanning.

To enable Face ID:

1. **Open Settings** and navigate to **Face ID & Passcode**.
2. **Enter your current passcode** if prompted.
3. Tap **Set Up Face ID** and follow the on-screen instructions.
4. Position your face inside the circular frame.
5. Move your head **slowly in a circular motion** to complete the scan.
6. Once the first scan is complete, repeat the motion for a second scan.
7. Tap **Done** when finished.

Now, Face ID is active and can be used to:

- **Unlock your iPhone** without typing a passcode.
- **Authorize Apple Pay transactions** with a glance.
- **Sign into apps and websites** securely.

💡 Tip: If you wear glasses or frequently change your look, you can add an **Alternate Appearance** under Face ID settings to improve recognition.

## Setting Up a Strong Passcode: Your Backup Security Layer

Even with Face ID, a passcode is essential. It acts as a backup in case Face ID fails or if your iPhone restarts.

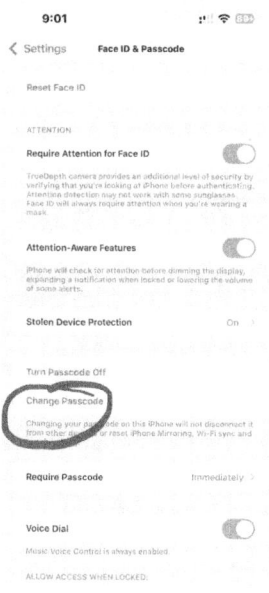

CREATING A SECURE PASSCODE

A strong passcode should be:

- **At least six digits** (longer is better).
- **Not an obvious combination** (avoid birthdays, "123456," or repeating digits).
- **Unique** (don't reuse the same code for other devices or accounts).

To set or change your passcode:

1. **Go to Settings > Face ID & Passcode**.
2. Tap **Change Passcode** (or **Turn Passcode On** if it's not enabled).
3. Enter your current passcode, then your new passcode twice.
4. Tap **Done** to confirm.

💡 Tip: For maximum security, choose **Custom Alphanumeric Code** instead of numbers.

## Two-Factor Authentication: Keeping Your Apple ID Safe

Your Apple ID is the key to your iPhone's data—iCloud, App Store purchases, backups, and more. If someone gains access to it, they can reset your device, steal your information, or even lock you out. That's where Two-Factor Authentication (2FA) comes in.

## What is Two-Factor Authentication?

With 2FA, even if someone knows your Apple ID password, they can't log in without a secondary verification code sent to a trusted device.

## How to Enable Two-Factor Authentication

1. **Go to Settings > [Your Name] > Password & Security**.
2. Tap **Turn On Two-Factor Authentication**.
3. Follow the on-screen instructions and **add a trusted phone number**.
4. When prompted, **enter the verification code sent to your phone**.

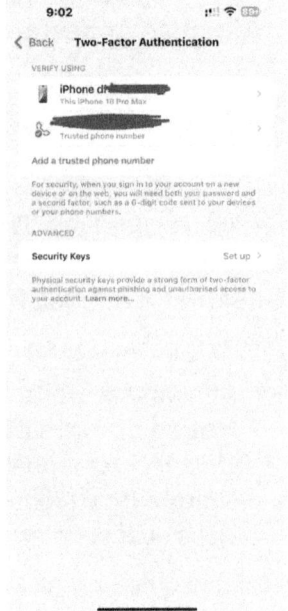

Once enabled, anytime you (or someone else) tries to log into your Apple ID from a new device, you'll receive a 6-digit verification code.

## Why Face ID, Passcodes, and 2FA Matter

Without these security measures, your iPhone could be:

- **Unlocked by someone else** if you leave it unattended.
- **Hacked if your Apple ID password is leaked**.
- **Used for unauthorized purchases** on the App Store or Apple Pay.

> 📍 **Example:** Susan, our buyer persona, **receives a phishing email pretending to be from Apple**, asking her to log in with her Apple ID. Thanks to **Two-Factor Authentication**, the hacker can't access her account without the verification code sent to her iPhone.

## Extra Tips for Maximum Security

To ensure your iPhone remains protected, consider these additional steps:

- **Turn on Auto-Lock**: Set your iPhone to lock quickly when not in use (**Settings > Display & Brightness > Auto-Lock**).
- **Enable Erase Data**: This will **erase all data** after **10 failed passcode attempts** (Settings > Face ID & Passcode > Erase Data).
- **Use Security Keys**: If you're extra cautious, you can **set up a physical security key** for Apple ID login (**Settings > Password & Security > Security Keys**).

> **♥ Tip:** Never share your **Face ID, passcode, or 2FA codes** with anyone—not even Apple Support.

By combining Face ID, a strong passcode, and Two-Factor Authentication, you're layering multiple security protections for your iPhone, keeping your personal information safe from unauthorized access.

# Understanding Privacy Settings to Protect Your Personal Data

Your iPhone isn't just a device—it's a digital vault filled with personal photos, messages, payment details, and browsing history. If you're not careful, apps and websites can track your behavior, share your data, or even compromise your privacy. That's why Apple's privacy settings give you powerful tools to control what gets shared and with whom.

By understanding how these settings work, you can keep your personal data safe while still enjoying the convenience of a connected world. Let's dive into the key privacy settings you need to know.

### Checking Your Privacy Dashboard

Before you tweak individual settings, it's helpful to get a big-picture view of your privacy status.

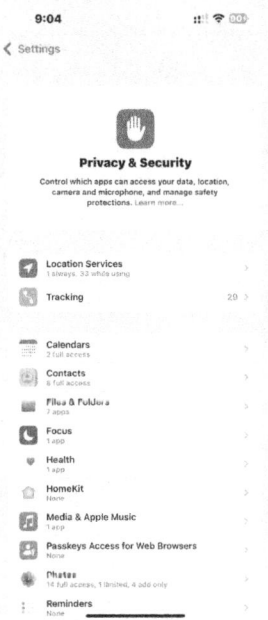

To access your Privacy Dashboard:

1. **Open Settings** on your iPhone.
2. Scroll down and tap **Privacy & Security**.
3. Explore different sections, such as **Location Services, Tracking, Microphone, Camera, and Analytics & Improvements**.

Here, you can see which apps have requested access to your data and decide whether to revoke permissions.

> **♥ Tip:** Make it a habit to **check your privacy settings every few months**, especially after downloading new apps.

## Managing Location Services: Who Knows Where You Are?

Many apps request access to your location—even when they don't need it. While this can be useful for navigation apps like Google Maps or Uber, some apps track your movements unnecessarily.

### HOW TO CONTROL LOCATION ACCESS

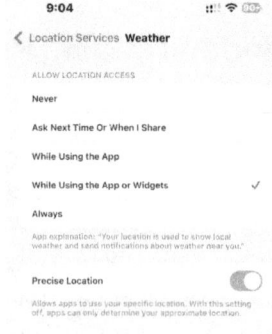

1. **Go to Settings > Privacy & Security > Location Services**.
2. You'll see a list of apps with their **location permissions**:

- **Never:** The app can't access your location.
- **Ask Next Time or When I Share:** The app asks for permission each time.
- **While Using the App:** The app can track you only when it's open.
- **Always:** The app tracks your location even when it's closed (use with caution!).

3. Tap an app to change its setting.

> 📍 **Example:** If you have a **weather app** installed, it might be set to "Always" track your location. Change it to **"While Using the App"** to limit unnecessary tracking.

## App Tracking Transparency: Stopping Apps from Following You

Ever searched for a product online and then saw ads for it everywhere? That's app tracking at work.

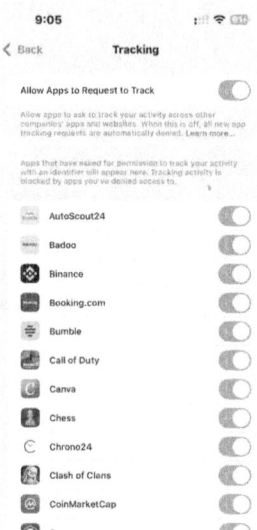

With App Tracking Transparency, Apple forces apps to ask for your permission before tracking your activity across other websites and apps.

### HOW TO DISABLE TRACKING REQUESTS

1. **Go to Settings > Privacy & Security > Tracking**.
2. Toggle off **"Allow Apps to Request to Track"**.

This prevents apps from even asking for permission to track you. If you prefer to allow certain apps, you can keep the setting on and approve or deny individual requests when prompted.

> ♥ **Tip:** If an app refuses to work unless you allow tracking, it's a **red flag**—consider finding an alternative app that respects your privacy.

## Microphone and Camera Access: Controlling What Apps Can Hear and See

Your iPhone's microphone and camera are prime targets for apps that might overstep their boundaries.

### HOW TO MANAGE MICROPHONE AND CAMERA ACCESS

1. **Go to Settings > Privacy & Security**.
2. Tap **Microphone** and **Camera** to see which apps have access.
3. If an app **doesn't need** to record audio or video, toggle off its access.

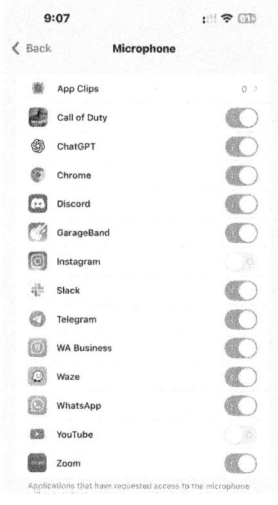

> ♥ **Example:** A **photo editing app** doesn't need **microphone access**, so you can disable it.

## Safari Privacy Settings: Preventing Websites from Tracking You

Safari includes several privacy-focused features to prevent websites from tracking your online activity.

### KEY SAFARI PRIVACY SETTINGS TO ENABLE

1. **Go to Settings > Safari**.
2. Enable **"Prevent Cross-Site Tracking"**—this stops advertisers from tracking you across different sites.
3. Turn on **"Hide IP Address"** (select "Trackers and Websites") to prevent sites from identifying you.
4. Use **"Block All Cookies"** (optional, but it may affect site functionality).

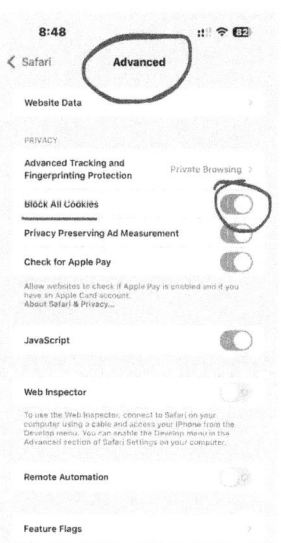

> ♥ **Tip:** If you want an even more **private browsing experience**, use **Safari's Private Mode**, which doesn't save history or cookies.

## Controlling Which Apps Can Access Your Contacts and Photos

Some apps request access to your contacts or photos, but do they really need it?

### How to Manage Access

1.  **Go to Settings > Privacy & Security**.
2.  Tap **Contacts** and **Photos**.
3.  Review which apps have access, and disable access for any apps that don't need it.

> 💡 **Example:** If a **calculator app** is requesting access to your contacts, that's a **red flag**—remove the permission immediately.

## Revoking Data Sharing with Apple and Third-Party Services

Apple collects some data to improve services like Siri and Maps, but you can choose to limit how much is shared.

### How to Limit Data Sharing

1.  **Go to Settings > Privacy & Security > Analytics & Improvements**.
2.  Toggle off options like **"Share iPhone Analytics"** and **"Improve Siri & Dictation"** if you prefer not to share usage data.

## Final Thoughts: Take Control of Your Digital Privacy

Understanding your iPhone's privacy settings isn't just about security—it's about having control over your personal data. By tweaking these settings, you can:

*   **Prevent apps from tracking your activity**.
*   **Limit access to sensitive data** like your microphone, camera, and location.
*   **Ensure websites don't follow you across the internet**.

Taking a few minutes to review these settings now will keep your personal data safe and secure for the long run.

# Using "Find My iPhone" to Keep Your Device Secure

Losing your iPhone can be stressful, but thanks to Apple's Find My iPhone feature, you don't have to panic. Whether you misplaced your device under a couch cushion or left it at a coffee shop, Find My iPhone gives you the power to locate, lock, and protect your device remotely.

Understanding how this feature works and ensuring it's set up correctly is crucial for your security. Let's explore how to activate it, use it in emergencies, and what to do if your iPhone is stolen.

## Setting Up "Find My iPhone"

Find My iPhone is enabled by default on all Apple devices when you sign in with your Apple ID. However, it's always a good idea to double-check that it's turned on.

### How to Enable Find My iPhone

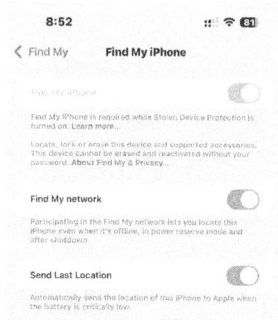

1. **Open Settings** on your iPhone.
2. Tap **[Your Name] > Find My**.
3. Tap **Find My iPhone**.
4. Ensure that **Find My iPhone** is toggled **on**.
5. Enable **Find My Network**—this allows your device to be located even when it's offline.
6. Turn on **Send Last Location**—this sends your iPhone's last known location before the battery dies.

> 💡 **Tip:** Enabling **Find My Network** means that even if your iPhone is turned off or out of battery, nearby Apple devices can still **detect its location** and send updates to iCloud.

## Locating Your iPhone Using Another Apple Device

If you lose your iPhone, you can use another Apple device (like an iPad or Mac) to track it.

### How to Find Your iPhone on Another Apple Device

1. Open the **Find My** app on an iPad, Mac, or another iPhone.
2. Tap the **Devices** tab.
3. Select your missing iPhone from the list.
4. The app will display its last known location on a map.

> 📍 **Example:** You left your phone at the grocery store. When you open the Find My app, it shows your iPhone's location at the store's address—problem solved!

## Using iCloud to Find Your iPhone

Even if you don't have another Apple device, you can still track your iPhone from any web browser.

### HOW TO FIND YOUR IPHONE USING ICLOUD

1. Go to **iCloud.com/find** and sign in with your Apple ID.
2. Click **All Devices** and select your missing iPhone.
3. iCloud will **display its location on a map**.

> 📍 **Tip:** If your iPhone is nearby but you can't see it, click **Play Sound** to make it ring—even if it's on silent.

## Using Lost Mode to Secure Your iPhone

If you suspect that your iPhone is lost in a public place, you should immediately activate Lost Mode to protect your data.

### HOW TO ACTIVATE LOST MODE

1. Open the **Find My** app or go to **iCloud.com/find**.
2. Select your iPhone and tap **Mark As Lost**.
3. Enter a phone number where you can be reached (optional).
4. Type a **custom message** that will appear on the iPhone's screen (e.g., "This iPhone is lost. Please call me at [your number]").
5. Tap **Enable**.

Once Lost Mode is activated:

- **Your iPhone will be locked**, preventing anyone from accessing your data.
- Apple Pay and other sensitive features are **disabled**.
- The location will **continue updating**, so you can track its movements.

## Erasing Your iPhone Remotely (If Necessary)

If you believe your iPhone has been stolen and you don't expect to recover it, your best option is to erase it remotely to protect your personal information.

### How to Erase Your iPhone from Find My

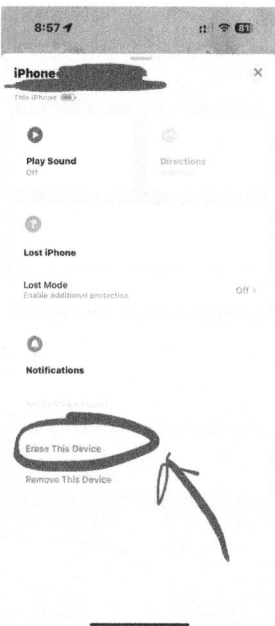

1. Open the **Find My** app or go to **iCloud.com/find**.
2. Select your iPhone from the device list.
3. Tap **Erase This Device**.
4. Confirm your choice.

⚠ *Warning:* Once you erase your iPhone, you won't be able to track it anymore. Use this option only as a last resort.

> 💡 Tip: If your iPhone is later found, you can restore it from your most recent **iCloud backup**.

## What Happens If Someone Tries to Use a Stolen iPhone?

Thanks to Apple's Activation Lock, a stolen iPhone is practically useless to thieves.

- If someone resets your iPhone, they **can't activate it without your Apple ID and password**.
- Even if they replace the SIM card, the phone remains **linked to your Apple ID**.
- Lost Mode **prevents unauthorized access**, keeping your data safe.

> 💡 Example: Someone steals your iPhone, resets it, and tries to sell it. Since **Activation Lock is still enabled**, the new owner **can't use it without your Apple ID**, making it worthless to thieves.

## Preventing Future iPhone Loss or Theft

While Find My iPhone is a lifesaver, it's better to prevent losing your device in the first place.

### Best Practices to Keep Your iPhone Safe

- **Use a secure passcode**: A strong passcode prevents unauthorized access.
- **Enable Face ID or Touch ID**: Biometric security ensures only you can unlock your phone.

- **Be mindful in public places**: Keep your phone **in a secure pocket or bag** when traveling.
- **Use an Apple Watch**: If your iPhone goes out of range, your Apple Watch can notify you.
- **Consider AirTag tracking**: Attach an **AirTag** to your iPhone case for an extra layer of security.

> 💡 **Example**: You're in a crowded subway, and your iPhone **slips out of your pocket**. With **AirTag alerts** and **Find My iPhone**, you can locate it before it's lost for good.

Using Find My iPhone is essential for protecting your device. Whether you misplace it at home or lose it in a public place, Apple's security features help you track it, secure it, and even erase it remotely if necessary. By setting up Find My iPhone today, you're taking a major step toward keeping your personal data safe and your device secure.

# Avoiding Scams, Spam Calls, and Unwanted Messages

Spam calls, phishing texts, and scam emails are more sophisticated than ever, making it crucial to protect yourself from fraudsters attempting to steal your information. With your iPhone's built-in security features and a few proactive measures, you can significantly reduce the risk of falling victim to scams, blocking spam, and keeping your inbox clutter-free.

Let's explore how to recognize scams, filter out spam calls and messages, and use Apple's security features to your advantage.

### Recognizing Common iPhone Scams

Scammers are always evolving their tactics, making it important to stay informed about the latest tricks they use. Some of the most common iPhone-related scams include:

1. Phishing Texts and Emails ("Smishing")

- You receive a text claiming to be from **Apple, your bank, or a delivery service**, urging you to click a link to update information or track a package.
- The link leads to a **fake login page** designed to steal your credentials.
- A common red flag: **Urgency and threats**, such as "Your Apple ID will be locked in 24 hours unless you verify now."

> 💡 **Tip**: Apple **never** sends texts or emails asking for your password or account details.

2.  Fake Tech Support Calls ("Vishing")

•   You receive a call from someone **pretending to be Apple Support**, claiming your iPhone is compromised.
•   The scammer might **request remote access to your device** or ask for payment to "fix" a nonexistent issue.

> 💡 Tip: Apple **does not** make unsolicited support calls. If in doubt, hang up and contact Apple Support directly.

3.  Fake Lottery or Gift Card Scams

•   You receive an email or text saying you've **won a giveaway** or need to pur-chase **Apple gift cards** to claim a prize.
•   The scammer asks you to **send gift card codes**, which can't be recovered once used.

> 💡 Tip: If you didn't enter a contest, you didn't win anything. **Ignore and delete.**

## Blocking and Filtering Spam Calls

Spam calls have become one of the biggest annoyances for iPhone users. Fortunately, Apple provides several tools to help block them.

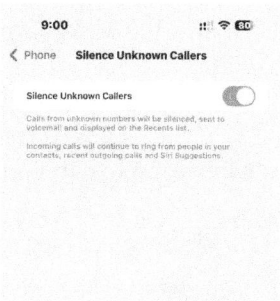

1.  Enable "Silence Unknown Callers"

This feature automatically silences calls from numbers not in your contacts, sending them to voicemail.

How to Enable Silence Unknown Callers:

1.  Open **Settings**.
2.  Scroll to **Phone**.
3.  Tap **Silence Unknown Callers** and toggle it **on**.

> 💡 Tip: This is **great for avoiding robocalls**, but keep in mind that calls from **doctors, delivery services, or other important contacts** may also be silenced.

2.  Use the "Report Junk" Feature

When you receive a spam call from an unknown number:

1.  Open the **Phone app** and go to **Recents**.
2.  Tap the **"i" (info) icon** next to the number.
3.  Select **Report Junk** and then tap **Block Caller**.
3.  Enable Carrier Spam Filtering

Most carriers provide free spam filtering. You can check if your carrier supports it by:

- Visiting your carrier's website or app.

- Looking for settings like **"Call Protect" (AT&T)**, **"Scam Shield" (T-Mobile)**, or **"Call Filter" (Verizon)**.

## Stopping Spam Texts and Phishing Messages

Spam texts can be annoying and dangerous if they contain phishing links. Here's how to filter them out and avoid clicking malicious links.

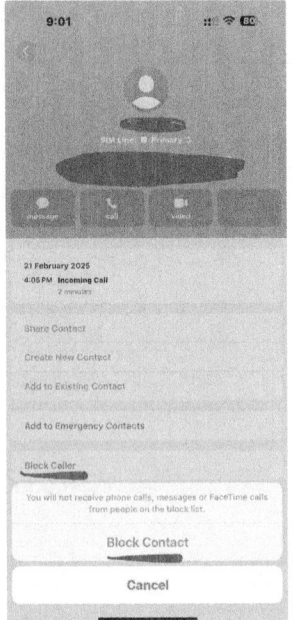

1. Filter Unknown Senders

This setting moves texts from people not in your contacts to a separate tab in Messages.

How to Enable Message Filtering:

1. Open **Settings**.
2. Tap **Messages**.
3. Scroll to **Filter Unknown Senders** and toggle it **on**.

> 📍 **Tip:** This doesn't block messages completely but **keeps them out of your main inbox** so they don't distract you.

2. Block Spam Numbers and Contacts

If you keep receiving spam messages from the same number, block it directly:

1. Open the **Messages app**.
2. Select the conversation from the spam sender.
3. Tap the **contact name or number** at the top.
4. Tap **Block this Caller**.

> 📍 **Tip:** Blocking a number **stops calls, texts, and FaceTime** from that contact.

3. Report Junk Messages to Apple

If you receive an iMessage spam text, Apple lets you report it directly:

1. Open the **Messages app**.
2. Find the spam text.
3. Tap **Report Junk** and select **Delete and Report Junk**.

## Preventing Email Scams on iPhone

Apple's Mail app includes smart filtering tools to detect junk emails, but you can take additional steps for security.

1. Enable Mail Privacy Protection

This feature hides your IP address and prevents senders from tracking your email activity.

How to Enable Mail Privacy Protection:

1. Open **Settings**.
2. Tap **Mail**.
3. Select **Privacy Protection**.
4. Turn on **Protect Mail Activity**.

> 💡 **Tip:** This blocks senders from knowing **when you open emails**, reducing tracking.

2. Use Hide My Email (iCloud+ Users)

iCloud+ users can create random email addresses for sign-ups, keeping their real email private.

How to Use Hide My Email:

1. Open **Settings**.
2. Tap **[Your Name] > iCloud**.
3. Select **Hide My Email**.
4. Tap **Create New Address** and use it for websites that require email sign-ups.

## Best Practices to Stay Safe from Scams

Beyond Apple's security features, staying vigilant is key to protecting yourself.

- **Never click unknown links:** If a message urges you to **act quickly**, it's likely a scam.
- **Avoid sharing personal information:** Legitimate companies **never** ask for sensitive info via text or email.
- **Use strong passwords:** A **password manager** can help generate and store unique passwords.
- **Enable two-factor authentication:** Adds an extra layer of security to your accounts.
- **Regularly update iOS:** Each update patches security vulnerabilities.

> 💡 **Example:** If you get a text saying, "Your Apple ID is locked. Click here to verify," **don't click the link!** Instead, go directly to **Apple's website** or contact support to check your account status.

By following these steps, you can filter out spam, block scammers, and keep your iPhone safe from fraudulent activity. Apple provides powerful tools, but being aware and proactive is your best defense against scams.

# Emergency Features: SOS, Medical ID, and More

In a crisis, seconds matter. Your iPhone is equipped with powerful emergency features that can help you call for help, share vital medical information, and even alert your emergency contacts automatically. Whether it's an accident, a sudden health issue, or a dangerous situation, knowing how to use Emergency SOS, Medical ID, and other life-saving features could make all the difference.

Let's explore how to set up and use these essential safety tools.

## Activating Emergency SOS: Call for Help Instantly

Emergency SOS allows you to quickly call for help and alert emergency services without needing to unlock your phone. Depending on your settings, it can also notify your emergency contacts, providing them with your location.

### How to Use Emergency SOS on iPhone

There are two ways to activate Emergency SOS, depending on your iPhone model:

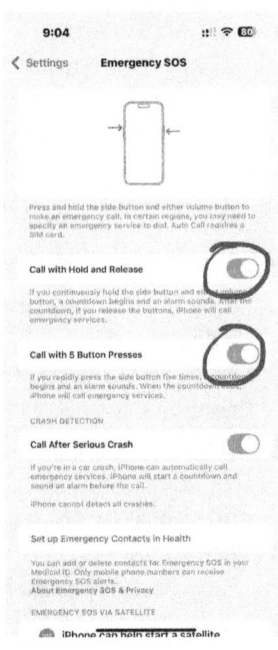

1. **For iPhones with Face ID (iPhone X and later)**
   » **Press and hold the Side button + one of the Volume buttons u**ntil the Emergency SOS slider appears.
   » Slide to ca**ll emergency services,** or kee**p holding b**oth buttons if you want the phone to ca**ll automatically.**

2. **For iPhones with a Home button (iPhone 7 and earlier)**
   » Ra**pidly press the Side (or Top) button five times t**o bring up the Emergency SOS slider.
   » Slide to ca**ll emergency services.**

> 🔌 **Tip:** If you want Emergency SOS to call automatically without sliding, you can enable Auto Call in Settings.

1. Open **Settings**.
2. Tap **Emergency SOS**.
3. Toggle **Call with Hold** or **Call with 5 Presses** to **on**.

### WHAT HAPPENS WHEN YOU ACTIVATE EMERGENCY SOS?

- Your iPhone **automatically calls 911** (or the equivalent emergency service for your country).
- If enabled, your **emergency contacts** receive a **text with your current location**.
- If your location changes, they receive an **update** after a short period.
- Your phone **disables Face ID** temporarily for added security, requiring your passcode to unlock.

> 💡 Example: If you're in a **dangerous situation** and can't speak, holding the Side and Volume buttons **calls 911 discreetly**, allowing you to get help without alerting potential threats.

## Setting Up Your Medical ID for First Responders

Medical ID is a lifesaver in medical emergencies, allowing paramedics and doctors to access critical health information even when your phone is locked.

### HOW TO SET UP MEDICAL ID

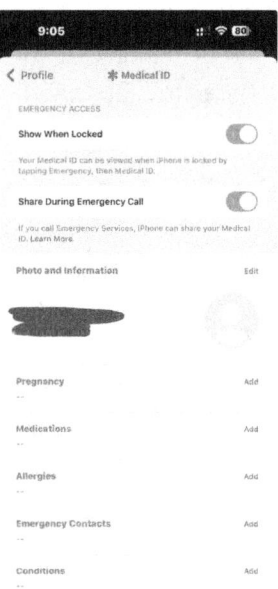

1. Open the **Health app**.
2. Tap your **profile picture** (top right corner).
3. Select **Medical ID → Edit**.
4. Fill in **important details**, such as:
   » Name and date of birth
   » Medical conditions (e.g., diabetes, heart disease)
   » Allergies and medications
   » Emergency contacts
   » Blood type and organ donor status
5. Toggle **Show When Locked** to **on** so first responders can access it from your Lock Screen.
6. Tap **Done** to save your information.

> 💡 Tip: If you have **serious allergies** or take essential medications, make sure they are **clearly listed** in Medical ID.

### How to Access Medical ID in an Emergency

If someone needs to see your Medical ID:

- From the Lock Screen, tap **Emergency → Medical ID**.
- If **Emergency SOS is activated**, responders automatically see your Medical ID.

> 💡 **Example:** If you **pass out from low blood sugar**, paramedics can check your iPhone's Medical ID for crucial details about your condition and **administer proper treatment faster**.

## Adding and Managing Emergency Contacts

Your iPhone allows you to add trusted emergency contacts who will be automatically notified if you use Emergency SOS.

### How to Add Emergency Contacts

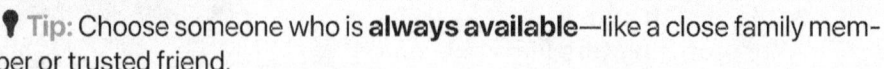

1. Open the **Health app**.
2. Tap your **profile picture → Medical ID → Edit**.
3. Scroll to **Emergency Contacts → Add Emergency Contact**.
4. Choose a contact from your phonebook and select their **relationship** to you.
5. Tap **Done** to save.

> 💡 **Tip:** Choose someone who is **always available**—like a close family member or trusted friend.

## Crash Detection and Fall Detection (iPhone and Apple Watch)

If you own a newer iPhone (iPhone 14 and later) or an Apple Watch, your device can automatically detect serious accidents and falls and call emergency services for you.

### Crash Detection (iPhone 14 and later)

If your iPhone detects a severe car accident, it will:

- **Sound an alarm** and display an emergency screen.
- Give you **10 seconds to respond** before calling emergency services.
- Alert your **emergency contacts** automatically.

## Fall Detection (Apple Watch Series 4 and later)

If you take a hard fall, your Apple Watch:

- Asks if you **need help**.
- If you **don't respond**, it **calls emergency services automatically**.

> **Tip:** If you **live alone or have a health condition**, enabling **Fall Detection** on your Apple Watch is a great precaution.

## Enabling Location Sharing in Emergencies

Your iPhone can share your location automatically with trusted contacts or emergency responders.

### Share My Location with Family and Friends

1. Open **Settings** → Tap **Privacy & Security**.
2. Select **Location Services** → **Share My Location**.
3. Toggle **Share My Location** to **on**.
4. Choose people to **share your live location with**.

> **Tip:** If you frequently travel alone, sharing your **live location** with a trusted contact can provide peace of mind.

## Best Practices for Staying Prepared

In an emergency, preparation is key. Here's how to ensure your iPhone's emergency features work when you need them most:

- **Test Emergency SOS:** Make sure you know how to trigger it quickly.
- **Keep Medical ID Updated:** Review your health info and emergency contacts regularly.
- **Enable Auto Call for SOS:** If you want to skip the slider, turn on **Auto Call** in settings.
- **Charge Your iPhone:** Emergency features don't work if your battery is dead!
- **Know Your Emergency Contacts' Numbers:** If your phone is lost, you should still be able to reach them.

By setting up Emergency SOS, Medical ID, and other safety features, your iPhone becomes a powerful tool for protecting your health and security. Whether you're in an accident, experiencing a medical emergency, or in a dangerous situation, these features could save your life.

CHAPTER 8

# Extending Battery Life and Optimizing Performance

## Understanding Battery Health and Charging Tips

Your iPhone's battery is the heartbeat of the device, determining how long you can stay connected, productive, and entertained before needing to recharge. Understanding battery health and following best practices for charging can extend its lifespan, ensuring that your device runs efficiently for years.

Let's dive deep into how iPhone batteries work, how to monitor their health, and the best charging habits to keep your iPhone powered longer.

### How iPhone Batteries Work: The Basics

Your iPhone is powered by a lithium-ion battery, the same technology used in most modern electronics. Unlike older battery types, lithium-ion batteries are designed to be lightweight, efficient, and fast-charging. They hold a charge longer, have a higher energy density, and don't suffer from the "memory effect" that plagued older nickel-based batteries.

However, like all batteries, they degrade over time. This means that after a certain number of charge cycles, your iPhone's battery won't hold as much energy as it once did.

### What is a charge cycle?

A charge cycle occurs when your battery discharges and recharges the equivalent of 100%. This doesn't have to happen in one go—if you use 50% of your battery today and recharge, then use 50% tomorrow, that counts as one full charge cycle.

Apple estimates that iPhone batteries are designed to retain up to 80% of their original capacity after 500 full charge cycles.

## Checking Your Battery Health

Your iPhone provides built-in tools to monitor battery health. Here's how you can check yours:

1. Open **Settings**.
2. Tap **Battery → Battery Health & Charging**.
3. Look at **Maximum Capacity**—this percentage indicates how much charge your battery can still hold compared to when it was new.

### UNDERSTANDING BATTERY HEALTH INDICATORS

- **Maximum Capacity**: If this number is **close to 100%**, your battery is in great shape. If it has dropped below **80%**, you might notice reduced battery life.
- **Peak Performance Capability**: This shows whether your battery can deliver peak power. If your iPhone has unexpectedly shut down before, Apple may enable **performance management** to prevent future shutdowns.
- **Optimized Battery Charging**: This feature helps slow battery aging by learning your charging habits and reducing wear on your battery.

> 💡 **Tip:** If your battery health is below **80%** and you're experiencing **faster battery drain**, consider **getting the battery replaced** at an Apple Store or authorized service provider.

## Best Practices for Charging Your iPhone

Your charging habits significantly impact battery lifespan. Follow these expert-recommended dos and don'ts to keep your battery healthy.

### ⬛ DO: CHARGE SMARTLY

- **Keep your battery between 20% and 80% most of the time.**
  - » Avoid fully depleting or charging to 100% too often, as this stresses the battery.
- **Use Optimized Battery Charging.**
  - » This feature delays charging beyond 80% until you need it. To enable it:
  - » Go to Settings → Battery → Battery Health & Charging → Toggle Optimized Battery Charging ON.
- **Use official or certified chargers.**
  - » Apple's **Lightning to USB-C cable** and MagSafe are ideal. If using third-party options, ensure they are MFi **(Made for iPhone) certified.**

## ✖ Don't: Overheat Your Battery

- **Avoid charging in extreme heat.**
  - » Ideal charging temperature: **62°F – 72°F (16°C – 22°C)**.
  - » High temperatures over 95**°F (35°C)** degrade battery health fa**ster**.
- **Never leave your iPhone in a hot car or direct sunlight while charging.**
  - » Heat is a major enemy of lithium-ion batteries.

> 🔦 **Example:** If you're charging your iPhone in the car during summer and the dashboard is baking under the sun, your battery could degrade **faster than normal**.

## Fast Charging: When and How to Use It

Fast charging is convenient, but frequent use can slightly stress your battery. iPhones support up to 50% charge in 30 minutes with a 20W or higher charger.

To reduce battery wear, use fast charging only when needed, and for daily charging, stick to standard 5W or wireless charging.

## Wireless vs. Wired Charging: Which Is Better?

Both charging methods have pros and cons:

| CHARGING METHOD | PROS | CONS |
| --- | --- | --- |
| **Wired Charging** | Faster, less heat buildup | Requires cable |
| **Wireless Charging (MagSafe, Qi)** | Convenient, cable-free | Generates more heat, slightly slower |

> 🔦 **Tip:** If using wireless charging overnight, place your iPhone **on a ventilated surface** to prevent overheating.

## How to Avoid Battery Drain Overnight

Many people leave their iPhones plugged in overnight, which is fine thanks to Optimized Battery Charging, but there are better ways to preserve battery life:

- **Enable Airplane Mode** or **Do Not Disturb** to prevent background activity.
- **Close unused apps** before bed.
- **Use a slower charger (5W or 10W)** instead of fast charging overnight.

## Battery Myths Debunked

There's a lot of misinformation about iPhone batteries. Let's clear up some common myths:

✖ Myth: You must fully drain your battery before recharging.

⬛ Truth: Modern lithium-ion batteries perform better with partial charging.

✖ Myth: Using a third-party charger will always damage your battery.

⬛ Truth: As long as it's MFi-certified, third-party chargers are safe.

✖ Myth: Closing apps will significantly improve battery life.

⬛ Truth: iOS manages background apps efficiently—closing them manually has minimal effect.

## Signs It's Time for a Battery Replacement

If your iPhone is experiencing any of these issues, it might be time to replace the battery:

- **Battery drains too fast** (e.g., drops from 50% to 10% suddenly).
- **Your iPhone shuts down unexpectedly, even with a charge left.**
- **Battery health is below 80% in Settings → Battery.**
- **Performance feels slow, even after restarting your iPhone.**

> 💡 Solution: Visit an **Apple Store** or authorized repair center for a **battery replacement**.

By following these battery health and charging best practices, you can ensure your iPhone lasts longer on a single charge and stays healthy for years. A well-maintained battery means fewer interruptions, less stress over low battery warnings, and a more reliable iPhone experience every day.

# Customizing Settings to Save Power Throughout the Day

Your iPhone is a powerhouse of productivity, entertainment, and communication, but it all comes down to battery life. If your device constantly runs out of charge before the end of the day, tweaking your settings can make all the difference. By making a few smart adjustments, you can significantly extend battery life without sacrificing performance or convenience.

This section will guide you through power-saving settings, background activity management, and everyday habits that help maximize battery efficiency while ensuring your iPhone works smoothly throughout the day.

## Optimizing Display Settings for Battery Efficiency

Your iPhone's display is one of the biggest power consumers. Bright, vibrant, and responsive screens are great, but they also drain battery faster. Here's how to strike a balance between visibility and efficiency.

### REDUCE SCREEN BRIGHTNESS

Lowering your screen brightness can drastically improve battery life. The good news? Your iPhone can adjust brightness automatically, but you can also take control manually.

To adjust brightness manually:

1. Open **Settings → Display & Brightness**.
2. Drag the **Brightness** slider down to a comfortable level.

Alternatively, swipe down from the top-right corner of your screen (or swipe up on older models) to access Control Center, then adjust the brightness slider.

### ENABLE AUTO-BRIGHTNESS

This feature automatically dims your screen in darker environments and brightens it when needed, helping conserve energy.

To enable Auto-Brightness:

1. Open **Settings → Accessibility**.
2. Tap **Display & Text Size**.
3. Scroll down and toggle **Auto-Brightness** ON.

> 💡 **Tip:** If you're in **low-light environments** like indoors or at night, keeping brightness low can **greatly extend battery life**.

### USE DARK MODE

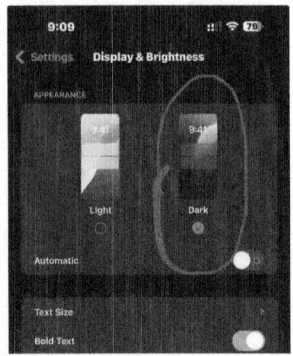

Dark Mode not only looks sleek but also reduces power consumption, especially on OLED displays (iPhone X and later).

To enable Dark Mode:

1. Open **Settings → Display & Brightness**.
2. Select **Dark Mode**.

## Managing Background Activity to Save Battery

Many apps continue to run in the background, consuming battery even when you're not actively using them. By tweaking background activity, you can prevent unnecessary power drain.

### Turn Off Background App Refresh

Background App Refresh allows apps to update content in the background (e.g., social media feeds, news updates). While useful, it drains battery quickly.

To disable Background App Refresh:

1.   Open **Settings → General → Background App Refresh**.
2.   Select **Off** or **Wi-Fi Only** (to refresh only when connected to Wi-Fi).

> ♥ Tip: You can disable Background App Refresh **individually for apps** you don't need constantly updating.

### Limit Location Services

GPS tracking can severely drain battery if too many apps constantly access your location.

To manage Location Services:

1.   Open **Settings → Privacy & Security → Location Services**.
2.   Scroll through the list and set apps to **While Using the App** or **Never**, instead of **Always**.

> ♥ Tip: Apps like **weather, maps, and fitness trackers** need location access, but social media and shopping apps **rarely require it**.

## Controlling Notifications to Minimize Battery Drain

Every notification wakes your screen, reducing battery life. If you receive hundreds of notifications daily, managing them efficiently can make a difference.

### Turn Off Unnecessary Notifications

1.   Open **Settings → Notifications**.
2.   Scroll through the list and disable notifications for apps you don't need re-al-time alerts from.
3.   Set important notifications to **Deliver Quietly** (so they appear in Notification Center without waking the screen).

## Battery-Friendly Connectivity Settings

Your iPhone constantly searches for Wi-Fi, Bluetooth, and cellular signals—each consuming power. Adjusting these settings can help extend battery life.

### ENABLE WI-FI INSTEAD OF CELLULAR DATA

Wi-Fi uses less power than cellular data, so when possible, connect to a trusted Wi-Fi network.

To connect to Wi-Fi:

1. Open **Settings → Wi-Fi**.
2. Select a trusted network and ensure **Auto-Join** is enabled.

### TURN OFF BLUETOOTH AND AIRDROP WHEN NOT IN USE

If you're not actively using Bluetooth accessories, disable Bluetooth to conserve power.

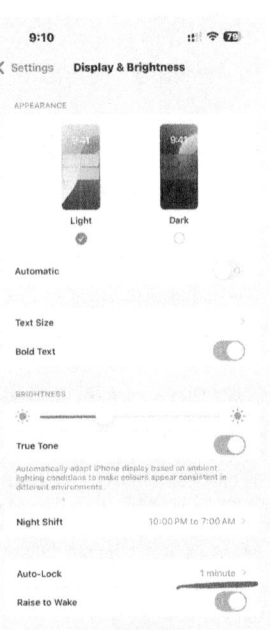

To turn off Bluetooth:

1. Open **Settings → Bluetooth**.
2. Toggle Bluetooth **OFF** when not needed.

> 💡 **Tip:** Avoid turning off Bluetooth from **Control Center**—this only **disconnects devices temporarily** instead of fully disabling Bluetooth.

## Optimizing Auto-Lock and Raise to Wake

Your screen staying on longer than necessary can drain battery quickly.

### SET AUTO-LOCK TO THE SHORTEST TIME POSSIBLE

1. Open **Settings → Display & Brightness → Auto-Lock**.
2. Set it to **30 seconds** or **1 minute**.

### DISABLE RAISE TO WAKE

Raise to Wake automatically turns on your screen when you lift your iPhone—useful, but it can drain battery if your phone moves frequently in a bag or pocket.

1. Open **Settings** → **Display & Brightness**.

2. Toggle **Raise to Wake** OFF.

## Using Smart Power-Saving Features

### Enable Low Power Mode (When Needed)

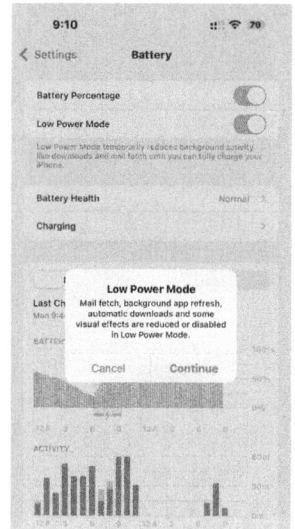

Low Power Mode reduces power consumption by dis-abling background tasks like mail fetch, auto-downloads, and visual effects.

To enable Low Power Mode manually:

1. Open **Settings** → **Battery**.
2. Toggle **Low Power Mode** ON.

> 💡 Tip: Your iPhone will **automatically prompt you** to enable Low Power Mode when battery drops to 20%, but you can turn it on **anytime** to extend battery life.

## Summary of Key Power-Saving Tweaks

| FEATURE | BENEFIT | HOW TO ENABLE |
|---------|---------|---------------|
| Lower screen brightness | Reduces battery drain | Control Center → Adjust Brightness |
| Enable Dark Mode | Saves power on OLED displays | Settings → Display & Brightness |
| Turn off Background App Refresh | Prevents unnecessary background activity | Settings → General → Background App Refresh |
| Limit Location Services | Stops apps from overusing GPS | Settings → Privacy & Security → Location Services |
| Disable Raise to Wake | Prevents accidental screen wake-ups | Settings → Display & Brightness |

| | | |
|---|---|---|
| Turn off Bluetooth when not in use | Saves battery from unnecessary connections | Settings → Bluetooth |
| Use Wi-Fi instead of Cellular Data | Consumes less power than 5G/LTE | Settings → Wi-Fi |
| Enable Low Power Mode | Extends battery by reducing system activity | Settings → Battery |

By implementing these simple yet effective changes, you can ensure your iPhone battery lasts all day without constantly reaching for a charger. Adjusting just a few settings can make a noticeable impact, letting you focus on using your iPhone without battery anxiety.

## Managing Apps and Background Activity for Better Performance

Your iPhone is designed to be fast, responsive, and efficient, but mismanaged apps and background activity can quickly lead to sluggish performance and battery drain. If you've ever noticed your device feeling slower than usual, apps taking longer to open, or your battery mysteriously running low by midday, background processes could be the culprit.

Fortunately, iOS provides powerful tools to control how apps run in the background, allowing you to strike the perfect balance between convenience and performance. This section will guide you through smart app management techniques, background activity control, and best practices to keep your iPhone running smoothly and efficiently throughout the day.

### Understanding How Background Activity Affects Performance

When you close an app on your iPhone, it doesn't always fully shut down—many apps continue running in the background, using resources such as:

- **CPU power** (slowing down performance).

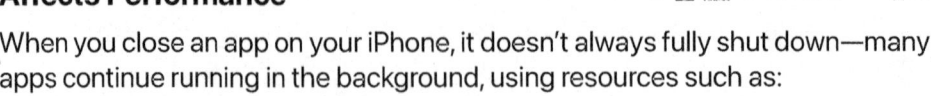

- **Battery life** (draining charge even when you're not actively using them).
- **Data/Wi-Fi usage** (refreshing content, fetching emails, updating social feeds).

This background activity is useful for certain apps (like messaging services and navigation), but others can unnecessarily drain your phone's resources. Knowing which apps to control—and how to do it—will make a noticeable difference in both performance and battery life.

## Checking Which Apps Are Consuming the Most Power

Before you start tweaking settings, it's helpful to identify which apps are consuming the most battery and background resources.

To check battery usage by app:

1. Open **Settings → Battery**.
2. Scroll down to see a **list of apps and their battery usage**.
3. Tap an app to see detailed breakdowns, including **screen time vs. background activity**.

> 💡 **Tip:** If an app shows **high background activity**, it's a sign that it's **refreshing data when you're not using it**, which can slow down your device and drain battery.

## Disabling Background App Refresh to Save Power and Improve Speed

One of the biggest culprits of battery drain and sluggish performance is Background App Refresh—a feature that allows apps to update content in the background even when they're not open.

While this is useful for some apps (like news and messaging apps), many apps don't need constant updates.

How to Disable Background App Refresh

1. Open **Settings → General → Background App Refresh**.
2. Choose **Wi-Fi & Cellular Data** (default) or **Wi-Fi Only** to limit refresh when connected to Wi-Fi.
3. To completely disable for certain apps, **toggle off individual apps** that don't require background updates.

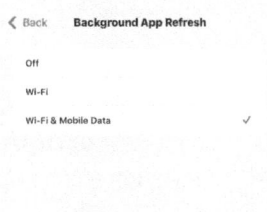

> 💡 **Example:** Apps like **Facebook, Instagram, and TikTok** don't need constant updates in the background. **Disabling them** can prevent unnecessary battery and data usage.

## Managing Location Services to Improve Performance

Many apps track your location in the background, which can significantly impact performance and battery life.

To control Location Services:

1. Open **Settings → Privacy & Security → Location Services**.
2. Scroll through the list of apps and adjust each one to:
   » **Never (**if the app doesn't need location access).
   » **While Using the App (**recommended for most apps).
   » **Always (**only for essential apps like Maps and Find My iPhone).

> 💡 **Tip: Weather apps, food delivery services, and social media apps** often request **constant location tracking**, even when not in use—this is **unnecessary and drains power**.

## Closing Unused Apps: Does It Help or Hurt?

There's a common myth that force-quitting apps (swiping them away from the App Switcher) improves performance. In reality, this can sometimes do more harm than good.

### WHEN SHOULD YOU FORCE-QUIT APPS?

- If an app **freezes or crashes**.
- If an app is **stuck in an error state** (e.g., draining battery abnormally).
- If an app **refreshes content too aggressively** and consumes too much power.

Otherwise, iOS is designed to manage apps intelligently, suspending inactive ones without using extra power.

How to force-quit an app (only when necessary):

1. Swipe up from the bottom of the screen (or double-click the Home button).
2. Swipe **left or right** to find the app you want to close.
3. Swipe **up** on the app to close it.

> 💡 **Tip:** Avoid force-quitting apps **you use frequently**—reopening them **from scratch** actually uses **more energy** than resuming them from suspension.

## Optimizing App Notifications for Efficiency

Every notification wakes up your screen and uses battery power. If you receive dozens of alerts from social media, email, or shopping apps, managing notifications can free up system resources.

To manage notifications:

1. Open **Settings → Notifications**.
2. Select an app and choose **None, Banners, or Alerts**.
3. Use **Scheduled Summary** to group non-urgent notifications.

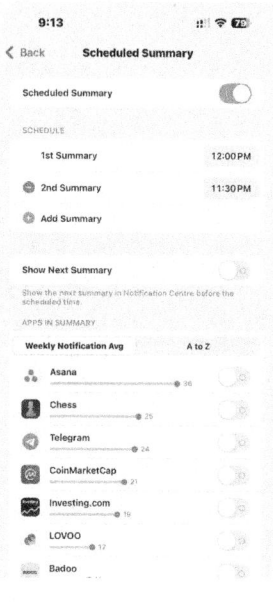

> 💡 **Example:** News apps, shopping apps, and **games** tend to **send frequent, unnecessary alerts**—limiting them reduces distractions and saves power.

## Clearing Safari and App Cache for Better Performance

Over time, cached files accumulate, slowing down your iPhone and consuming storage. Clearing cache periodically helps boost speed.

### How to Clear Safari Cache

1. Open **Settings → Safari**.
2. Tap **Clear History and Website Data**.
3. Confirm your choice.

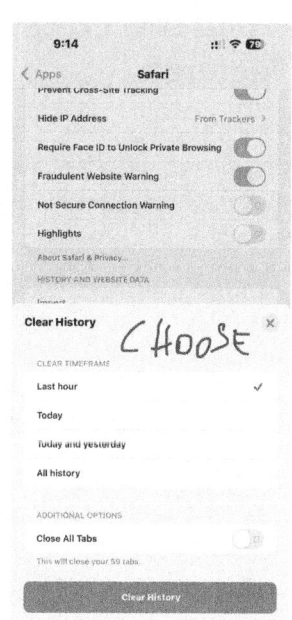

> 💡 **Tip:** This also **logs you out of websites**, so be sure to save important passwords first.

### Clearing Cache in Other Apps

- Some apps (like YouTube, Facebook, and Twitter) **store large amounts of cached data**.
- The best way to clear their cache is by **uninstalling and reinstalling the app**.

## Final Tips for Managing Apps Efficiently

| FEATURE | WHAT IT DOES | HOW TO OPTIMIZE |
|---|---|---|
| **Background App Refresh** | Updates apps when not in use | Disable for non-essential apps |
| **Location Services** | Tracks your GPS location | Set to "While Using" for most apps |
| **App Notifications** | Sends alerts that wake screen | Limit to essentials only |
| **Cache & Temporary Files** | Stores browsing and app data | Clear Safari and uninstall cache-heavy apps |
| **Force-Closing Apps** | Stops an app from running | Only do this if an app is misbehaving |

By managing apps wisely, reducing unnecessary background activity, and controlling notifications and location tracking, you'll extend battery life, improve performance, and ensure your iPhone runs smoothly throughout the day.

# Using Low Power Mode and Optimized Charging Features

Your iPhone is packed with smart energy-saving features that can extend battery life and preserve its long-term health. Among these, Low Power Mode and Optimized Battery Charging stand out as two of the most effective tools for maximizing efficiency and keeping your device powered up when you need it most.

Whether you're trying to get through a long day without a charger or simply want to prolong your iPhone's battery lifespan, understanding how these features work—and when to use them—can make all the difference.

## What Is Low Power Mode and How Does It Work?

Low Power Mode (LPM) is designed to conserve battery life when your charge gets low. When activated, it reduces background activity and certain system functions to extend your remaining power.

Here's what happens when Low Power Mode is enabled:

- **Background app refresh is paused** (apps won't update until you open them).
- **Mail fetch is turned off** (you'll need to manually check emails).
- **Auto-downloads and some visual effects are reduced**.
- **Hey Siri is disabled** (you can still activate Siri manually).
- **Processor performance is slightly reduced** (to balance power and efficiency).
- **Screen brightness and auto-lock timers are adjusted** (your screen turns off more quickly).

Think of it as a power-saving emergency mode—it slows things down slightly, but helps you stretch your remaining battery life significantly.

## When Should You Use Low Power Mode?

- **At 20% Battery or Lower**: Your iPhone will automatically prompt you to turn on Low Power Mode when you reach **20% battery**, and again at **10%**.
- **Before a Long Day**: If you know you'll be **away from a charger for an extended period**, enabling Low Power Mode early can **help your battery last longer**.
- **In Cold Temperatures**: Batteries drain **faster in extreme cold**. If you're outdoors during winter, activating Low Power Mode can **help prevent sudden shutdowns**.
- **If Your Battery Is Aging**: If your iPhone battery health is below **80%**, using Low Power Mode regularly can **help it hold a charge longer**.

> 💡 Example: If you're traveling and realize you left your charger at home, turning on **Low Power Mode early in the day** can help you get **several more hours** of battery life.

## How to Enable Low Power Mode

MANUALLY VIA SETTINGS

1. Open **Settings → Battery**.
2. Toggle **Low Power Mode** ON.

QUICKLY VIA CONTROL CENTER

1. Swipe **down from the top-right corner** (on Face ID models) or **up from the bottom** (on Touch ID models).
2. Tap the **Low Power Mode** icon (if it's not there, you can add it in Settings → Control Center).

> 💡 **Tip:** Your iPhone will automatically **disable Low Power Mode** when you **charge past 80%**, restoring normal performance. If you want it to stay on, you'll need to **re-enable it manually**.

## What Is Optimized Battery Charging?

Apple introduced Optimized Battery Charging to help extend the lifespan of your battery by reducing wear from repeated full charges.

### How It Works

- The feature **learns your charging habits** and **delays charging past 80%** until just before you need to use your phone.
- This reduces the time your battery spends at **100% charge**, which helps slow **chemical aging**.
- It's especially useful for people who charge overnight—your iPhone will wait until morning to complete the last **20% of the charge**, so it's fresh when you wake up.

> 💡 **Example:** If you charge your phone every night at 11 PM and wake up at 7 AM, Optimized Battery Charging will **pause charging at 80% and only complete the charge around 6 AM**.

## How to Enable Optimized Battery Charging

1. Open **Settings → Battery → Battery Health & Charging**.
2. Toggle **Optimized Battery Charging** ON.

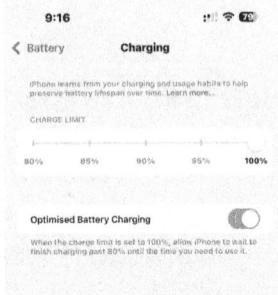

> 💡 **Tip:** You can **disable Optimized Battery Charging temporarily** if you need a full charge **immediately**. Just tap **Turn Off Until Tomorrow** when prompted.

# Low Power Mode vs. Optimized Battery Charging: What's the Difference?

| FEATURE | PURPOSE | WHEN TO USE | EFFECT ON PERFOR-MANCE |
|---------|---------|-------------|------------------------|
| Low Power Mode | Temporarily reduces power usage | When battery is low or you need extra battery life | Some slowdown (reduces background processes and brightness) |
| Optimized Battery Charging | Extends long-term battery health | All the time (enabled automatically) | No effect on daily performance |

Think of Low Power Mode as an "emergency battery saver" and Optimized Battery Charging as a "battery lifespan protector."

## Additional Tips for Battery Optimization

If you want to go beyond these built-in features, here are a few extra tricks to maximize your iPhone's battery life:

- **Keep iOS Updated**: Apple **frequently improves battery efficiency** in software updates, so make sure you're running the latest iOS version.
- **Avoid Extreme Temperatures**: Heat is the **biggest enemy of lithium-ion batteries**—never leave your iPhone in direct sunlight or inside a hot car.
- **Use Original Apple Chargers**: Cheap third-party chargers **can degrade battery health faster**. Stick to MFi-certified accessories.
- **Unplug When Fully Charged**: Leaving your phone plugged in overnight every day **can shorten battery lifespan** over time (Optimized Battery Charging helps with this).

## Final Thoughts on Battery Optimization

By leveraging Low Power Mode when needed and using Optimized Battery Charging every day, you can extend your iPhone's daily battery life while also preserving its long-term performance.

These two features work hand-in-hand—one helps you get more out of each charge, while the other ensures your battery lasts for years to come. Mastering them will keep your iPhone running efficiently no matter where your day takes you.

# Diagnosing and Fixing Common Battery Issues

Even with Apple's advanced battery optimization features, iPhone battery issues can still happen. Maybe your device isn't holding a charge like it used to, or it's draining way too fast for no clear reason. Perhaps it's shutting down unexpectedly, overheating, or taking forever to charge.

Whatever the case, diagnosing and fixing these problems can make a huge difference in your iPhone's usability. The good news? Most battery issues are easy to fix, and even if they require more serious intervention, Apple provides tools to help you assess your battery's health before making any decisions.

## Step 1: Check Your Battery Health

Your iPhone has a built-in tool that lets you check the overall health of your battery. Since lithium-ion batteries naturally degrade over time, knowing where yours stands can help you determine if your battery needs replacing or if there's just an app or setting draining it too fast.

### How to Check Battery Health

1. Open **Settings → Battery → Battery Health & Charging**.
2. Look at the **Maximum Capacity** percentage.
3. Check the **Peak Performance Capability** section.

What It Means:

- **100% - 85%:** Battery health is **still strong**—issues are likely due to software or app settings.
- **84% - 75%:** Battery is **aging**—you may notice **faster drains**, but you don't necessarily need a replacement yet.
- **Below 75%:** Your battery **won't hold a charge as well**, and Apple may suggest a **battery replacement**.

> 🔋 Tip: If your battery capacity is below **80%**, your iPhone might slow down performance **to prevent unexpected shutdowns**.

## Step 2: Identify Battery-Draining Apps

Some apps consume way more battery than others—especially social media, streaming, and location-based apps. Luckily, iOS makes it easy to spot the culprits.

### How to See Battery Usage by App

1. Open **Settings → Battery**.
2. Scroll down to see the **Battery Usage by App** list.

3.  Tap on any app to get more details about **how much battery it's using**.

What to Look For:

*   If an app is using **over 20% of your battery**, it's worth investigating.
*   **Background Activity** means an app is running even when you're not using it—turn it off in **Settings → General → Background App Refresh**.
*   **High Screen Time** suggests you're spending a lot of time in an app, and reducing usage may help save battery.

> 💡 **Tip:** If you see an app draining **an abnormal amount of battery**, try up-dating it or reinstalling it.

## Step 3: Fix Common Battery Drain Issues

Once you've identified the cause of your battery drain, try these fixes:

1.  Adjust Display & Brightness Settings

*   Lower your **screen brightness** (**Settings → Display & Brightness**).
*   Set **Auto-Lock** to **30 seconds** (**Settings → Display & Brightness → Auto-Lock**).
*   Use **Dark Mode** (**Settings → Display & Brightness → Dark Mode**).

2.  Turn Off Unnecessary Location Services
1.  Open **Settings → Privacy & Security → Location Services**.
2.  Scroll through the list and **disable location access** for apps that don't need it.
3.  Set frequently used apps to **"While Using"** instead of **"Always"**.
3.  Manage Background App Activity
1.  Go to **Settings → General → Background App Refresh**.
2.  Turn off **Background App Refresh** for apps that **don't need to run in the background**.
4.  Enable Low Power Mode When Needed
1.  Open **Settings → Battery →** Toggle **Low Power Mode** ON.
2.  Or add **Low Power Mode** to your **Control Center** for quick access.

> 💡 **Tip: Low Power Mode** can **extend battery life significantly** by reducing background tasks, mail fetch, and system animations.

## Step 4: Solve Charging Problems

Sometimes the problem isn't battery drain, but charging issues. Here's how to fix them:

1.  Check Your Charging Cable & Adapter

- Use an **Apple-certified cable and adapter**. Cheap third-party chargers **can damage your battery**.
- Try **switching cables or adapters** to see if the issue persists.

2.  Inspect the Charging Port

- **Lint or debris** in the charging port can **prevent proper charging**.
- Use a **toothpick or compressed air** to gently clean the port.

3.  Restart Your iPhone Before Charging

- If your iPhone **isn't charging**, restart it and try again.
- **Soft Reset:** Hold **Power + Volume Down** (on Face ID models) or **Power + Home Button** (on older models) until you see the Apple logo.

## Step 5: What If Your iPhone Overheats?

Overheating can drain your battery quickly and damage internal components.

HOW TO PREVENT OVERHEATING:

- **Avoid charging in direct sunlight** or hot environments.
- **Remove your case** while charging—some thick cases **trap heat**.
- If overheating occurs, **put your iPhone in Airplane Mode** and let it cool down.

> 💡 Tip: If your iPhone **shuts down due to overheating, let it cool completely** before turning it back on—forcing a restart can cause damage.

## Step 6: When to Consider a Battery Replacement

If you've tried all these fixes and your battery life is still terrible, it may be time to replace your battery.

Signs You Need a Battery Replacement:

- **Battery drains extremely fast**, even on Low Power Mode.
- **Phone shuts down unexpectedly**, even with 20-30% battery remaining.
- **Your iPhone feels sluggish**, and Battery Health says **"Performance Management Applied."**

HOW TO REPLACE YOUR BATTERY

- Check if you're **eligible for Apple's free battery replacement program** (*Apple occasionally offers free replacements for certain models*).
- If your warranty has expired, Apple offers **battery replacements starting at around $69**.
- You can also go to a **certified Apple repair center** for a **genuine battery replacement**.

## Final Battery Troubleshooting Checklist

- Check **Battery Health** in settings.
- Identify and **limit battery-draining apps**.
- Reduce **screen brightness** and **background activity**.
- **Manage Location Services** for apps that don't need GPS.
- Use **Low Power Mode** when needed.
- Fix **charging issues** by checking cables, ports, and restarting.
- Prevent **overheating** by avoiding direct sunlight while charging.
- Consider **battery replacement** if your iPhone no longer holds a charge.

By following these diagnostic steps, you can pinpoint and fix common battery problems, making your iPhone more efficient and reliable in the long run.

# CHAPTER 9

# Troubleshooting Made Easy

## Fixing Wi-Fi, Bluetooth, and Cellular Connection Problems

Staying connected is an essential part of using your iPhone, whether you're browsing the web, making a call, streaming your favorite music, or connecting Bluetooth devices like AirPods or a smartwatch. However, when Wi-Fi, Bluetooth, or cellular connections stop working, it can be frustrating—especially when you're in a hurry.

The good news? Most connectivity issues can be fixed quickly and easily with a few troubleshooting steps. Whether your Wi-Fi won't stay connected, your Bluetooth devices aren't pairing, or your cellular data isn't working, this guide will help you diagnose the issue and get back online fast.

### Step 1: Troubleshooting Wi-Fi Issues

Wi-Fi problems are among the most common connection issues on an iPhone. Maybe your device won't
connect to Wi-Fi, keeps disconnecting, or shows full
bars but won't load anything.

QUICK FIXES FOR WI-FI NOT WORKING

1. **Toggle Wi-Fi Off and On:**
   - » Open **Settings** → **Wi-Fi** → Toggle **Wi-Fi off,** wait **10 seconds,** and turn it back on.

2. **Forget the Network and Reconnect:**
   - » Open **Settings** → **Wi-Fi** → Tap on the network name.
   - » Tap **Forget This Network** and confirm.
   - » Reconnect by selecting the Wi-Fi network and entering your password.

3. **Restart Your iPhone and Router:**
   - » Turn your iPhone **off and back on.**
   - » Unplug your Wi-Fi router **for 30 seconds,** then plug it back in.

4. **Check for Wi-Fi Interference:**

   » If your Wi-Fi is **slow or unstable,** move closer to your router.
   » Avoid walls, metal objects, and other electronics that **could cause interference.**

5. **Reset Network Settings (As a Last Resort):**

   » Open **Settings → General → Transfer or Reset iPhone → Reset → Reset Network Settings.**
   » This **erases all Wi-Fi networks and passwords,** so make sure to **write down y**our Wi-Fi password first.

---

> 💡 **Tip:** If your iPhone **connects to Wi-Fi but doesn't have internet**, the issue might be with **your router or internet service provider (ISP)**, not your iPhone. Try connecting another device to the same Wi-Fi and see if it works.

---

## Step 2: Troubleshooting Bluetooth Issues

Bluetooth is essential for wireless headphones, car connections, smartwatches, and more. But when Bluetooth refuses to connect, it can be frustrating.

QUICK FIXES FOR BLUETOOTH NOT CONNECTING

1. **Turn Bluetooth Off and On:**

   » Open **Settings → Bluetooth →** Toggle **Bluetooth off,** wait **10 seconds,** and turn it back on.

2. **Forget and Re-pair the Device:**

   » Go to **Settings → Bluetooth.**
   » Tap the (i) **info button** next to the device name.
   » Select **Forget This Device,** then try reconnecting.

3. **Restart Your iPhone and Bluetooth Device:**

   » Turn off both your **iPhone and the Bluetooth device,** wait **30 seconds,** and turn them back on.

4. **Ensure the Device is in Pairing Mode:**

   » Some Bluetooth devices require **manual pairing mode.**
   » Check the **user manual** for instructions on how to **enter pairing mode.**

5. **Reset Network Settings (If Nothing Else Works):**

   » Go to **Settings → General → Transfer or Reset iPhone → Reset → Reset Network Settings.**

> 💡 **Tip:** If your Bluetooth **connects but keeps disconnecting**, check if the device is **fully charged** or **too far from your iPhone** (Bluetooth works best within **30 feet**).

## Step 3: Fixing Cellular Data Problems

If your cellular data isn't working, you won't be able to browse the web, send iMessages, or use apps like Maps or Weather when you're not on Wi-Fi.

QUICK FIXES FOR CELLULAR DATA NOT WORKING

1. **Check Airplane Mode:**
   » Open **Control Center** and make sure **Airplane Mode is off.**
   » If it's on, turn it off and wait for your signal to return.

2. **Turn Cellular Data Off and On:**
   » Go to **Settings → Cellular →** Toggle **Cellular Data off,** wait **10 seconds,** then turn it back on.

3. **Check Carrier Updates:**
   » Go to **Settings → General → About.**
   » If an **update for your carrier settings** is available, you'll see a pop-up. Tap **Update.**

4. **Reinsert Your SIM Card:**
   » If your iPhone **says "No Service" or "Searching",** try removing and reinserting the **SIM card.**
   » Use a **SIM ejector tool o**r a paperclip to open the SIM tray.

5. **Reset Network Settings:**
   » Open **Settings → General → Transfer or Reset iPhone → Reset → Reset Network Settings.**

> 💡 **Tip:** If your **cellular data still isn't working**, contact your **mobile carrier** to check for **network outages or SIM card issues**.

## Step 4: Fixing Slow Internet Speeds

If your Wi-Fi or cellular data is slow, try these tricks:

- **Turn Off VPNs** – If you use a VPN, it could be slowing down your internet. Disable it in **Settings → VPN**.
- **Limit Background App Activity** – Apps running in the background can **slow down your connection**. Go to **Settings → General → Background App Refresh** and turn off unnecessary apps.

- **Try Another Wi-Fi Network** – If your home Wi-Fi is slow, connect to a **different network** to see if the issue is your internet provider.

### Final Troubleshooting Checklist

- Wi-Fi Issues
- Bluetooth Problems
- Cellular Data Not Working
- Slow Internet Speeds

By following these step-by-step solutions, you can quickly diagnose and fix any connectivity problems on your iPhone.

# Solving Issues with Apps That Freeze or Crash

Few things are more frustrating than an app freezing or crashing in the middle of something important. Maybe you're drafting an email, editing a photo, or just scrolling through social media when suddenly, the app stops responding, crashes to the home screen, or refuses to open altogether.

If this sounds familiar, don't worry—you're not alone. App crashes can happen for various reasons, from software glitches and outdated versions to insufficient storage or even a misbehaving iOS update. Thankfully, there are several troubleshooting steps that can get things back on track quickly.

### Step 1: Force Close the App and Reopen It

When an app freezes or becomes unresponsive, the first and easiest fix is to force close it and restart.

How to Force Close an App:

- On **iPhones with Face ID**:
    - » Swipe up from the bottom and **pause i**n the middle of the screen.
    - » Find the app causing the issue and sw**ipe it up t**o close it.
- On **iPhones with a Home Button**:
    - » Double-press the Ho**me button t**o open the App **Switcher.**
    - » Swipe up on the pr**oblematic app t**o close it.
- Open the app again and see if it works properly.

> 💡 **Tip:** If the issue happens often with a **specific app**, check if it **freezes only in certain scenarios**—like when uploading a file or using a particular feature.

## Step 2: Restart Your iPhone

If force closing the app didn't work, try a simple restart. This can help clear temporary glitches that may be affecting app performance.

### HOW TO RESTART YOUR IPHONE:

1. Press and hold the **Side button + Volume Up (or Down)** until the **power-off slider appears**.
2. Drag the **slider to turn off your iPhone**.
3. Wait **30 seconds**, then **turn it back on** by holding the Side button.

> 💡 *Why does this help?* Restarting your iPhone **clears temporary memory (RAM)**, which can fix issues with apps **stuck in a bad state**.

## Step 3: Update the App to the Latest Version

Outdated apps may not work properly, especially if they aren't optimized for the latest iOS version.

### HOW TO CHECK FOR APP UPDATES:

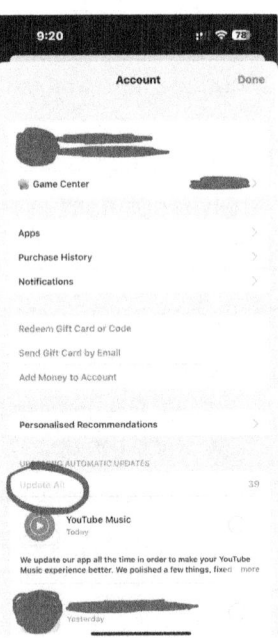

- Open the **App Store** → Tap your **profile picture** in the top right.
- Scroll down to the **Upcoming Updates** section.
- Tap **Update** next to the app (or **Update All** for multiple apps).

> 💡 **Tip:** If an app **hasn't been updated in months**, the developer may have **stopped supporting it**. Check the **App Store description** to see if it's still **actively maintained**.

## Step 4: Delete and Reinstall the App

If the app continues to freeze or crash, uninstalling and reinstalling it may help.

### HOW TO DELETE AND REINSTALL AN APP:

1. Press and hold the app **until it jiggles**.
2. Tap the **minus (-) icon** and select **Delete App**.
3. Open the **App Store**, search for the app, and **redownload it**.

> **Warning:** Deleting an app may remove **saved data** unless the app stores it in iCloud. Make sure to check before uninstalling!

## Step 5: Check iPhone Storage Space

Apps may freeze or crash if your iPhone is low on storage.

### HOW TO CHECK YOUR STORAGE:

- Open **Settings → General → iPhone Storage**.
- If your storage is almost full, **delete unnecessary files**, apps, or photos.

> **Tip:** Apps like **Photos, Messages, and Safari** can take up **hidden storage**. Clearing cache and deleting old downloads can **free up space**.

## Step 6: Check for iOS Updates

Sometimes, an iOS update fixes app-related issues—especially if many users report similar problems.

### HOW TO UPDATE IOS:

- Go to **Settings → General → Software Update**.
- If an update is available, tap **Download and Install**.

> **Tip:** If an app **crashes after an iOS update**, check the **developer's website** or **App Store page** for compatibility issues.

## Step 7: Reset All Settings (If the Problem Persists)

If none of the previous steps work, resetting all settings can help resolve deeper issues without deleting your files.

### HOW TO RESET ALL SETTINGS:

1. Open **Settings → General → Transfer or Reset iPhone**.
2. Tap **Reset → Reset All Settings**.

This will reset Wi-Fi passwords, wallpapers, and system settings, but will not erase apps or personal data.

> **Warning:** This should be a **last resort**, as it resets all **custom settings** like notifications and Face ID preferences.

## Final Troubleshooting Checklist

- **Force Close and Reopen the App**
- **Restart Your iPhone**
- **Update the App to the Latest Version**
- **Delete and Reinstall the App**
- **Check iPhone Storage Space**
- **Update iOS**
- **Reset All Settings (Last Resort)**

By following these step-by-step solutions, you can quickly fix most app freezing or crashing issues on your iPhone.

# Recovering Lost Data with iCloud Backup and Restore

Losing data on your iPhone can feel like a nightmare—whether it's priceless photos, important notes, or crucial contacts. Fortunately, iCloud Backup and Restore provides a reliable way to recover lost data quickly and effortlessly.

If you've accidentally deleted files, switched to a new iPhone, or experienced unexpected data loss, this guide will walk you through the steps to restore your information using iCloud.

## Step 1: Understanding How iCloud Backup Works

Before we dive into recovery, let's clarify how iCloud Backup functions.

- **Automatic Backups**: Your iPhone can back up **automatically** when connected to Wi-Fi, locked, and charging.
- **Storage Limitations**: Apple provides **5GB of free iCloud storage**, but additional storage is available through **iCloud+ plans**.
- **What's Included in iCloud Backup?**
  - » Photos and videos (if iCloud Photos is not enabled).
  - » Messages, including iMessage, SMS, and MMS.
  - » App data, device settings, and home screen layout.
  - » Health data, Apple Watch backups, and more.

> 📍 **Tip:** If you **don't see a recent backup**, check if your iPhone has iCloud Backup enabled (**Settings → [Your Name] → iCloud → iCloud Backup**).

## Step 2: Restoring from an iCloud Backup

If you need to recover lost data, the best way is to restore your iPhone from a previous iCloud backup.

IMPORTANT NOTES BEFORE RESTORING:

- **Restoring from iCloud requires erasing your iPhone first**. This means all current data will be erased, and your iPhone will return to the state of your last backup.
- **Ensure you have a backup available** before proceeding.

HOW TO RESTORE FROM ICLOUD BACKUP:

1. Open **Settings** → **General** → **Transfer or Reset iPhone**.
2. Tap **Erase All Content and Settings** → Confirm the reset.
3. Once your iPhone restarts, follow the **on-screen setup instructions**.
4. When you reach the **Apps & Data** screen, select **Restore from iCloud Backup**.
5. Sign in to your Apple ID and **choose the most recent backup**.
6. Wait for the restoration process to complete.

> 💡 **Tip:** The restore process **may take time** depending on the backup size and your internet speed. Make sure you're on **Wi-Fi** and keep your iPhone plugged in.

## Step 3: Recovering Specific Data Without a Full Restore

If you don't want to erase your iPhone but need to recover only certain files, there are alternative solutions.

METHOD 1: RECOVERING PHOTOS AND VIDEOS FROM ICLOUD PHOTOS

If iCloud Photos is enabled, your pictures and videos aren't included in iCloud Backup but instead sync to iCloud Photos.

To check if your photos are available in iCloud:

- Open the **Photos app** → Tap **Albums** → Scroll down to **Recently Deleted**.
- If your photos are missing, go to **iCloud.com** on a browser and check your **Photos Library**.

> 💡 **Tip:** Recently deleted photos stay in the **Recently Deleted** folder for **30 days** before being permanently erased.

## Method 2: Restoring Messages, Contacts, and Notes

If your contacts, messages, or notes are missing, they might still be stored in iCloud.

- Open **Settings → [Your Name] → iCloud**.
- Toggle off **Contacts, Messages, or Notes**, then turn them back on to force a **re-sync**.

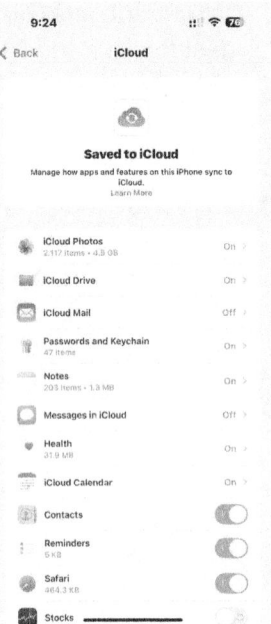

> ♥ **Tip:** If a contact or note was deleted recently, try checking the **"Recently Deleted" folder** in the Notes app.

## Step 4: Using Third-Party Tools for Data Recovery

If your data isn't in iCloud Backup, third-party recovery tools like Dr.Fone, Tenorshare UltData, or PhoneRescue may help retrieve lost files without erasing your iPhone.

- These tools scan your iPhone and **attempt to re-cover deleted files**, including messages, contacts, and app data.
- They work best when **data hasn't been overwritten**—so use them **as soon as possible** after data loss.

> ♥ Warning: Always use **trusted software** and avoid scams promising **"100% recovery"**. Not all lost data is retrievable.

## Step 5: Preventing Future Data Loss

Once you've recovered your lost data, it's crucial to set up safeguards to prevent it from happening again.

1. Enable Automatic iCloud Backup

- Go to **Settings → [Your Name] → iCloud → iCloud Backup**.
- Turn on **Back Up This iPhone**.
- Tap **Back Up Now** to create a **manual backup immediately**.

2. Upgrade iCloud Storage if Needed

If you're running out of space, consider upgrading your iCloud storage plan:

- **50GB ($0.99/month) – Ideal for most users.**
- **200GB ($2.99/month) – Great for families.**
- **2TB ($9.99/month) – For power users with lots of data.**

3. Use an Alternative Backup Method (Mac or PC)

- **Mac Users:** Connect your iPhone to a Mac and use **Finder** to create a **local backup**.
- **Windows Users:** Use **iTunes** to back up your iPhone manually.

> 🔆 Tip: A **Mac or PC backup** is useful if you **don't have enough iCloud storage** or need a **complete local copy** of your iPhone.

### Final Troubleshooting Checklist

- **Check if a recent iCloud backup exists.**
- **Restore from iCloud Backup if full recovery is needed.**
- **Recover individual photos, contacts, or notes without erasing your iPhone.**
- **Use third-party recovery tools if necessary.**
- **Enable automatic backups and upgrade storage if needed.**

By following these steps, you can recover lost data efficiently and ensure your important information is always backed up and secure.

# Updating iOS Without Stress: Step-by-Step Guide

Keeping your iPhone updated is essential to ensure security, performance, and access to new features. However, iOS updates can sometimes feel overwhelming—from fears of losing data to concerns about longer download times. If you've ever hesitated before tapping that "Download and Install" button, this guide will help you update iOS with confidence while avoiding common pitfalls.

### Step 1: Why Updating iOS Matters

Apple regularly releases iOS updates that bring new features, security improvements, and bug fixes. Updating your iPhone is not just about getting the latest emojis—it's about keeping your device running smoothly and securely.

Here's why updates are important:

- **Security Fixes**: Apple frequently patches vulnerabilities that hackers could exploit.
- **Performance Enhancements**: New updates often **improve battery life and system stability**.
- **Bug Fixes**: If you've experienced crashes or glitches, an update might fix them.

- **New Features**: From redesigned apps to **enhanced widgets and AI improvements**, Apple often introduces **game-changing features** in iOS updates.

> 🔑 **Tip:** Major iOS updates (like iOS 18) **arrive annually in September**, while smaller updates are released throughout the year to fix bugs and security vulnerabilities.

## Step 2: Preparing Your iPhone for an iOS Update

Before installing an update, take a few precautionary steps to avoid issues like failed updates, lost data, or a frozen screen.

1. Check Your iPhone's Compatibility

Every new iOS version drops support for older devices. To check if your iPhone is compatible:

- Open **Settings → General → About** → Find your **Model Name**.
- Visit Apple's website or search **"iOS [version] compatibility list"** to confirm if your device supports the update.

2. Back Up Your Data (Just in Case!)

While updates rarely cause data loss, it's always a good idea to back up your iPhone before installing.

To back up via iCloud:

1. Open **Settings → [Your Name] → iCloud**.
2. Tap **iCloud Backup** → Toggle on **Back Up This iPhone**.
3. Tap **Back Up Now** and wait for the process to finish.

Alternatively, you can back up using your Mac or PC:

- **Mac users**: Connect your iPhone, open **Finder**, select your device, and choose **Back Up Now**.
- **Windows users**: Use **iTunes** and follow the same steps.

3. Free Up Storage Space (If Needed)

If your iPhone has low storage, the update might fail. To check your storage:

- Open **Settings → General → iPhone Storage**.
- If storage is nearly full, delete **unused apps, large videos, or old messages** before updating.

> 🔑 **Tip:** If you need more space **without deleting important files**, try offloading apps (**Settings → General → iPhone Storage → Offload Unused Apps**).

4. Plug in Your iPhone and Connect to Wi-Fi

- **Your iPhone must have at least 50% battery** or be connected to a charger to start the update.
- Updates **can be large (1GB+), so using Wi-Fi instead of cellular data is recommended** to avoid high data usage.

## Step 3: How to Update iOS

Once your iPhone is backed up and ready, follow these steps to install the latest iOS version effortlessly.

METHOD 1: UPDATING OVER-THE-AIR (OTA) VIA SETTINGS

1. Open **Settings → General → Software Update**.
2. Your iPhone will check for updates. If available, tap **Download and Install**.
3. Enter your **passcode** if prompted.
4. The update will download, then tap **Install Now**.

> 💡 Tip: If you see **"Update Requested" for a long time**, Apple's servers might be busy. Try again later or restart your iPhone.

METHOD 2: UPDATING VIA A MAC OR PC (IF OTA FAILS)

If the OTA method doesn't work or you experience update errors, try updating using a computer.

1. **Mac users**: Connect your iPhone to your Mac → Open **Finder** → Click on your iPhone under "Locations" → Click **Check for Update** → Install.
2. **Windows users**: Open **iTunes**, select your iPhone, then click **Check for Update**.

> 💡 Tip: If your update keeps failing, try **putting your iPhone into recovery mode** before updating via a Mac or PC.

## Step 4: What to Do If an iOS Update Fails

Even with preparation, sometimes updates don't go smoothly. If you encounter an issue, here's how to fix it:

1. Not Enough Storage Error?
- Free up space as mentioned in **Step 2**.
- Try updating via **a Mac or PC**, which doesn't require as much free space.
2. Stuck on "Verifying Update"?
- If your iPhone is stuck for more than 10 minutes, restart it and try again.

3. iPhone Won't Turn On After Update?

- **Force restart your iPhone**: Press and quickly release **Volume Up**, then **Volume Down**, then press and hold the **Side Button** until the Apple logo appears.

4. Update Stuck at "Preparing Update"?

- Go to **Settings** → **General** → **iPhone Storage** → Locate the iOS update and **delete it**.
- Restart your iPhone and re-download the update.

> 💡 **Tip:** If none of these work, try **putting your iPhone in DFU (Device Firmware Update) mode** and restoring it via a Mac or PC.

### Step 5: Enabling Automatic Updates (Optional but Recommended)

If you want iOS to update automatically overnight without manual effort:

1. Open **Settings** → **General** → **Software Update**.
2. Tap **Automatic Updates**.
3. Toggle on **Download iOS Updates** and **Install iOS Updates**.

> 💡 **Tip:** Automatic updates **only install when your iPhone is charging and connected to Wi-Fi overnight**, so you won't be interrupted during the day.

### Final Troubleshooting Checklist

- **Check iPhone compatibility before updating.**
- **Back up your iPhone to iCloud or a computer.**
- **Ensure enough free storage before installing the update.**
- **Keep your iPhone charged and connected to Wi-Fi.**
- **Use a Mac or PC if OTA updates fail.**
- **Enable automatic updates to stay up-to-date effortlessly.**

By following these steps, you can update iOS stress-free and keep your iPhone running at its best.

## When to Contact Apple Support and How to Get Help

Despite all the troubleshooting methods available, sometimes your iPhone just won't cooperate. Maybe your screen has frozen, your device won't turn on, or a persistent issue keeps coming back no matter what you try. At this point, you might be wondering: *Is it time to contact Apple Support?*

Reaching out for help doesn't have to be a frustrating experience. Apple offers several convenient ways to get assistance, from online chat support to in-person

Genius Bar appointments. This guide will help you determine when you should contact Apple, how to do it efficiently, and what to expect.

## Step 1: When Should You Contact Apple Support?

Before calling Apple, ask yourself these questions:

- Have you **tried basic troubleshooting** and the issue persists?
- Is your iPhone **physically damaged** (e.g., a cracked screen, water damage, or battery swelling)?
- Are you seeing **persistent error messages** that don't go away?
- Has your **iPhone completely stopped responding** (won't turn on, won't charge, or stuck on the Apple logo)?
- Did a **recent update cause major problems** that you can't fix?

If you answered yes to any of the above, it's time to get help from Apple Support.

> 💡 Tip: If your issue is minor or common, try searching Apple's Support website support.apple.com or Apple's **user community forums** before calling. There's a good chance someone else has had the same issue, and the solution is already available.

## Step 2: Choosing the Right Way to Contact Apple Support

Apple offers multiple ways to get support, so you can choose the one that best fits your needs.

1. Apple Support App (Fastest & Easiest Method)

The Apple Support app provides personalized troubleshooting, lets you chat with an expert, schedule repairs, and even check your warranty.

- **How to Use It:**

1. Download the **Apple Support** app from the App Store.
2. Open the app, sign in with your Apple ID, and select your **iPhone** from the list of devices.
3. Browse common problems, request chat support, or schedule an in-store appointment.

> 💡 Tip: If you need **live chat support**, the app is the fastest way to connect with an Apple representative.

2. Online Support via Apple's Website

Apple's Support website ([support.apple.com](https://support.apple.com)) allows you to search for solutions and connect with Apple via chat, email, or phone.

- **How to Use It:**
1. Visit **[support.apple.com](https://support.apple.com)** and click **iPhone**.
2. Select your issue from the list or type it in the search bar.
3. Follow troubleshooting steps or choose **Contact Support** to chat or request a call.

> 🔦 **Tip:** If you prefer **chat over a phone call**, this is a great option.

3. Call Apple Support (For Urgent Issues)

If your iPhone isn't working at all, calling Apple directly is the best option.

- **Apple's support number (U.S.):** 1-800-MY-APPLE (1-800-692-7753).
- **Hours:** Typically available **24/7**, but response times may vary.

> 🔦 **Tip:** If your issue is complex, request a **call-back** through the Apple Support website instead of waiting on hold.

4. In-Person Help at an Apple Store (Genius Bar)

If your iPhone has a hardware issue (broken screen, faulty battery, or charging problems), visiting an Apple Store or Apple Authorized Service Provider is the best choice.

- **How to Schedule a Genius Bar Appointment:**
1. Open the **Apple Support app** or visit **[getsupport.apple.com](https://getsupport.apple.com)**.
2. Choose your iPhone issue and select **Bring in for Repair**.
3. Pick the nearest Apple Store and schedule a time.

> 🔦 **Tip:** Apple Stores can be **very busy**, so book your appointment in advance to avoid long wait times.

5. Twitter & Social Media Support (For Quick Questions)

Apple has an official Twitter support account (@AppleSupport) where you can send quick questions via DM. While they won't help with complex issues, they're great for basic troubleshooting tips.

## Step 3: Checking Your Warranty and Repair Options

If your iPhone needs repair, the cost depends on whether it's covered under warranty or AppleCare+.

1. Open **Settings → General → About**.
2. Tap **Coverage** (or visit **[checkcoverage.apple.com](https://checkcoverage.apple.com)** and enter your serial number).

> 💡 **Tip:** If your iPhone is out of warranty, you can still get it repaired, but costs will apply. AppleCare+ customers may qualify for **discounted repairs or free replacements**.

APPLECARE+ VS. STANDARD WARRANTY

| COVERAGE TYPE | STANDARD WAR-RANTY | APPLECARE+ |
|---|---|---|
| Duration | 1 year | 2-3 years |
| Phone Support | 90 days | Full term |
| Accidental Damage | Not covered | Discounted repairs |
| Battery Replace-ment | Only for defects | Included |

> 💡 **Tip:** If your iPhone is out of warranty and repair costs are too high, consider **Apple's Trade-In Program** to get credit towards a new iPhone.

## Step 4: What to Bring to an Apple Store Appointment

If you're going to an Apple Store or Authorized Repair Center, make sure to bring the following:

- Your **iPhone**
- A **photo ID** (if your device is linked to your Apple ID)
- **Proof of purchase** (if claiming a warranty repair)
- Your **charging cable** (if experiencing charging issues)
- **Backup your data!** Repairs may require wiping your device

> 💡 **Tip:** If your iPhone **won't turn on**, Apple may **offer a loaner device** while it's being repaired.

## Final Troubleshooting Checklist Before Contacting Apple

Before reaching out to Apple Support, try these final troubleshooting steps:

- Restart your iPhone.
- Ensure your iOS is updated to the latest version.
- Try resetting settings (**Settings → General → Transfer or Reset iPhone → Reset All Settings**).
- Check Apple's **System Status** ([Apple System Status](https://www.apple.com/support/systemstatus/)) to see if services like iCloud or App Store are down.

If your issue still isn't resolved, it's time to get in touch with Apple Support using one of the methods above.

CHAPTER 10

# Making Siri Work for You

## Setting Up and Customizing Siri for Your Needs

Siri is more than just a voice assistant—it's your personalized digital helper that can simplify tasks, manage your schedule, send messages, and even control smart home devices. But to get the most out of Siri, you'll want to set it up properly and customize it to match your daily habits.

Whether you're new to Siri or just looking to fine-tune its capabilities, this guide will take you through everything you need to know to set up, personalize, and optimize Siri for a seamless experience.

### Step 1: Enabling Siri on Your iPhone

Before you can use Siri, you need to make sure it's turned on. By default, Siri is enabled on new iPhones, but if you've skipped the setup or disabled it previously, here's how to get it running again.

1. Open **Settings**.
2. Scroll down and tap **Siri & Search**.
3. Toggle on the following options:
   » **Listen for "Hey Siri"** (or just "Siri" if you're using iOS 17 and later).
   » **Press Side Button for Siri** (or Home button on older iPhones).
   » **Allow Siri When Locked** (if you want to use Siri without unlocking your phone).

> 💡 Tip: If you don't want to say *"Hey Siri"* every time, you can just say *"Siri"* in newer iOS versions to activate it.

### Step 2: Training Siri to Recognize Your Voice

To ensure Siri responds only to your voice, you'll need to complete a quick voice recognition setup.

1. When you enable "Listen for 'Hey Siri,'" a setup screen will appear.

2.  Follow the on-screen prompts to **repeat specific phrases**, allowing Siri to learn your voice.
3.  Once completed, Siri will be **more accurate in recognizing your commands**.

> 💡 **Tip:** If Siri isn't responding well to your voice, **reset voice recognition** by turning off "Listen for 'Hey Siri'" and setting it up again.

## Step 3: Choosing Siri's Voice and Language

Siri's voice is fully customizable, so you can choose a different accent, gender, or even language.

### How to Change Siri's Voice:

1.  Go to **Settings → Siri & Search → Siri Voice**.
2.  Select a **variety (American, Australian, British, etc.)**.
3.  Choose a **voice** (male or female).

> 💡 **Tip:** The first time you switch voices, **Siri will download the voice files**. Make sure you're connected to Wi-Fi to avoid using cellular data.

### How to Change Siri's Language:

1.  Go to **Settings → Siri & Search → Language**.
2.  Choose a language from the list.
3.  Restart Siri to apply the change.

> 💡 **Note:** Siri's features may vary depending on the **language and region**. Some languages don't support **certain voice commands** like sending messages or scheduling reminders.

## Step 4: Customizing Siri's Responses and Behavior

You can fine-tune how Siri interacts with you by adjusting response settings.

1.  Choose When Siri Speaks

If you prefer Siri to respond only in certain situations, you can control whether Siri talks back to you or remains silent.

1.  Go to **Settings → Siri & Search → Siri Responses**.

2. Select one of the following options:

» **Automatic** – Siri decides when to speak based on context.
» **Prefer Spoken Responses** – Siri always responds out loud.
» **Prefer Silent Responses** – Siri shows results on screen without speaking.

> 📍 **Tip:** If you use **AirPods** or **CarPlay**, Siri will automatically **speak out responses**, even if you have Silent Mode enabled.

2. Enable Type to Siri (For Silent Use)

If you'd rather type commands instead of speaking, you can enable Type to Siri mode.

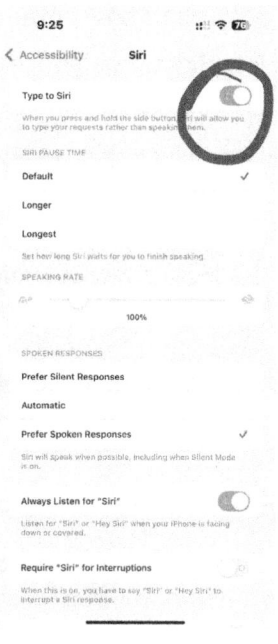

1. Go to **Settings → Accessibility → Siri**.
2. Turn on **Type to Siri**.

Now, instead of talking, you can type queries directly into Siri's interface.

> 📍 **Great for:** People who **prefer silent interactions** or need Siri in **quiet environments like meetings or libraries**.

## Step 5: Personalizing Siri's Suggestions and App Integration

Siri can provide smart suggestions based on your habits and frequently used apps. If you want to control what Siri suggests, follow these steps.

1. Manage Siri's App Suggestions
1. Open **Settings → Siri & Search**.
2. Scroll down to **Siri Suggestions** and toggle on/off:

» **Suggestions on Lock Screen (**shows relevant Siri shortcuts).
» **Suggestions in Search (**suggests apps when you search).
» **Suggestions in Look Up (**provides contextual suggestions).

2. Customize App-Specific Siri Settings

Siri works differently with different apps, and you can manage which apps Siri has access to.

1. Open **Settings → Siri & Search**.
2. Scroll down and **tap on an app** (e.g., Messages, Photos, Maps).
3. Toggle on/off **Use with Siri** depending on your preferences.

> 💡 **Tip:** If you don't want Siri **suggesting embarrassing past searches** or messages, disable Siri for specific apps.

### Step 6: Setting Up Siri for Hands-Free Use

If you want to control your iPhone without touching it, Siri can automate tasks like sending messages, making calls, and reading notifications.

1. Enable Announce Notifications (Great for AirPods Users)
1. Go to **Settings → Siri & Search → Announce Notifications**.
2. Toggle on **Announce Notifications** and select apps.

Now, Siri will read out notifications when you're using AirPods or CarPlay.

2. Enable Siri with CarPlay

If you use Apple CarPlay, you can enable Siri for hands-free navigation and music controls.

1. Connect your iPhone to **CarPlay**.
2. Hold down the **voice command button** on your steering wheel.
3. Ask Siri for directions, music, or messages.

> 💡 **Tip:** If you have **"Hey Siri" enabled**, you can **ask for help hands-free while driving** without pressing any buttons.

### Final Siri Customization Checklist

- **Enabled Siri** (Hey Siri or Press Side Button)
- **Trained Siri to recognize your voice**
- **Customized Siri's language, voice, and responses**
- **Enabled Type to Siri (if needed)**
- **Managed Siri's suggestions and app integration**
- **Set up hands-free controls for notifications and CarPlay**

Now that you've fully set up and customized Siri, you're ready to start using it like a pro. Whether it's checking the weather, setting reminders, or controlling smart home devices, Siri can make your life easier with just a simple voice command.

## Everyday Siri Commands to Save Time and Simplify Tasks

Siri isn't just a voice assistant—it's a powerful tool that can help you streamline your daily routine, boost productivity, and make multitasking easier. Whether you need to send messages hands-free, check the weather, or control your smart home devices, Siri can handle it all with a simple voice command.

This guide will walk you through the most useful Siri commands for different aspects of daily life, helping you save time and reduce effort when using your iPhone.

## Step 1: Using Siri for Basic Information and Quick Lookups

Sometimes you need information right away—whether it's the current time, your next appointment, or a quick calculation. Siri makes it easy to get answers without opening an app.

1. Get the Time, Date, and Weather

- **"Hey Siri, what time is it?"**
- **"Hey Siri, what's today's date?"**
- **"Hey Siri, what's the weather like today?"**

> 💡 Bonus Tip: If you need weather details for another city, just specify the location:

- **"Hey Siri, what's the weather like in Paris?"**

2. Quick Calculations and Conversions

- **"Hey Siri, what's 25% of 175?"**
- **"Hey Siri, convert 10 miles to kilometers."**
- **"Hey Siri, how many cups are in a liter?"**

These quick math functions can be a lifesaver, whether you're splitting a bill at dinner or converting measurements while cooking.

## Step 2: Making Calls and Sending Messages Hands-Free

Siri is fantastic for hands-free communication, especially when driving, cooking, or simply when your hands are full.

1. Making Phone Calls

- **"Hey Siri, call Mom."**
- **"Hey Siri, dial 555-123-4567."**
- **"Hey Siri, redial the last number."**

> 💡 Bonus Tip: If you want to use speakerphone automatically, say:

- **"Hey Siri, call Dad on speaker."**

2. Sending Text Messages and Emails

- **"Hey Siri, send a message to Sarah: 'I'll be there in 10 minutes.'"**
- **"Hey Siri, send an email to John with the subject 'Meeting Update' and say 'Let's reschedule to 4 PM.'"**

> 📍 Tip: Siri will read back your message before sending it. If you want to send it immediately, just say:

- **"Hey Siri, send it."**

## Step 3: Managing Your Schedule with Siri

Siri is your personal assistant when it comes to organizing your day. You can set reminders, schedule appointments, and check your calendar effortlessly.

1. Setting Reminders and Alarms

- **"Hey Siri, remind me to take my medicine at 8 AM."**
- **"Hey Siri, remind me to water the plants every Monday at 6 PM."**
- **"Hey Siri, wake me up at 7 AM."**

> 📍 Bonus Tip: You can set location-based reminders like:

- **"Hey Siri, remind me to buy milk when I get to the grocery store."**

2. Checking and Adding Calendar Events

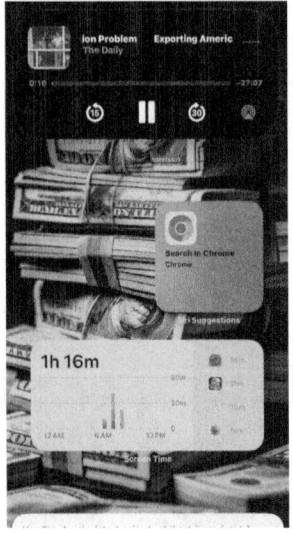

- **"Hey Siri, what's on my calendar for today?"**
- **"Hey Siri, schedule a meeting with Tom tomorrow at 3 PM."**

> 📍 Tip: If you made a mistake, you can ask Siri to **reschedule or cancel events**.

## Step 4: Controlling Your Music and Podcasts

Whether you're driving, working out, or just relaxing, Siri can play your favorite music or podcasts with a simple command.

1. Playing Music

- **"Hey Siri, play some jazz."**
- **"Hey Siri, play my workout playlist."**
- **"Hey Siri, skip this song."**

- **"Hey Siri, play 'Imagine' by John Lennon."**

2. Controlling Podcasts and Audiobooks

- **"Hey Siri, play the latest episode of 'The Daily' podcast."**
- **"Hey Siri, skip ahead 30 seconds."**

## Step 5: Navigating with Siri

Siri is an excellent travel companion, whether you're driving, walking, or using public transport.

1. Getting Directions

- **"Hey Siri, give me directions to the nearest coffee shop."**
- **"Hey Siri, how long will it take to get home?"**

2. Checking Traffic and Nearby Locations

- **"Hey Siri, what's the traffic like on my way to work?"**
- **"Hey Siri, where's the nearest gas station?"**

## Step 6: Managing Smart Home Devices with Siri

If you use HomeKit-enabled smart devices, Siri can control them with your voice.

1. Controlling Lights and Appliances

- **"Hey Siri, turn off the living room lights."**
- **"Hey Siri, set the thermostat to 72 degrees."**

2. Using Siri with Security Devices

- **"Hey Siri, lock the front door."**
- **"Hey Siri, show me the front door camera."**

## Step 7: Fun and Hidden Siri Features

Siri isn't just practical—it can be fun and entertaining too. Try these commands when you need a laugh!

- **"Hey Siri, tell me a joke."**

- "Hey Siri, what's your favorite movie?"
- "Hey Siri, beatbox for me."

> 💡 **Bonus Easter Egg:** Ask Siri **"What does the fox say?"** for a fun response.

## Final Siri Commands Cheat Sheet

- Basic Information: Time, date, weather, calculations.
- Calls & Messages: Hands-free communication.
- Scheduling & Reminders: Stay organized effortlessly.
- Music & Podcasts: Play songs, skip tracks, control volume.
- Navigation: Directions, traffic updates, nearby places.
- Smart Home Control: Lights, appliances, security systems.
- Entertainment & Fun: Jokes, trivia, hidden easter eggs.

By using these everyday Siri commands, you can save time, simplify tasks, and make your iPhone experience truly hands-free. Whether you're looking to be more productive or just have a little fun, Siri is ready to help—just ask!

# Creating Custom Shortcuts for Frequently Used Features

Siri is already a powerful assistant, but when you start creating custom shortcuts, it transforms into a personalized automation tool tailored to your daily routine. With Siri Shortcuts, you can streamline repetitive tasks, launch multiple actions with a single phrase, and even connect multiple apps for a seamless, hands-free experience.

If you've ever thought, *"I wish Siri could do this faster!"*—good news: it can. Whether you want to text your spouse when you leave work, turn on Do Not Disturb before a meeting, or create a morning routine that starts your favorite playlist and pulls up the weather—Siri Shortcuts can do it all.

## Step 1: Understanding Siri Shortcuts

Siri Shortcuts are custom voice commands that trigger one or more automated tasks. These can be as simple as "Hey Siri, I'm on my way" (which sends a text and opens Maps) or as advanced as running a multi-step sequence that adjusts your smart home, starts a workout, and sends a reminder—all at once.

TYPES OF SIRI SHORTCUTS

1. **Basic Shortcuts (Pre-Suggested by iOS)**
   - » iOS **automatically suggests shortcuts b**ased on your activity. For example:

- » If you often text "On my way" to a contact, Siri will suggest a shortcut for that.
- » If you frequently open a specific app in the morning, it may suggest creating a shortcut.

2. **Custom Shortcuts (Created in the Shortcuts App)**

- » With Apple's Sh**ortcuts app,** you can bu**ild multi-step automations** u**sing** if**-then conditions, time triggers, and app integrations.**

3. **App-Specific Shortcuts**

- » Many apps (like Google Maps, Spotify, and HomeKit-enabled apps) provide built-in Siri Shortcuts that you can activate.

## Step 2: Creating a Basic Siri Shortcut

Before diving into advanced automations, let's create a simple shortcut—one that sends a text message and opens Maps when you say, *"Hey Siri, I'm leaving home."*

1. Open the Shortcuts App

- Open **Shortcuts** on your iPhone.
- Tap **Create Shortcut**.

2. Add an Action

- Tap **Add Action → Apps → Messages**.
- Choose **Send Message** and type your recipient and message (e.g., "I'm on my way!").

3. Add a Second Action (Optional)

- Tap **+ Add Action** again.
- Select **Maps** and choose **Get Directions to Home/Work**.

4. Set a Siri Voice Command

- Tap the **Share icon** at the bottom, then tap **Add to Siri**.
- Record your custom command (e.g., *"I'm leaving home."*).

5. Save and Test

- Tap **Done**, then **test** by saying *"Hey Siri, I'm leaving home."*

## Step 3: Advanced Shortcuts for Daily Use

Once you master basic shortcuts, you can create more complex automations that integrate multiple apps. Here are a few powerful shortcuts to try:

1. A Morning Routine Shortcut

With one voice command, Siri can:

- Read today's weather

- Announce your calendar events
- Start a news podcast
- Turn on smart lights

How to create it:

- Open **Shortcuts** → Tap **+ Add Action** → **Choose "Get Weather"**.
- Add **Calendar** → **Get Today's Events**.
- Add **Podcasts** → **Play Latest Episode**.
- Add **HomeKit** → **Turn On Smart Lights**.
- Tap **Add to Siri**, then record **"Good morning!"**.

> 💡 Tip: You can also **set this shortcut to run automatically at a scheduled time each morning** (without needing to say "Hey Siri").

2. Do Not Disturb Mode for Meetings

If you frequently forget to turn on Do Not Disturb during meetings, create a shortcut that:

- Activates **Do Not Disturb**
- Sends a **"I'm in a meeting"** auto-reply to texts
- Ends **after 1 hour**

How to create it:

- Open **Shortcuts** → Tap **+ Add Action** → **Set Do Not Disturb Until End of Event**.
- Add **Send Auto-Reply in Messages**.
- Tap **Add to Siri**, then record **"I'm in a meeting."**

## Step 4: Creating Location-Based Shortcuts

Another way to trigger Siri Shortcuts automatically is by setting location-based triggers. For example:

1. **Text Your Family When You Arrive at Work/Home**
   - » Open Sh**ortcuts** → Au**tomation** → Create **Personal Automation.**
   - » Choose Ar**rive** → Se**lect Location (**Home or Work).
   - » Add Se**nd Message a**nd type your preferred text.

2. **Turn On Wi-Fi When You Get Home**
   - » Create an automation that tu**rns on Wi-Fi and Bluetooth w**hen you arrive home, and tu**rns them off w**hen you leave.

> 💡 Tip: Location-based automations can **run silently in the background**—so Siri takes care of tasks without you even asking.

### Step 5: Siri Shortcuts for Health and Fitness

Siri can also help with your health goals by automating fitness routines and reminders.

1.   Start a Workout with One Command

- Open **Shortcuts → Add Action → Apple Fitness+ or Strava**.
- Choose **Start Workout**.
- Tap **Add to Siri**, then record **"Let's work out!"**.

2.   Track Your Water Intake

- Open **Shortcuts → Add Action → Health**.
- Select **Log Water Intake** and set a default amount.
- Assign a Siri command like **"Log my water"**.

> 💡 Tip: Pair this with **Reminder notifications** to encourage daily habits.

### Final Siri Shortcuts Cheat Sheet

- **Basic Commands:** One-step actions like sending texts or opening apps.
- **Multi-Step Automations:** Combine tasks like weather, news, and music.
- **Location-Based Shortcuts:** Automate actions based on where you are.
- **Health & Fitness Shortcuts:** Track workouts, water intake, or reminders.
- **Smart Home Integrations:** Control lights, locks, and thermostats hands-free.

By setting up custom Siri Shortcuts, you can simplify daily tasks, increase efficiency, and personalize your iPhone experience like never before. Whether it's saving time, reducing manual effort, or just making life more convenient, Siri is ready to work for you—exactly the way you want it to.

# Using Siri with Smart Home Devices for Hands-Free Living

Imagine walking into your home and simply saying, *"Hey Siri, I'm home,"* and instantly the lights turn on, the thermostat adjusts to your preferred temperature, and your favorite playlist starts playing in the background. With Siri and Apple's HomeKit, this futuristic vision is a reality today.

Siri makes hands-free smart home control incredibly easy, whether you're managing lights, adjusting the thermostat, locking doors, or even running entire automated routines. The best part? You don't need to be tech-savvy to set it up. If you have an iPhone, iPad, or HomePod, you're already halfway there.

## Step 1: Understanding HomeKit and Siri Integration

Apple's HomeKit is the system that allows smart home devices to communicate with your iPhone. If a smart device is HomeKit-compatible, it means you can control it through Siri—either with your voice, via the Home app, or even using automations.

### WHAT CAN SIRI CONTROL IN YOUR SMART HOME?

Siri can manage a wide range of smart devices, including:

- **Lights** – Turn lights on/off, dim them, or change colors.
- **Thermostats** – Adjust heating and cooling settings.
- **Locks** – Lock or unlock doors securely.
- **Security Cameras** – Check live feeds or playback recordings.
- **Blinds/Shades** – Raise or lower blinds automatically.
- **Appliances** – Control smart plugs and outlets.
- **Speakers & TVs** – Adjust volume, switch channels, or play music.

## Step 2: Setting Up Siri with HomeKit Devices

Before Siri can control your smart home, you need to connect your smart devices to Apple HomeKit.

1.  Open the Home App

- On your iPhone, open the **Home app**.
- Tap **Add Accessory** (the + icon in the upper-right corner).

2.  Scan the HomeKit Code

- Look for the **HomeKit QR code** on your smart device or its packaging.
- Scan it using your iPhone camera.

3.  Assign the Device to a Room

- Give your device a **custom name** (e.g., "Living Room Lights").
- Assign it to a specific **room** (this helps when controlling multiple devices).

4.  Enable Siri Control

- Once added, you can now use Siri commands like:

    » *"Hey Siri, turn on the living room lights."*
    » *"Hey Siri, set the thermostat to 72 degrees."*

## Step 3: Essential Siri Commands for Smart Home Control

Once your devices are set up, you can use Siri hands-free to control your home. Here are some everyday Siri commands you can try:

### LIGHTS & POWER

- *"Hey Siri, turn off all the lights."*
- *"Hey Siri, dim the bedroom lights to 50%."*
- *"Hey Siri, turn on the kitchen lights in 10 minutes."*

### THERMOSTAT & TEMPERATURE

- *"Hey Siri, set the temperature to 72 degrees."*
- *"Hey Siri, make it cooler in the living room."*

### SECURITY & DOORS

- *"Hey Siri, lock the front door."*
- *"Hey Siri, is the garage door closed?"*

### ENTERTAINMENT & MUSIC

- *"Hey Siri, play my favorite playlist in the living room."*
- *"Hey Siri, turn on the Apple TV and start Netflix."*

> 💡 Tip: **Use personalized names** for your devices so you don't have to remember default names. For example, renaming **"Thermostat"** to **"Living Room Heat"** makes it more natural to say, *"Hey Siri, turn up the Living Room Heat."*

## Step 4: Creating Smart Home Routines with Siri

Beyond simple commands, Siri can combine multiple actions into one phrase using HomeKit Scenes and Automations.

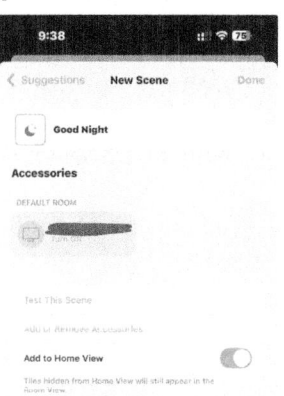

1. Create a Scene (Multiple Actions in One Command)

Scenes allow you to control multiple devices with a single voice command.

Example: Good Night Scene

- Turns off all the lights.
- Locks the doors.
- Adjusts the thermostat.

How to Create a Scene:

- Open the **Home app** → Tap **+ Add Scene**.
- Name it **"Good Night"**.
- Add devices (e.g., lights, thermostat, locks).
- Tap **Done**, then say: *"Hey Siri, good night!"*

2.   Automate Actions Based on Time or Location

You can also set automatic triggers, so Siri doesn't even need a voice command.

Example: "Leave Home" Automation

- When your iPhone detects you **leaving home**, it:
  - » Turns off all lights.
  - » Locks the front door.
  - » Adjusts the thermostat.

How to Set Up Automations:

- Open **Home app** → **Automation** → **Create Personal Automation**.
- Choose **"When I Leave Home"**.
- Select actions (e.g., turn off lights, lock doors).
- Tap **Done**.

Now, Siri will automatically run this routine when you leave the house—no voice command needed!

**9:39**

**Automation**
Have your accessories react to changes at home.

Make Apple TV (4th generation or later) or HomePod the centre of your home. Control HomeKit-enabled accessories remotely, grant access to the people you trust, and automate accessories to do what you want, when you want.

## Step 5: Using Siri with HomePod for a True Smart Home Hub

If you have a HomePod mini or Apple TV, it can act as a HomeKit hub, allowing you to control your smart home even when you're not home.

What a HomeKit Hub Enables:

- **Remote control** of smart home devices.
- **Automations** that run even when your phone is off.
- **Secure access** to smart locks and security cameras.

> 📍 Tip: If you travel often, **set up a HomeKit hub** so you can control everything from anywhere in the world—just say *"Hey Siri, turn off the lights at home."*

## Final Siri Smart Home Cheat Sheet

- **Turn lights on/off, dim them, or change colors.**
- **Adjust thermostat, heating, or cooling settings.**
- **Lock/unlock doors securely.**

- **Check security cameras and garage doors.**
- **Control music, Apple TV, and speakers.**
- **Set up automation routines like "Good Morning" or "Good Night".**
- **Use a HomePod or Apple TV for remote control access.**

By setting up Siri with your smart home devices, you can create a hands-free experience that saves time, increases convenience, and even boosts home security. Whether it's turning off the lights without getting out of bed or checking if you locked the door from miles away, Siri makes home automation feel effortless.

# Troubleshooting Siri: When Things Don't Work as Expected

Siri is designed to make life easier, handling everything from sending messages to setting reminders, controlling smart devices, and even answering random trivia questions. But let's be honest—sometimes Siri doesn't quite get it right. Maybe she misinterprets what you said, refuses to respond, or stops working entirely. If you're finding yourself saying, *"Siri, why aren't you listening to me?"* more than you'd like, this guide will help you diagnose and fix the problem.

### Step 1: Checking Basic Siri Settings

Before diving into advanced troubleshooting, start with the basics. Sometimes, Siri's issues stem from simple settings that aren't enabled or accidental changes in your iPhone's configuration.

1.  Make Sure Siri is Enabled

If Siri isn't responding, the first thing to check is whether it's actually turned on.

- Open **Settings → Siri & Search**
- Ensure **Listen for "Hey Siri"** and **Press Side Button for Siri** are both toggled ON.

If Siri was off, turning it on should resolve your issue! But if it was already on and still isn't working, continue to the next step.

2.  Restart Your iPhone

Yes, the classic *"Have you tried turning it off and on again?"* applies to Siri too.

- Press and hold the **Side Button + Volume Down**, then slide to **Power Off**.
- Wait **30 seconds**, then turn your iPhone back on.
- Try activating Siri again.

> 💡 **Tip:** If your iPhone has been on for weeks without a restart, temporary glitches might be affecting Siri's performance. A quick reboot often fixes these problems.

## Step 2: Fixing Siri's Microphone and Audio Issues

Siri relies on your iPhone's microphone to hear your commands. If the microphone isn't working properly, Siri won't be able to detect your voice or might misunderstand your requests.

1.   Test Your Microphone

Try using Voice Memos to record yourself speaking:

*   Open the **Voice Memos** app.
*   Record a short message and play it back.

If the audio sounds muffled, Siri might not be hearing you clearly. Clean your microphone:

*   Gently remove dust using a **soft-bristle brush** or compressed air.
*   Make sure your iPhone case isn't **blocking the microphone**.

If Siri still isn't responding, try using wired or wireless headphones (like AirPods) and activating Siri. If Siri works fine through a headset, the issue is likely with your iPhone's built-in microphone.

## Step 3: Fixing Siri's Connection Issues

Siri relies on an active internet connection to process most commands. If your internet is slow or disconnected, Siri might struggle to respond.

1.   Check Your Wi-Fi or Cellular Data

Try opening Safari and loading a webpage. If it's slow or not loading:

*   Toggle **Wi-Fi off and on** (Settings → Wi-Fi).
*   If on cellular, ensure **Cellular Data is enabled** (Settings → Cellular → Toggle "Cellular Data" ON).

> 📍 Tip: If you see *"Siri is not available"*, it usually means your connection is too weak for Siri to process requests. Try switching to a **different Wi-Fi network** or **resetting your router**.

## Step 4: Fixing Siri's Misinterpretations

If Siri doesn't understand your requests or keeps misinterpreting what you say, there are a few tricks to improve accuracy.

1.   Retrain Siri's Voice Recognition

Siri might struggle to recognize your voice, especially if you've had a cold, changed your speech patterns, or if background noise interferes.

To retrain Siri:

- Open **Settings → Siri & Search**
- Toggle **Listen for "Hey Siri"** OFF and back ON
- Follow the on-screen instructions to **retrain Siri with your voice**.

2.  Speak Clearly and Naturally

While Siri is smart, it's not perfect. Try to:

- Speak **clearly and at a normal pace**.
- Avoid **background noise** like TV or loud music.
- Use **specific phrases** (e.g., "Set an alarm for 7 AM" instead of "Wake me up at 7").

> 📍 Tip: If Siri consistently **misunderstands names**, go to **Contacts**, find the person, tap **Edit**, scroll to **Add Field**, and select **Phonetic Name** to help Siri pronounce it correctly.

## Step 5: Resetting Siri and iPhone Settings

If nothing has worked so far, a reset might be necessary.

1.  Reset Siri's Settings

- Open **Settings → Siri & Search**
- Toggle **all Siri options OFF**, restart your iPhone, then turn Siri back ON.

2.  Reset Network Settings (For Connectivity Issues)

- Go to **Settings → General → Transfer or Reset iPhone → Reset → Reset Network Settings**.
- This clears all **Wi-Fi networks, cellular settings, and VPN configurations**, but sometimes fixes Siri's **internet connection problems**.

> 📍 Warning: This will **erase all saved Wi-Fi passwords**, so be prepared to reconnect to your networks.

## Step 6: Checking for iOS Updates

Apple frequently improves Siri's performance through software updates. If Siri is acting strangely, it might be due to a bug that Apple has already fixed.

To check for updates:

- Go to **Settings → General → Software Update**.
- If an update is available, tap **Download and Install**.

> 📍 Tip: If you notice Siri stopped working **after an iOS update**, Apple might release a **fix in the next update**, so check back frequently.

## Step 7: When to Contact Apple Support

If Siri still isn't working after all these steps, you may be dealing with a hardware issue or a deeper software problem.

SIGNS YOU SHOULD CONTACT APPLE SUPPORT:

- Siri **stopped working after a recent update**, and resets didn't help.
- The microphone **works in some apps but not with Siri**.
- Siri's **responses are delayed or never load**, even on a strong internet connection.

To get help:

- Visit **support.apple.com** and select **Siri** for troubleshooting guides.
- Use the **Apple Support app** (pre-installed on iPhones).
- Book a **Genius Bar appointment** at an Apple Store.

## Siri Troubleshooting Cheat Sheet

- **Make sure Siri is enabled in settings.**
- **Restart your iPhone to clear temporary glitches.**
- **Check the microphone and clean it if needed.**
- **Ensure Wi-Fi or cellular data is working.**
- **Retrain Siri to recognize your voice.**
- **Reset Siri settings if commands aren't recognized.**
- **Update iOS to fix known Siri issues.**
- **Contact Apple Support if nothing else works.**

By following these troubleshooting steps, you should be able to get Siri back up and running smoothly—so you can go back to setting reminders, controlling your smart home, and getting those random trivia answers without frustration!

# CHAPTER 11

# Exploring Hidden Features and Advanced Tips

## Using Widgets, Focus Modes, and Live Activities for Efficiency

Your iPhone isn't just a device—it's your personal assistant, digital planner, and productivity hub all in one. With features like Widgets, Focus Modes, and Live Activities, you can customize your home screen, reduce distractions, and stay on top of real-time events without even opening an app.

These features are designed to make your iPhone work smarter, helping you save time and boost efficiency. Whether you want at-a-glance information, an environment free of distractions, or a real-time feed of live updates, let's dive into how you can leverage these tools to take control of your day.

### Enhancing Productivity with Widgets

Widgets provide quick access to essential information right from your Home Screen or Lock Screen, eliminating the need to open apps repeatedly.

1. Adding and Customizing Widgets

Widgets can be added to your Home Screen and Lock Screen to display weather updates, upcoming events, battery levels, and more. Here's how:

- **To add a widget:**
  - » Press and hold on your Home Screen until the apps start jiggling.
  - » Tap the (+) **icon in** the top-left corner.
  - » Browse through available widgets and tap one to select it.
  - » Choose a size (small, medium, or large) and tap Add **Widget.**
  - » Drag it to your preferred location and tap Done.

💡 Tip: You can also **stack multiple widgets** together by dragging them on top of each other. Swiping through stacked widgets keeps your Home Screen clean while providing **quick access to multiple pieces of information**.

2. Best Widgets for Productivity

- **Calendar**: Shows upcoming meetings and appointments.
- **Reminders**: Displays tasks due for the day.
- **Battery**: Tracks battery levels of your iPhone, AirPods, and Apple Watch.
- **Weather**: Provides real-time weather updates.
- **News**: Displays the latest headlines at a glance.
- **Notes**: Allows quick access to important notes and to-do lists.

> 💡 **Tip:** If you frequently use **Apple Maps** or a ride-sharing app, adding a **travel widget** can help you track travel times, upcoming rides, or estimated arrival times without opening the app.

## Reducing Distractions with Focus Modes

If you ever feel overwhelmed by notifications, Focus Modes help filter them based on what you're doing. Whether you're working, sleeping, or driving, Focus Modes silence unnecessary notifications while allowing important ones through.

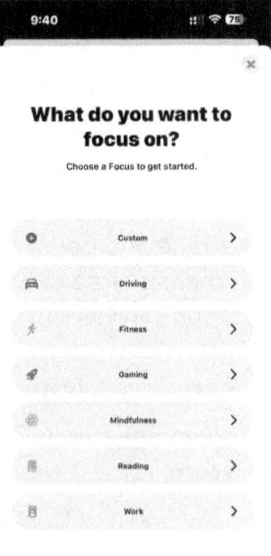

1. Setting Up Focus Mode

- Open **Settings → Focus**.
- Tap **+ Add Focus** to create a new mode.
- Choose a preset (Work, Sleep, Personal, Driving) or create a **Custom Focus**.
- Select which apps and contacts **can notify you** during this Focus Mode.
- Customize your **Home Screen and Lock Screen** to match your Focus Mode.

> 💡 **Tip:** You can also **schedule Focus Modes** to turn on automatically at specific times or when you arrive at certain locations.

2. Creating Different Focus Modes for Maximum Productivity

- **Work Mode**: Blocks distractions like social media while allowing work-related notifications (emails, Slack, etc.).
- **Sleep Mode**: Mutes all notifications except emergency contacts.
- **Driving Mode**: Silences notifications and automatically replies to messages with "I'm driving."
- **Personal Mode**: Lets you enjoy downtime by muting work-related apps.

## Staying Updated with Live Activities

Live Activities are real-time notifications that stay on your Lock Screen and Dynamic Island, updating continuously without requiring you to open an app.

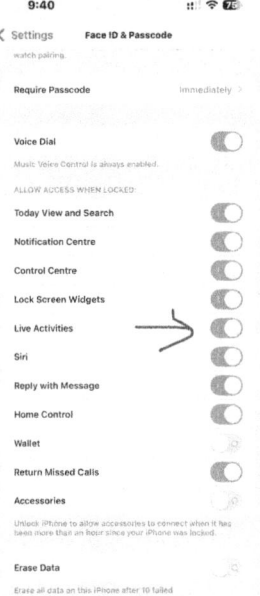

1. How Live Activities Work

Live Activities are perfect for tracking ongoing events like:

- **Food deliveries** (e.g., Uber Eats, DoorDash).
- **Ride-sharing apps** (e.g., Lyft, Uber).
- **Workout tracking** (e.g., Apple Fitness).
- **Sports scores** (e.g., NBA, NFL games).
- **Flight updates** (e.g., Flighty, airline apps).

2. Enabling Live Activities

To enable Live Activities:

- Go to **Settings → Face ID & Passcode**.
- Scroll to **Allow Access When Locked** and toggle ON **Live Activities**.
- Open **Settings → Live Activities** and enable them for apps like Uber, ESPN, or Apple Maps.

## Maximizing Your iPhone's Efficiency

By combining Widgets, Focus Modes, and Live Activities, you can create an iPhone experience that is tailored to your daily routine. Instead of being constantly distracted, these tools help you stay organized, informed, and in control—all with minimal effort.

# Discovering Picture-in-Picture Mode and Multitasking

We live in an era of constant multitasking, where juggling different tasks at once is almost a necessity. Whether you're watching a YouTube tutorial while taking notes, FaceTiming a friend while checking your schedule, or following a recipe while replying to messages, Picture-in-Picture (PiP) mode and multitasking features on your iPhone can significantly improve efficiency.

Apple has integrated powerful multitasking tools that allow you to seamlessly switch between apps, stay productive, and minimize interruptions. If you haven't fully explored these features yet, you're about to discover how to get the most out of your iPhone's ability to do multiple things at once.

## What is Picture-in-Picture Mode?

Picture-in-Picture (PiP) mode lets you continue watching a video or participating in a FaceTime call while using other apps. Instead of pausing what you're doing or keeping an app open, the video shrinks into a floating window that you can move around the screen, allowing you to interact with other apps simultaneously.

1.   How to Use Picture-in-Picture Mode

PiP is automatically enabled for apps that support it. Here's how to use it:

- **For Videos:**
  - » Start playing a video in a supported app (such as Safari, Apple TV, or YouTube Premium).
  - » Swipe up or press the Home button (on iPhones with a Home button).
  - » The video will sh**rink into a floating window t**hat you can drag anywhere on the screen.

- **For FaceTime Calls:**
  - » While on a FaceTime call, swipe up to go to the Home Screen.
  - » Your video call will c**ontinue in a small window,** allowing you to use other apps.

> 💡 Tip: You can **resize the PiP window** by pinching in and out or hide it off-screen by dragging it to the edge.

2.   Best Apps That Support Picture-in-Picture

Not every app supports PiP, but some of the most useful ones include:

- **Safari** – Watch videos from websites while browsing other tabs.
- **Apple TV** – Keep watching movies while replying to messages.
- **YouTube (Premium users)** – Play videos while using other apps.
- **FaceTime** – Multitask during calls.
- **Netflix, Hulu, Disney+** – Stream your favorite shows in a floating window.

> 💡 Tip: If PiP isn't working, **go to Settings → General → Picture in Picture** and make sure it's enabled.

## Mastering Multitasking on Your iPhone

Beyond PiP, your iPhone has built-in multitasking features that help you seamlessly switch between apps and work more efficiently.

1.   Quick Switching Between Apps

When you're using multiple apps, switching between them quickly saves time and effort. Here's how:

- **Swipe left or right on the bottom edge** of the screen to cycle through recent apps.
- **Use the App Switcher** by swiping up and pausing in the middle of the screen, then selecting the app you need.

> **Tip:** This is **especially useful** when copying and pasting between apps or keeping track of multiple conversations.

2.   Drag and Drop for Seamless Productivity

Did you know you can drag and drop text, images, and files between apps?

- Hold your finger on a **photo, link, or text snippet** until it lifts off the screen.
- With another finger, swipe up to access another app.
- Drop the item into a **message, note, or email**.

> **Example:** Drag a **photo from Photos** into a **WhatsApp conversation** or move **a Safari link** directly into a **Notes document**.

## Using Split View and Slide Over (iPad-Exclusive Features)

If you also use an iPad, Apple offers advanced multitasking features that iPhones don't have:

- **Split View**: Run two apps side by side.
- **Slide Over**: Open a secondary app in a floating window over another app.

While these aren't available on iPhones, some third-party apps offer similar multitasking experiences through app-specific pop-up windows or split-screen browsing.

## Combining Picture-in-Picture with Multitasking for Maximum Efficiency

Imagine how much time you can save by using PiP alongside multitasking features:

- **FaceTime + Notes**: Take notes while in a video call.
- **Safari + Calendar**: Browse flights while checking your schedule.
- **YouTube + Messages**: Watch a tutorial while discussing it with a friend.

> 💡 **Tip:** If you're **reading an article or watching a video and want to copy key points**, use **PiP + Drag and Drop** to move text into your Notes app without switching screens.

## Final Thoughts on PiP and Multitasking

By mastering Picture-in-Picture mode, quick app switching, and drag-and-drop, you can turn your iPhone into a powerful multitasking machine. These features eliminate unnecessary steps, reduce distractions, and keep everything within reach, making your digital life more seamless than ever.

# Mastering iCloud: Syncing Data Across All Devices

If you own more than one Apple device—whether it's an iPhone, iPad, Mac, or even an Apple Watch—iCloud is your best friend when it comes to keeping everything in sync. With Apple's seamless cloud-based system, you can access your photos, contacts, messages, and even your Safari tabs from any device effortlessly.

But while iCloud works in the background for most users, many don't realize its full potential. In this section, we'll break down how to make the most of iCloud, troubleshoot common syncing issues, and ensure your data is always available when you need it.

## Understanding How iCloud Syncing Works

iCloud is more than just a backup system—it's a real-time syncing tool that keeps your files, photos, contacts, and app data consistent across all Apple devices.

- When you take a **photo on your iPhone**, it appears instantly on your Mac and iPad via iCloud Photos.
- If you **edit a document in Pages**, the updated file is automatically available on all linked devices.
- Messages, Safari bookmarks, and even Wi-Fi passwords are **shared securely across your Apple ecosystem**.

> 💡 **Tip:** iCloud **requires an internet connection** to sync data. If syncing seems slow or doesn't work, check that Wi-Fi or cellular data is enabled.

## Setting Up iCloud on Your iPhone

To make sure iCloud is syncing everything properly, follow these steps:

1. **Go to Settings** → Tap your **Apple ID (your name at the top)**.
2. **Select iCloud** → You'll see a list of apps and services that use iCloud.

3. **Enable the features you want to sync** (Photos, Contacts, iCloud Drive, Safari, etc.).

## Essential iCloud Features for Syncing Data

Now that you've turned on iCloud, let's go over the key features you should be using.

1. iCloud Photos: Keep Your Pictures Everywhere

iCloud Photos automatically uploads every photo and video to the cloud so you can access them on any device.

- **To enable it:**
  - » Go to Se**ttings** → Ph**otos** → Toggle on iC**loud Photos.**
- **Optimize Storage:** If your iPhone is low on space, enable **Optimize iPhone Storage** to store smaller versions of photos on your device while keeping the full-resolution ones in iCloud.

> **Tip:** Deleted photos stay in **Recently Deleted** for **30 days** before being permanently erased.

2. iCloud Drive: Access Files Across Devices

iCloud Drive is your built-in cloud storage, perfect for syncing documents, PDFs, and app data.

- Open **Settings** → **iCloud** → Toggle on **iCloud Drive**.
- You can access files in the **Files app** on iPhone or **Finder** on a Mac.

> **Tip:** You can also **share iCloud Drive files** with others, making collaboration easier.

3. Syncing Contacts, Calendars, and Notes

One of the biggest benefits of iCloud is that it automatically syncs contacts, calendars, and notes across all devices.

- Go to **Settings** › **iCloud** › Enable **Contacts, Calendars, and Notes**.
- Any update you make to a contact or event **instantly reflects** on your iPad or Mac.

> **Tip:** If contacts or calendar events aren't syncing, check that **you're signed into the same Apple ID** on all devices.

4. Messages in iCloud: Keep Conversations Up-to-Date

Ever wished your text messages would sync between devices? With Messages in iCloud, your entire chat history stays updated everywhere.

- Go to **Settings** → **Messages** → Toggle on **Messages in iCloud**.

> 🎙 Tip: Deleting a message on one device **removes it from all synced devices**—so be careful before deleting anything important!

5.  Safari and Keychain: Syncing Browsing Data and Passwords

With iCloud, your browsing history, tabs, and saved passwords sync across all your Apple devices.

- **Safari Syncing:** Go to **Settings** → **iCloud** → Enable **Safari** to sync bookmarks and tabs.
- **Keychain:** Saves passwords and Wi-Fi networks across devices. Toggle it on under **iCloud Settings**.

> 🎙 Tip: You can access saved passwords by going to **Settings** → **Passwords**.

## Troubleshooting iCloud Syncing Issues

If your data isn't syncing properly, try these steps:

1.  **Check iCloud Status:** Apple services sometimes experience outages. Visit **Apple's System Status page** to check.
2.  **Ensure You're Signed into the Same Apple ID:** If your devices aren't using the same iCloud account, syncing won't work.
3.  **Turn iCloud Off and Back On:** Go to **Settings** → **iCloud**, toggle off the service that isn't syncing, then turn it back on.
4.  **Restart Your Device:** A simple restart often fixes iCloud syncing delays.
5.  **Check Storage Space:** If iCloud is full, new files **won't sync**. Go to **Settings** → **iCloud** → **Manage Storage** to check.

> 🎙 Tip: If iCloud is full, **delete old backups, remove unnecessary files, or upgrade storage** via Apple's iCloud+ plans.

## iCloud Backup: Keeping Your Data Safe

Beyond syncing, iCloud is critical for backups. If you ever lose your iPhone or need to switch to a new device, iCloud Backup ensures you don't lose important data.

- **To enable backups:**
  - » Go to Settings → iCloud → iCloud Backup → Toggle it on.
  - » Tap Back Up Now to create a fresh backup.

> 🎙 Tip: iCloud automatically **backs up your iPhone daily** when connected to Wi-Fi and charging.

## Maximizing iCloud for Seamless Syncing

iCloud makes managing data across devices effortless—as long as it's set up correctly. Whether you're syncing photos, messages, or Safari tabs, keeping iCloud optimized ensures everything stays connected in real time.

By following these steps, you'll unlock the full potential of iCloud, making your Apple experience smoother, safer, and more efficient than ever.

# Creating Automations with Shortcuts for a Smarter iPhone

Your iPhone is already a powerful tool, but what if it could anticipate your needs and perform tasks automatically—without you lifting a finger? That's exactly what Shortcuts and Automations allow you to do. Whether it's having your phone automatically turn on Do Not Disturb when you start a workout, dimming your lights when you're about to sleep, or sending a text to your family when you leave work, Automations make your iPhone work for you.

In this section, we'll explore how to set up iPhone Automations using the Shortcuts app, covering real-world examples, practical use cases, and troubleshooting tips.

### What Are iPhone Automations?

Automations allow your iPhone to perform actions automatically based on triggers like time of day, location, app usage, or even device status. Unlike regular Shortcuts, which you run manually, Automations execute on their own, making your device more intuitive and responsive to your routine.

Examples include:

- **Automatically turning on Low Power Mode** when your battery drops below 20%.
- **Starting your favorite playlist** when you connect Bluetooth headphones.
- **Sending a "Leaving Work" text** when you exit your office location.

> ♥ Tip: Automations can be **completely hands-free**, but some require user confirmation to run. We'll cover how to disable these prompts later.

### How to Create an Automation in Shortcuts

To set up an automation:

1. **Open the Shortcuts app** on your iPhone.
2. Tap **Automation** at the bottom.

3. Tap **Create Personal Automation** (or **New Automation** if you already have some set up).
4. Select a **trigger** (e.g., "Time of Day," "When I Leave Home," or "Wi-Fi Connects").
5. Choose the **action(s)** you want to automate.
6. Tap **Next**, review your settings, and tap **Done**.

## Best iPhone Automations for Everyday Use

Now that you know how to create Automations, let's look at some of the most useful and time-saving ones you can set up today.

### 1. Automate Your Morning Routine

Mornings can feel rushed, but Automations can help streamline your start to the day.

- **Trigger:** Time of Day → Set for when you wake up.
- **Actions:**
  » Read **today's weather** aloud.
  » Launch **your favorite morning playlist.**
  » Open **the News app t**o check headlines.

> 💡 Tip: You can even make Siri read out your **calendar events** for the day!

### 2. Auto-Enable Low Power Mode at a Certain Battery Level

If you find yourself always turning on Low Power Mode manually, automate it.

- **Trigger:** Battery Level → **20% or lower**.
- **Action:** Enable **Low Power Mode**.

> 💡 Tip: You can also add a **notification** that reminds you to charge your phone when this automation runs.

### 3. Set Up a "Leaving Work" Notification

Want to let your family know when you're heading home without sending a text every day? Automate it!

- **Trigger:** Location → When you leave **your workplace**.
- **Action:** Send a text like **"On my way home!"** to your family.

> 💡 Tip: This also works for **arriving home**, so your smart lights or thermostat can turn on as you pull into the driveway.

### 4. Silence Notifications During Focus Time

Need distraction-free work sessions? Automate Focus Mode based on time or app usage.

- **Trigger:** Time of Day (e.g., **9 AM to 12 PM** for deep work).
- **Action:** Enable **Work Focus Mode** → Silence notifications.

> 💡 Tip: You can also trigger this **when opening certain apps** like Notes or Google Docs.

5.  Enable Dark Mode at Sunset

Prefer Dark Mode in the evening? Make it happen automatically.

- **Trigger: Sunset** (uses your local time).
- **Action: Enable Dark Mode**.

> 💡 Tip: If you use **Night Shift**, you can **combine it** with Dark Mode for less eye strain at night.

6.  Lock Social Media After a Certain Time

If you're trying to limit distractions, you can automatically close apps after a set time.

- **Trigger:** Time of Day (e.g., **11 PM**).
- **Action:** Close **Instagram, TikTok, or YouTube**.

> 💡 Tip: Combine this with **Downtime in Screen Time settings** for more control.

## How to Disable "Ask Before Running" in Automations

By default, most Automations require user confirmation before running. This can be annoying, especially for hands-free tasks. Here's how to turn it off:

1.  Open **Shortcuts** → Go to the **Automation tab**.
2.  Select the **Automation you want to edit**.
3.  Toggle off **Ask Before Running** → Confirm **Don't Ask**.

> 💡 Tip: Not all Automations allow this option—location-based triggers still require confirmation due to privacy rules.

## Troubleshooting Common Automation Issues

If your Automations aren't running as expected, try these fixes:

- **Check if Shortcuts has permission** → Go to **Settings** → **Shortcuts** → Ensure **Allow Untrusted Shortcuts** is on.

- **Ensure background app refresh is enabled** → Some Automations need this to run in the background.
- **Restart your iPhone** → A simple restart can resolve most issues.
- **Update iOS** → Some bugs in older versions might prevent Automations from working properly.

## Taking Automations to the Next Level

Once you've mastered basic Automations, you can combine multiple actions for even smarter workflows:

- **"Good Night" Automation:**
  - » Turn on Do **Not Disturb.**
  - » Set Low **Power Mode.**
  - » Play white **noise or a sleep playlist.**
- **"Gym Mode" Automation:**
  - » Launch Spotify **w**hen you connect your AirPods.
  - » Turn on Do **Not Disturb.**
  - » Open Workout app.

> 💡 Tip: **Use Siri voice commands** to trigger Shortcuts manually when needed!

## Final Thoughts on iPhone Automations

With Shortcuts and Automations, your iPhone can anticipate your needs and handle everyday tasks without effort. Whether it's setting the mood for a workout, keeping distractions at bay, or sending location-based messages, Automations help your device work smarter, not harder.

# Unlocking Hidden Camera and Editing Tricks

Your iPhone's camera is packed with hidden features and powerful editing tools that can turn everyday moments into stunning, professional-looking photos and videos. Whether you're capturing family memories, shooting artistic portraits, or creating content for social media, mastering these tricks can elevate your photography game.

Let's explore some of the best-kept secrets of the iPhone camera, along with hidden editing tools that will transform your photos and videos in seconds.

# Hidden iPhone Camera Tricks You Need to Know

Your iPhone's camera is capable of much more than just pointing and shooting. Here are some of the most useful hidden camera features that can take your photos to the next level.

1.    Use the Hidden Level for Perfectly Straight Shots

Ever struggled to keep your horizon perfectly level when taking photos? The iPhone has a built-in leveling tool that helps you line up your shots with precision.

How to enable it:

1.    Open **Settings → Camera**.
2.    Scroll down and turn on **Grid**.
3.    Now, when you tilt your iPhone, you'll see a **hidden crosshair** in the center of the screen, helping you align your shot.

   💡 Tip: This is especially useful for taking **flat lays** (photos of objects arranged on a flat surface) and **architectural shots** where symmetry is important.

2.    Capture Photos While Recording a Video

Sometimes, while recording a video, you might see a perfect photo opportunity. Instead of stopping the recording, you can take a photo while shooting a video.

How to do it:

•    While recording a video in the **Camera app**, look for the **white shutter button** on the screen.
•    Tap it to capture a photo **without interrupting the video**.

   💡 Tip: The photos taken during video recording will **not be as high-resolution** as normal photos but still retain great quality.

3.    Use Burst Mode for Fast-Moving Subjects

Trying to capture kids playing, pets running, or sports action? Burst mode allows you to take multiple photos in rapid succession so you can choose the perfect shot.

How to use it:

•    Hold down the **shutter button** in the Camera app.
•    Your iPhone will take a **burst of photos** at high speed.
•    Open the **Photos app**, select the burst, and choose the best images.

   💡 Tip: You can also enable **Volume Up for Burst Mode** under **Settings → Camera**, making it easier to activate.

4.    Shoot in ProRAW for Maximum Detail (For iPhone Pro Models)

If you have an iPhone Pro, you can shoot in Apple ProRAW, which captures more detail, better color, and higher dynamic range for professional editing.

How to enable ProRAW:

1. Open **Settings → Camera → Formats**.
2. Turn on **Apple ProRAW**.
3. In the Camera app, tap **RAW** at the top of the screen before taking a photo.

> 💡 Tip: ProRAW files are **much larger than standard photos**, so use this only when needed.

## Hidden Editing Tricks in the Photos App

The Photos app isn't just for viewing your pictures—it's packed with powerful editing tools that can make your photos look professionally retouched without needing third-party apps.

1. Remove Reflections and Glare from Photos

Have you ever taken a photo through glass and ended up with annoying reflections? iPhone's editing tools can reduce glare with just a few taps.

How to do it:

1. Open the **Photos app** and select a photo.
2. Tap **Edit → Exposure**.
3. Reduce the **Highlights** and adjust the **Shadows** to minimize glare.

> 💡 Tip: This works well for **photos taken through car windows or storefront glass**.

2. Enhance Portrait Mode Blur (or Remove It)

Portrait mode creates a beautiful blurred background, but did you know you can adjust or remove the blur after taking the photo?

How to do it:

1. Open a **Portrait Mode photo** in the **Photos app**.
2. Tap **Edit** → Adjust the **f/number slider** at the top.
3. A lower **f/stop (like f/1.4)** creates more blur, while a higher **f/stop (like f/16)** reduces it.

> 💡 Tip: If the blur looks unnatural around hair or edges, use the **Depth Control slider** to refine it.

3. Turn Live Photos into Long Exposures

Long exposure photography is usually done with a professional camera, but your iPhone can do it too using Live Photos!

How to create a long exposure:

1. Take a **Live Photo** (make sure the yellow "Live" icon is on).
2. Open the photo in **Photos** and swipe up.
3. Select **Long Exposure** from the effects list.

> 💡 Tip: This works best for **waterfalls, night traffic, and moving clouds**.

4. Use the "Brilliance" Tool for Instant Photo Enhancement

If your photo looks dull or underexposed, the Brilliance tool in the Photos app can instantly brighten shadows and improve contrast without over-editing.

How to use it:

1. Open a photo in **Photos → Edit**.
2. Scroll to **Brilliance** and adjust the slider.
3. Watch as your photo gains **more detail and natural contrast**.

> 💡 Tip: Unlike **Exposure**, which brightens the whole image, **Brilliance focuses on details**, making it more natural.

## Bonus: Hidden Video Editing Features

If you love shooting videos, the Photos app has powerful editing tools to enhance your footage without needing iMovie or third-party apps.

1. Trim and Cut Clips in Seconds

- Open **Photos → Select a video.
- Tap **Edit** → Drag the **yellow handles** on the timeline to trim the video.

> 💡 Tip: This is great for **removing unnecessary footage before sharing a video**.

2. Adjust Video Colors Like a Pro

- Open a video in **Edit Mode**.
- Adjust settings like **Brilliance, Exposure, Shadows, and Saturation** just like in photos.

> 💡 Tip: If your video looks **too warm or too cool**, use the **Tint** and **Temperature** sliders for a color-balanced look.

3. Add Slow Motion to Any Video (Even If You Didn't Record in Slo-Mo!)

Didn't record in Slow Motion but want that effect? You can add it afterward!

- Open the **Photos app** → Select a video.
- Tap **Edit** → Choose **Speed**.
- Adjust the **speed slider** to slow down or speed up the video.

> 💡 Tip: Use this to **emphasize action shots**, like jumping into a pool or a dramatic moment.

## Final Thoughts on iPhone Camera and Editing Tricks

With these hidden camera and editing tricks, your iPhone becomes a powerful photography tool—no expensive software required. Whether you're capturing stunning portraits, cinematic videos, or artistic long exposures, these features help unlock the full potential of your iPhone's camera.

CHAPTER 12

# Keeping Memories Alive with Photos and Videos

## Creating Slideshows and Movies with Your Photos

Your iPhone is more than just a tool for capturing photos and videos—it's also a powerful storytelling device. Whether you're reminiscing about a family vacation, celebrating a milestone, or simply organizing your memories, creating slideshows and movies is an easy and engaging way to bring your photos to life.

With just a few taps, you can compile your best moments, add music, apply transitions, and customize the flow to create a beautiful, shareable video that can be enjoyed on your iPhone, iPad, or even your TV.

### Using the Photos App to Create Automatic Slideshows

The Photos app comes with a built-in feature called Memories, which automatically selects and organizes pictures from a specific event, location, or time period and presents them in a stylish slideshow. But did you know you can customize and create your own slideshows too?

CREATING A QUICK SLIDESHOW FROM AN ALBUM

If you want a fast, hassle-free slideshow, this method is for you:

1. Open the **Photos app**.
2. Go to **Albums** and select an album or create a new one with the photos you want.
3. Tap the **More Options (...) button** in the top-right corner.
4. Choose **Play Memory Movie**.

Your iPhone will automatically generate a slideshow with music and transitions. You can watch it immediately or customize it.

> 🔦 Tip: The Photos app smartly selects moments, but you can **remove or rearrange photos** if you prefer more control.

## CUSTOMIZING A SLIDESHOW IN THE PHOTOS APP

Once your Memory Movie is created, you can fine-tune it to match your style:

1. Tap the **Edit** button while viewing the slideshow.
2. Choose a **different theme** (like "Happy," "Chill," or "Epic") to adjust the mood.
3. Change the **music** by selecting a different song from Apple's options or your **own music library**.
4. Adjust the **length and pacing** of the video.
5. Add or remove **specific photos or videos**.

> **Tip:** If you want **more precise editing tools**, consider using iMovie or a third-party app like Splice or CapCut.

## Creating a Custom Movie with iMovie

For more creative control, Apple's iMovie app is the best tool to turn your photos and videos into a profession-al-looking movie with titles, effects, and voiceovers.

### STEP-BY-STEP GUIDE TO MAKING A MOVIE IN IMOVIE

1. **Open iMovie** (free on the App Store) and tap **Create Project**.
2. Choose **Movie** (not Trailer, unless you want a pre-made format).
3. Select the **photos and videos** you want to include.
4. Tap **Create Movie**, and you'll be taken to the time-line.
5. Here's where the fun begins:
   » **Rearrange clips by** dragging them in the time-line.
   » Add transitions (like fade-ins and slide effects).
   » Insert text titles for captions or descriptions.
   » Overlay music from Apple's free soundtracks or your own library.
   » Use filters to give a cinematic touch.

> **Tip:** If you want to add a **voiceover**, tap the **+ button**, select **Voiceover**, and record directly into iMovie.

## Adding Music and Sound Effects

A slideshow or movie isn't complete without music that sets the mood. Here's how to add audio effectively:

- **In the Photos app**: Choose from built-in themes with matching music.
- **In iMovie**:
  - » Tap the + **button** → Select Au**dio.**
  - » Choose from So**undtracks (free Apple music),** My **Music,** or Sound **Effects.**

> 🍴 Tip: If you want a **royalty-free music option**, you can download tracks from **websites like Free Music Archive or YouTube Audio Library**.

## Advanced Editing Features in iMovie

Want to make your slideshow stand out? Here are some powerful tricks:

1.  Ken Burns Effect for Dynamic Photo Movement

The Ken Burns effect adds subtle zooming and panning to still images, making them feel more dynamic.

- In iMovie, select a photo → Tap the **Crop button** → Enable **Ken Burns**.
- Adjust the **start and end positions** for a smooth motion.

> 🍴 Tip: This is great for storytelling, like zooming into a **child's face in a family slideshow**.

2.  Overlaying Text and Captions

Adding text can provide context or emphasize emotions in your slideshow.

- In iMovie, tap the **T icon** and choose a **text style**.
- Drag and position the text where you want it.
- Adjust the **duration** to control how long it appears.

> 🍴 Tip: Use this for **anniversary dates, travel locations, or special messages**.

3.  Slow Motion and Speed Effects

Want to emphasize a key moment? Slow motion can add drama to an important scene.

- Select a video in iMovie.
- Tap **Speed (the speedometer icon)** and **adjust the slider**.
- Speed it up or slow it down as needed.

> **Tip:** This is great for **wedding videos, sports highlights, or action-packed moments**.

## Saving and Sharing Your Slideshow or Movie

Once your slideshow or movie is complete, you'll want to share it with family and friends.

### SAVING YOUR PROJECT

1. Tap the **Share button** in iMovie or Photos.
2. Choose **Save Video** (it will export to your Photos app).
3. Select the **resolution** (1080p is ideal for high-quality playback).

### SHARING OPTIONS

- **Airdrop**: Instantly send to another Apple device.
- **iMessage/WhatsApp**: Share directly with friends and family.
- **Social Media**: Upload to **Instagram, Facebook, or YouTube**.
- **Apple TV/AirPlay**: Watch on a big screen.

> **Tip:** If the video file is **too large to send via email**, upload it to **iCloud Drive or Google Drive** and share the link.

## Final Thoughts on Creating Slideshows and Movies

Turning your photos and videos into a beautifully crafted slideshow or movie isn't just about technology—it's about preserving memories that last a lifetime. Whether you're making a birthday surprise, a wedding montage, or a travel documentary, your iPhone provides all the tools you need to make something truly special.

# Organizing Family Albums and Sharing Them Safely

Capturing precious moments is effortless with an iPhone, but what happens after? If your photo library is cluttered with thousands of random pictures, it can be overwhelming to find the special memories that matter most. Organizing your family albums ensures that your best photos are easy to find, beautifully arranged, and ready to be shared with loved ones.

Apple's Photos app offers a range of powerful tools to keep your pictures organized, create shared albums, and safeguard your memories with privacy settings. Whether you want to build a digital scrapbook, share pictures with grandparents, or make sure your photos are secure and backed up, this guide will help you master the process.

## Creating and Organizing Family Albums in the Photos App

Instead of scrolling endlessly through your camera roll, organizing photos into albums can help you group images by events, people, or themes.

### STEP-BY-STEP GUIDE TO CREATING AN ALBUM

1. Open the **Photos app** on your iPhone.
2. Tap the **Albums** tab at the bottom.
3. Tap the **+ icon** in the top left corner and select **New Album**.
4. Give your album a **meaningful name** (e.g., "Summer Vacation 2024" or "Grandkids").
5. Select the **photos and videos** you want to add, then tap **Done**.

> 💡 Tip: You can always add more photos later by selecting an image, tapping **Add to Album**, and choosing where it belongs.

### SMART ALBUMS: LET YOUR IPHONE DO THE WORK

If manually sorting photos sounds tedious, let Apple's AI-powered organization help you.

- **People & Pets Albums**: The Photos app automatically recognizes faces and groups them into albums.
- **Location-Based Albums**: If you've enabled **Location Services**, your iPhone can categorize pictures by place (e.g., "Hawaii Trip" or "Family BBQ").
- **Memories & Suggestions**: Apple curates moments for you, like "Best of Last Year" or "Weekend Getaway," based on usage patterns.

> 💡 Tip: To **name a person in the People album**, tap the face, select **Add Name**, and type in their name. Your iPhone will now recognize them in future photos.

## Sharing Family Albums with Loved Ones

Once your albums are organized, you might want to share them securely with family members. Instead of texting individual pictures, use Apple's Shared Albums feature to create a private, interactive photo stream.

### HOW TO SET UP A SHARED ALBUM

1. Open the **Photos app** and go to the **Albums** tab.

2. Tap the **+ icon** and select **New Shared Album**.
3. Give it a **name** (e.g., "Grandkids' Adventures" or "Smith Family Updates").
4. Tap **Next**, then add **family members' Apple IDs** or phone numbers.
5. Once created, **invite them to contribute** by enabling **Subscribers Can Post**.

Now, everyone in the shared album can add photos, like images, and comment on memories—perfect for keeping grandparents or distant relatives updated.

> 💡 Tip: If someone in the family doesn't use an iPhone, **they can still view the album via a public link** (but won't be able to contribute).

## Privacy and Security: Keeping Your Photos Safe

Family photos often contain personal moments you wouldn't want to be shared outside your circle. Apple offers robust privacy controls to help protect your images.

### ADJUSTING SHARED ALBUM PRIVACY SETTINGS

- Open **Settings → Photos → Shared Albums**.
- Disable **Public Website** to prevent non-invited users from viewing.
- Enable **Subscribers Can Post** if you want trusted family members to add their own pictures.

### HIDING SENSITIVE PHOTOS

If you have private pictures (like gift ideas or personal documents), you can hide them from your main library:

1. Select the photo(s) in the **Photos app**.
2. Tap the **Share button** (square with an arrow).
3. Choose **Hide → Confirm**.

Your hidden images will be stored in the Hidden Album (found under Utilities in the Albums tab). For added security, you can lock this album behind Face ID or Touch ID in Settings → Photos → Use Face ID.

> 💡 Tip: This is **especially useful for surprise parties, gifts, or any private family moments** you want to keep hidden from kids or others.

## Best Practices for Keeping Family Photos Organized

To prevent your albums from becoming chaotic again, follow these best practices:

- **Delete Unnecessary Photos**: Regularly remove duplicates, blurry shots, or screenshots that no longer serve a purpose.

- **Tag People & Places**: This makes searching for specific moments easier later.
- **Use Favorites**: Tap the **heart icon** on important photos so they appear in the **Favorites album** for quick access.
- **Sort by Date or Event**: Name albums with specific dates (e.g., "Christmas 2023") to make chronological searches effortless.

> **Tip:** If you take a lot of screenshots, check the **Screenshots album** under **Media Types** and clean it out regularly.

## Backing Up Your Albums for Long-Term Safety

Nothing is worse than losing years of family memories due to a lost or damaged phone. Ensure your albums are always safe with iCloud Backup and external storage solutions.

### ENABLING ICLOUD BACKUP

1. Go to **Settings → [Your Name] → iCloud → Photos**.
2. Toggle on **iCloud Photos** to sync across all Apple devices.
3. Ensure **Optimize iPhone Storage** is enabled if you're running low on space.

> **Tip:** With **iCloud Family Sharing**, you can **share photo storage** with family members.

### USING EXTERNAL STORAGE FOR EXTRA PROTECTION

If you prefer offline backups, consider:

- **Transferring to a Mac or PC** via AirDrop or USB.
- **Using an external hard drive or SSD** with the **Files app**.
- **Uploading to Google Photos or Dropbox** for redundancy.

## Sharing Albums Without Compromising Privacy

If you want to share select photos without exposing your entire library, consider these methods:

### AIRDROP: FAST AND SECURE

- Great for quick **in-person transfers** between Apple devices.
- Keeps full-resolution quality intact.
- No need for third-party apps or cloud storage.

- Select photos → Tap **Share** → Choose **Copy iCloud Link**.
- Send the link via **text, email, or messaging apps**.
- **Expires after 30 days**, keeping shared images **temporary and secure**.

> 💡 **Tip: Never upload personal family photos to unsecured social media platforms** without adjusting privacy settings.

## Making Photo Organization a Habit

The best way to keep family albums organized and secure is to make it part of your routine:

- Spend **10 minutes each month** cleaning up your library.
- Regularly update shared albums to keep everyone involved.
- Use **AI-powered albums** to quickly access past events.
- Always have a **backup strategy**—iCloud, external storage, or both.

By following these steps, your family memories will be beautifully preserved, easy to find, and safely shared with the people who matter most.

# Using Live Photos and Burst Mode for Dynamic Shots

Capturing the perfect moment can be tricky. A second too early, and you miss the best expression. A second too late, and the magic is gone. That's where Live Photos and Burst Mode come in—two powerful iPhone features designed to help you capture movement, emotion, and action with precision.

Whether you want to snap the perfect shot of a child's laughter, capture an unforgettable vacation moment, or ensure no one in a group photo is blinking, mastering these features will take your photography skills to the next level.

## Live Photos: Bringing Still Images to Life

Live Photos aren't just static pictures—they're mini-videos that capture 1.5 seconds before and after you press the shutter button. This means you get a brief moving memory, complete with sound, giving you more context than a standard photo.

### HOW TO ENABLE LIVE PHOTOS

1. Open the **Camera app**.
2. Look for the **Live Photos icon** (a set of concentric circles in the top-right corner).
3. Tap it to enable (it will turn yellow when active).

4. Capture your photo as usual.

> **Tip:** Keep your phone **steady for a second before and after taking the shot** to ensure a smooth, clear Live Photo.

## Editing and Enhancing Live Photos

Live Photos offer more than just motion—they allow you to select the best frame and apply creative effects.

### CHOOSING A KEY PHOTO (BEST FRAME)

Sometimes, the perfect expression or moment happens just before or after you press the shutter. You can change the key photo to get the best possible frame:

1. Open the **Photos app** and select your Live Photo.
2. Tap **Edit** in the top-right corner.
3. Drag the **frame slider** to find the best still image.
4. Tap **Make Key Photo → Done**.

> **Tip:** This is great for **group photos**—if someone blinked in the original shot, you can pick a frame where everyone's eyes are open!

## Applying Live Photo Effects

Apple provides creative motion effects to make Live Photos even more dynamic:

- **Loop:** Creates an automatic GIF-like effect.
- **Bounce:** Rewinds and replays your motion continuously.
- **Long Exposure:** Blurs movement for a professional DSLR-like effect (great for waterfalls or light trails).

To access these:

1. Open your **Live Photo** in the **Photos app**.
2. Swipe up to reveal the **Effects menu**.
3. Select your preferred effect.

> **Tip: Long Exposure** is perfect for capturing city lights, fireworks, or silky smooth water effects.

## Burst Mode: Capture the Action, Pick the Best Shot

If you've ever tried to capture fast-moving subjects (kids playing, pets running, sports, or dance performances), you know one single photo is often not enough.

Burst Mode helps by taking a rapid sequence of photos—so you can choose the best one later.

## How to Use Burst Mode

- On **iPhones with a Home button:** Hold down the **shutter button**.
- On **newer iPhones (without a Home button):** Swipe the shutter button **to the left and hold**.
- Release to stop the burst.

Your iPhone will capture 10 photos per second, helping you freeze fast action.

> 💡 Tip: Use **Burst Mode for group photos**—someone **always** blinks at the wrong time!

## Selecting the Best Photo from a Burst

Since Burst Mode captures dozens of images, you'll want to pick the best one:

1. Open **Photos** and find your burst (it appears as a **stacked set**).
2. Tap **Select** to view all frames.
3. Scroll and choose the sharpest or best-timed shot.
4. Tap **Keep Only Favorites** to save space.

> 💡 Tip: Your iPhone suggests **the sharpest images with a gray dot**—a quick way to pick the best.

## When to Use Live Photos vs. Burst Mode

| FEATURE | BEST FOR | MOTION CAPTURE STYLE |
|---|---|---|
| Live Photos | Moments with subtle movement (laughing, hair blowing, pets wagging tails) | Captures **1.5 seconds before and after** |
| Burst Mode | Fast-moving action (kids running, sports, jumping, fireworks) | **10 photos per second** for precise selection |

> 💡 Tip: If unsure, **use both**—Live Photos for casual moments and Burst Mode for high-speed action.

## Combining Live Photos and Burst Mode for Dynamic Shots

For the ultimate multi-frame action shot, you can combine these features.

- **Step 1:** Use **Burst Mode** to capture a high-speed sequence.
- **Step 2:** Choose the best shot and convert it to a **Live Photo** using editing apps like Motion Stills.
- **Step 3:** Apply **Bounce or Long Exposure effects** to make your shot more artistic.

> 💡 **Tip:** If you're **shooting a child's first steps or a surprise reaction**, using both ensures you'll have the **best frame and a moving memory**.

## Editing Burst and Live Photos Like a Pro

Once you've taken amazing Live Photos or Burst shots, you can enhance them further with Apple's built-in editing tools:

1. Open the **Photos app** and select your photo.
2. Tap **Edit** → Adjust brightness, contrast, or color.
3. Apply filters to **enhance mood or correct lighting**.
4. Crop or straighten your photo for **better composition**.
5. Tap **Done** to save.

> 💡 **Tip:** Want even more control? Try third-party apps like **Snapseed** or **VSCO** for advanced color grading.

## Tips for Getting the Best Shots

- **Keep Your Hand Steady:** Even slight movement can blur the final image.
- **Use Natural Light:** Live Photos look best in well-lit conditions.
- **Experiment with Angles:** Try different perspectives—high, low, or close-up.
- **Use the Volume Button to Shoot:** A steadier alternative to tapping the screen.

> 💡 **Tip:** You can even use your Apple Watch as a **remote shutter** for steadier shots!

## Conclusion-Free Learning: Apply What You've Learned

Now that you've mastered Live Photos and Burst Mode, try them out:

1. Capture a **pet's reaction** in Live Photo mode.
2. Use Burst Mode at a **family gathering** to get the best group shot.
3. Apply a **Long Exposure effect** to moving water for a silky smooth result.

With these tools in your photography arsenal, you'll never miss the perfect moment again.

# Backing Up and Restoring Photos with iCloud and External Drives

Losing precious photos and videos can be devastating. Whether it's a technical glitch, accidental deletion, or a lost device, having a reliable backup system ensures your cherished memories are never truly gone. Fortunately, iPhones offer multiple ways to back up and restore photos, with iCloud and external drives being the most effective solutions.

This section will guide you through setting up automatic backups, restoring lost images, and using external storage devices to keep your media safe and accessible.

## Why Backing Up Your Photos is Essential

Most people take hundreds, if not thousands, of photos every year. Without a backup, a simple accident—like dropping your phone into water or an unexpected software issue—could wipe them out forever.

Regularly backing up your photos protects them from:

- **Accidental deletion:** We've all mistakenly deleted a photo we meant to keep.
- **Lost or stolen devices:** If your iPhone gets lost or stolen, your photos will still be accessible.
- **Software failures:** Bugs or failed updates can sometimes cause data loss.
- **Storage limitations:** If your iPhone is running out of space, transferring photos to an external drive can free up storage.

## Backing Up Photos with iCloud

iCloud is Apple's built-in cloud storage solution that allows you to automatically sync photos across all your Apple devices.

How to Enable iCloud Photo Backup

1. Open **Settings** on your iPhone.
2. Tap **[Your Name]** at the top of the screen.
3. Select **iCloud → Photos**.
4. Toggle **Sync this iPhone** to **On** (it will turn green).

This ensures that all your photos and videos are automatically uploaded to iCloud and available on all devices signed in with the same Apple ID.

> 💡 **Tip:** Enable **Optimize iPhone Storage** to save space. This keeps lower-resolution photos on your device while full-resolution versions are stored in iCloud.

## Restoring Photos from iCloud

If you accidentally delete a photo, don't panic—iCloud keeps deleted photos for 30 days in the Recently Deleted folder.

### RECOVERING DELETED PHOTOS

1. Open the **Photos app**.
2. Go to **Albums** → Scroll to **Recently Deleted**.
3. Select the photos you want to recover.
4. Tap **Recover** → **Confirm**.

> 💡 **Tip:** If 30 days have passed, the photo will be **permanently deleted** from iCloud unless you've backed it up elsewhere.

## Using iCloud Backup for Full Device Recovery

If your iPhone is lost, damaged, or replaced, you can restore all your photos (and other data) from an iCloud backup.

1. During **iPhone setup**, choose **Restore from iCloud Backup**.
2. Sign in with your Apple ID.
3. Select the most recent backup and wait for the process to complete.

> 💡 **Tip:** You can check the last backup date in **Settings** → **[Your Name]** → **iCloud** → **iCloud Backup**.

## Backing Up Photos to an External Drive

For those who prefer physical backups or need extra storage, an external drive is a great alternative to iCloud.

### COMPATIBLE EXTERNAL DRIVES

- **Lightning to USB Drives:** Plug directly into older iPhones (e.g., SanDisk iXpand).
- **USB-C Drives:** Compatible with newer iPhones (iPhone 15 series and later).
- **Portable SSDs (with adapter):** Fast and reliable (e.g., Samsung T7 SSD).

## How to Transfer Photos to an External Drive

1. Connect the drive to your iPhone using a **Lightning to USB adapter** or **USB-C cable**.
2. Open the **Files app** and select **Browse**.
3. Locate your **Photos folder** in the **Files app** or use the **Photos app**.
4. Select the photos/videos you want to transfer.
5. Tap **Share** → **Save to Files** → Choose the external drive.

> 💡 **Tip:** Always **eject the drive properly** before unplugging to avoid data corruption.

## Restoring Photos from an External Drive

If you ever need to restore photos from your external drive:

1. Connect the drive to your iPhone.
2. Open the **Files app** → Navigate to your stored photos.
3. Select the images you want to restore.
4. Tap **Share** → **Save Image** (this saves them back to the Photos app).

> 💡 **Tip:** Organize your photos into **folders labeled by year or event** for easy retrieval.

## Comparing iCloud and External Drive Backups

| FEATURE | ICLOUD BACKUP | EXTERNAL DRIVE BACKUP |
|---|---|---|
| **Storage Space** | Limited to iCloud plan (5GB free, paid plans available) | Limited to drive capacity |
| **Accessibility** | Available on all Apple devices | Requires physical connection |
| **Security** | Encrypted and stored on Apple's servers | Secure, but can be lost/damaged |
| **Automatic Syncing** | Yes | No (manual transfer required) |
| **Cost** | Monthly fee for extra storage | One-time purchase |

> 💡 **Tip:** Use **both iCloud and an external drive** for **double protection** against data loss.

## Additional Backup Options: Google Photos & Dropbox

If you need extra cloud storage beyond iCloud, consider:

- **Google Photos:** Free unlimited storage for compressed photos, or 15GB of free storage for original quality.
- **Dropbox:** Great for storing large video files with 2GB free storage (paid plans available).

**💡 Tip:** Enable **Auto Backup** in these apps to keep your photos synced without manual uploads.

## Key Takeaways for a Bulletproof Photo Backup Strategy

- **Use iCloud** for automatic syncing and easy recovery.
- **Regularly back up to an external drive** for extra security.
- **Keep a secondary cloud backup** (Google Photos or Dropbox) for redundancy.
- **Check your backup settings monthly** to ensure everything is working correctly.

**💡 Tip:** Set a **monthly reminder** on your iPhone to review your backups— better safe than sorry!

Now, go ahead and back up those precious memories—you'll thank yourself later.

# Printing Photos and Making Physical Albums

In today's digital world, it's easy to forget about printing photos. Most of us have thousands of pictures stored on our iPhones, but there's something special about holding a printed photograph in your hands. A physical album can become a family heirloom, a unique gift, or simply a way to bring your favorite memories to life in a tangible way.

This section will guide you through printing high-quality photos, choosing the best printing services, and creating stunning physical albums that preserve your cherished moments for years to come.

## Why Print Photos? The Beauty of Tangible Memories

While digital storage makes photos easy to access, printed pictures offer something a screen can't replicate—a physical connection to your memories.

Printing your photos allows you to:

- **Create family albums** that can be passed down for generations.
- **Decorate your home** with personalized art.

- **Give thoughtful gifts** like custom photo books or framed prints.
- **Preserve important moments** in a way that doesn't rely on technology.

> 📍 **Tip:** Digital photos can be lost due to accidental deletion, device failures, or forgotten passwords. Printed copies serve as an **extra layer of backup**.

## How to Print Photos from Your iPhone

Apple has made it incredibly easy to print directly from your iPhone, whether using an AirPrint-compatible printer or an online printing service.

### OPTION 1: PRINTING AT HOME WITH AN AIRPRINT PRINTER

If you own a printer that supports AirPrint, you can print directly from your iPhone.

1. **Open the Photos app** and select the photo(s) you want to print.
2. Tap **Share → Print**.
3. Choose your **AirPrint-compatible printer**.
4. Adjust settings (number of copies, paper size, etc.).
5. Tap **Print**.

> 📍 **Tip:** Use **photo paper** instead of regular printer paper for **higher-quality results**.

### OPTION 2: USING A PROFESSIONAL PHOTO PRINTING SERVICE

For better quality, consider using a professional online printing service. Many services have apps or websites where you can upload photos directly from your iPhone.

Popular printing services include:

- **Apple Photos** (built into macOS)
- **Shutterfly** (photo books, prints, and custom gifts)
- **Snapfish** (affordable, high-quality prints)
- **CVS/Walgreens Photo** (quick, same-day pickup available)

> 📍 **Tip:** Before uploading, **edit your photos** to adjust brightness, contrast, and sharpness for the best print quality.

## Choosing the Right Print Size and Quality

Not all print sizes work well for every photo. When choosing a print size, consider the resolution of your image to avoid blurry prints.

## Common Photo Print Sizes

| PRINT SIZE | BEST USE CASE |
|---|---|
| 4x6 inches | Standard photo size, fits in most albums |
| 5x7 inches | Great for framing small photos |
| 8x10 inches | Larger prints for home decor |
| 11x14 inches & above | Ideal for posters or canvas prints |

> 💡 Tip: For the sharpest prints, make sure your photo has a resolution of **at least 300 DPI (dots per inch)**.

## Creating Stunning Physical Photo Albums

A well-designed photo album tells a story—whether it's a family vacation, a child's first year, or a wedding. There are two main ways to create a physical album:

1. DIY Scrapbook-Style Albums

If you enjoy a hands-on approach, you can create a scrapbook-style album with printed photos, handwritten captions, and decorations.

What you'll need:

- **Photo prints** (printed at home or ordered online)
- **A blank scrapbook or photo album**
- **Adhesives** (photo tape, glue dots, or corner stickers)
- **Pens, stickers, and decorative elements**

> 💡 Tip: Write small **stories or captions** next to each photo to add a personal touch.

2. Custom Printed Photo Books

If you prefer a sleek, modern look, many online services let you create professionally printed photo books.

Popular services include:

- **Shutterfly** (custom layouts, hardcover & softcover options)
- **Mixbook** (beautiful themes and easy customization)
- **Blurb** (high-end, professional-quality books)

> **Tip:** Organize your photos by **theme or date** before creating the album to make the process easier.

## Framing and Displaying Printed Photos

Printing photos isn't just for albums—you can also use them for home decor.

CREATIVE WAYS TO DISPLAY PHOTOS

- **Classic frames:** Choose matching frames for a cohesive look.
- **Canvas prints:** Large-scale prints that look like paintings.
- **Photo walls:** Create a gallery wall with a mix of sizes.
- **Magnetic prints:** Stick your favorite moments to the fridge.
- **Wood or metal prints:** Modern and unique display options.

> **Tip:** When framing photos, choose **matte paper** to reduce glare and fingerprints.

## Protecting Printed Photos from Damage

Unlike digital files, printed photos are susceptible to wear and tear. To keep them in good condition:

- **Store albums in a cool, dry place** to prevent fading.
- **Use acid-free paper and albums** to avoid yellowing.
- **Keep photos away from direct sunlight** to prevent discoloration.
- **Laminate or frame important prints** for extra protection.

> **Tip:** Consider scanning old printed photos to create **a digital backup**.

## Digital vs. Physical: Which One is Right for You?

| FEATURE | DIGITAL PHOTOS | PRINTED PHOTOS |
|---|---|---|
| **Storage** | Unlimited (Cloud, iPhone storage) | Requires physical space |
| **Access** | Instant, accessible anywhere | Must be physically present |
| **Durability** | Susceptible to deletion/corruption | Can last generations if stored properly |
| **Aesthetic Appeal** | Viewable on screens | Tangible, can be framed/albums |

> 💡 **Tip:** The best approach is a **combination of both**—store digital copies for convenience and **print the most important moments**.

## Final Tips for Printing and Preserving Your Photos

- **Choose high-quality printing services** for vibrant, long-lasting prints.
- **Print only the best photos** to avoid clutter.
- **Label your albums** by year or event for easy organization.
- **Gift custom photo books** for birthdays, anniversaries, or holidays.
- **Keep a backup of digital copies** in iCloud or an external drive.

> 💡 **Tip:** Set a **reminder every few months** to print your favorite new photos so your albums stay updated!

Now, it's time to bring those digital memories to life—print your photos, create albums, and enjoy the beauty of holding your most cherished moments in your hands.

# CHAPTER 13

# Enhancing Your Digital Life with Accessibility

## Making Text Larger and Easier to Read

As technology becomes more integrated into our daily lives, readability and accessibility are more important than ever. If you find yourself squinting at your iPhone screen, struggling to read small text in emails, messages, or apps, you're not alone. Apple has built-in accessibility tools that make text larger, clearer, and easier to read—ensuring that your iPhone adapts to your needs rather than the other way around.

In this section, we'll explore different ways to enlarge text, enhance readability, and customize your iPhone for optimal comfort.

### Why Adjusting Text Size Matters

For many users, reading small text on a screen can be tiring or even frustrating. Whether due to aging eyes, visual impairments, or just personal preference, making text larger can significantly improve your experience.

Here's why it matters:

- **Reduces eye strain** when reading for long periods.
- **Prevents mistakes** caused by misreading small details.
- **Enhances overall usability** by improving contrast and clarity.
- **Supports accessibility needs**, particularly for those with low vision.

> 💡 Tip: Even if you don't think you need larger text now, **experimenting with these settings** might surprise you—it's all about finding what's most comfortable for you!

### Adjusting Text Size on Your iPhone

Apple provides multiple ways to increase text size system-wide, making everything from emails to web pages easier to read.

To increase the text size across most apps and menus:

1. **Open the Settings app**.
2. Tap **Accessibility → Display & Text Size**.
3. Tap **Larger Text**.
4. Adjust the **slider** to increase or decrease text size.
5. Toggle on **Larger Accessibility Sizes** for even bigger text options.

💡 **Tip**: Some apps (like Messages and Mail) allow you to increase text size **independently** from system-wide settings.

## Bold Text for Extra Clarity

If increasing the text size isn't enough, making it bold can improve readability by adding more contrast.

To enable Bold Text:

1. **Go to Settings → Accessibility → Display & Text Size**.
2. Toggle on **Bold Text**.

This will bold all system fonts, making everything from menu labels to notifications easier to distinguish.

💡 **Tip**: If you combine **Larger Text + Bold Text**, the readability improves significantly!

## Using the Zoom Feature for Extra Enlargement

If larger text still isn't enough, you can magnify portions of your screen using Zoom.

### HOW TO ENABLE ZOOM

1. **Go to Settings → Accessibility → Zoom**.
2. Toggle **Zoom** ON.
3. Use **three fingers to double-tap** the screen to activate the magnification window.
4. Drag the **Zoom Lens** around the screen to enlarge specific areas.
5. Adjust the **zoom level** using the slider.

> 💡 **Tip:** The **Zoom Controller** (a small on-screen button) lets you **quickly enable/disable Zoom** without triple-tapping every time.

## Customizing Display Settings for Better Readability

Apple includes several additional settings that enhance text clarity and reduce eye strain.

### INCREASE CONTRAST

1. **Go to Settings → Accessibility → Display & Text Size**.
2. Toggle on **Increase Contrast** to make text and background colors more distinct.

### REDUCE TRANSPARENCY

1. **Go to Settings → Accessibility → Display & Text Size**.
2. Toggle on **Reduce Transparency** to make text **more readable** on translucent backgrounds.

### SMART INVERT COLORS (DARK MODE ALTERNATIVE)

If you prefer lighter text on a dark background, Smart Invert can help.

1. **Go to Settings → Accessibility → Display & Text Size**.
2. Toggle on **Smart Invert** for a dark interface with **normal-looking photos and videos**.

> 💡 **Tip:** These settings **work well together**—try mixing **Larger Text + Bold Text + High Contrast** for the best effect.

## Text Size Shortcuts: Changing Text Size Quickly

Did you know you can adjust text size on the fly without going into Settings?

### ADDING TEXT SIZE TO THE CONTROL CENTER

1. **Go to Settings → Control Center**.
2. Tap **+ Text Size** to add it to **your quick settings**.

Now, you can swipe down from the top-right corner and adjust text size instantly!

> 💡 **Tip:** This shortcut lets you **increase text size for a specific app** without affecting system-wide settings.

# Text-to-Speech: Let Your iPhone Read for You

If enlarging text isn't enough, listening might be a better solution.

## ENABLE SPEAK SELECTION

1. **Go to Settings → Accessibility → Spoken Content**.
2. Toggle on **Speak Selection**.
3. Highlight any text → Tap **Speak** to have it read aloud.

> 📍 **Tip:** You can adjust the **voice speed** to make reading more natural.

## How This Helps Different Users

### 1. Older Adults

- Helps reduce **eye strain and fatigue**.
- Makes reading **menus, messages, and web pages easier**.
- Enhances **contrast and clarity** for better visibility.

### 2. Users with Low Vision

- Zoom and VoiceOver provide **alternative ways** to read content.
- High contrast and Smart Invert **improve readability**.

### 3. Everyday Users

- Perfect for **reading outdoors** in bright light.
- Reduces **mistakes from misreading small text**.

> 📍 **Tip:** Even users with perfect vision often **increase text size** for **better comfort**.

## Final Tips for a Better Reading Experience

- **Try different combinations** (Larger Text + Bold Text + High Contrast).
- **Use Siri** to read messages and web pages.
- **Adjust brightness** to reduce glare.
- **Use Reader View in Safari** to simplify web pages.
- **Keep a shortcut** in Control Center for quick adjustments.

By using these settings, you can customize your iPhone to be as readable and comfortable as possible—ensuring that you never struggle to read small text again.

# Using VoiceOver and Other Screen Reader Features

Apple's VoiceOver is a powerful accessibility tool designed for users who are blind or visually impaired, offering a way to navigate the iPhone through spoken feedback and touch gestures. But VoiceOver isn't just for those with vision loss—it can be useful for anyone who prefers auditory guidance, whether for reading emails, browsing the web, or getting real-time descriptions of images and objects.

In this section, we'll explore how to enable and use VoiceOver, customize its settings for the best experience, and take advantage of other screen reader features that can make your iPhone more intuitive and accessible.

## What is VoiceOver?

VoiceOver is a gesture-based screen reader that lets you navigate your iPhone without seeing the screen. Once enabled, VoiceOver reads aloud what's on your display, including:

- **App names** and icons
- **Text messages and emails**
- **Web pages and notifications**
- **Buttons and menus**
- **Images and objects using AI-generated descriptions**

Instead of tapping an item to activate it, you first select it by touching the screen, and VoiceOver will announce what it is. A second tap confirms the action. This changes the way you interact with your iPhone but gives you complete control with voice guidance.

## How to Enable VoiceOver

1. Go to **Settings → Accessibility → VoiceOver**.
2. Toggle **VoiceOver** ON.
3. Your iPhone will now **speak out loud** everything you touch.
4. Tap **VoiceOver Practice** to learn gestures.

> 💡 **Tip:** You can **quickly turn VoiceOver on/off** using Siri by saying, **"Turn on VoiceOver."**

## Mastering VoiceOver Gestures

Once VoiceOver is activated, your normal touch gestures change. Instead of directly tapping to open apps, you now use these gestures:

- **Single tap**: Selects an item (VoiceOver reads it aloud).
- **Double tap**: Activates the selected item (like opening an app).
- **Three-finger swipe up/down**: Scrolls through a page.
- **Two-finger tap**: Stops VoiceOver from speaking.
- **Three-finger double-tap**: Enables/Disables screen curtain (turns display off while keeping VoiceOver active for privacy).

> 💡 Tip: If you get lost, swipe **left or right with one finger** to move between elements!

## Customizing VoiceOver for a Better Experience

1. Adjusting Speaking Rate

By default, VoiceOver speaks at a moderate speed, but you can adjust it:

1. **Go to Settings → Accessibility → VoiceOver**.
2. Scroll to **Speaking Rate**.
3. Drag the **slider left or right** to decrease or increase the speed.

> 💡 Tip: Try **slowing down VoiceOver** when learning gestures, then speed it up once you're comfortable!

2. Enabling Image Descriptions

VoiceOver can describe photos, objects, and even text in images using Apple's AI.

1. **Go to Settings → Accessibility → VoiceOver → VoiceOver Recognition**.
2. Enable **Image Descriptions**.

> 💡 Tip: This feature is great for **identifying text in images** or getting details on unlabeled photos!

3. Using Braille Input

If you prefer typing in Braille, VoiceOver includes on-screen Braille input for messaging and browsing.

1. **Go to Settings → Accessibility → VoiceOver → Braille**.
2. Select **Six-Dot or Eight-Dot Braille Input**.

> 💡 Tip: This works best with **external Braille displays**, but the touchscreen method is surprisingly intuitive!

## Other Screen Reader Features for Accessibility

VoiceOver isn't the only tool available—Apple provides other screen-reading features that enhance accessibility.

1. Speak Screen: Read Everything Aloud

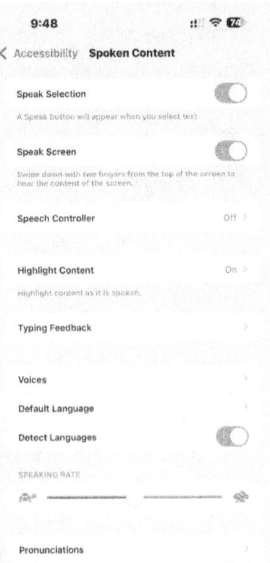

For users who don't need full VoiceOver functionality but want content read aloud, Speak Screen is perfect.

1. **Go to Settings → Accessibility → Spoken Content**.
2. Toggle on **Speak Screen**.
3. Swipe **down with two fingers** from the top of the screen to have text read aloud.

> 💡 Tip: Works well for **long emails, articles, and books**!

2. Select to Speak (Speak Selection)

If you only need occasional text read aloud, this feature lets you highlight what you want VoiceOver to read.

1. **Go to Settings → Accessibility → Spoken Content**.
2. Toggle on **Speak Selection**.
3. Highlight text in any app → Tap **Speak**.

> 💡 Tip: This is great for **reading text messages, emails, or news articles** without activating full VoiceOver.

3. Sound and Haptic Feedback for Navigation

Even with VoiceOver off, Apple provides audio cues and vibrations to assist navigation.

- **Enable Haptic Feedback** for physical confirmation when typing.
- **Use Siri to announce notifications** hands-free.
- **Enable Sounds for App Notifications** for audio alerts.

> 💡 Tip: These small changes **reduce reliance on visuals**, making navigation smoother!

## Real-World Benefits of VoiceOver and Screen Readers

Who Benefits?

- **Blind or Low-Vision Users**: Full iPhone navigation without needing to see the screen.
- **Seniors or Users with Eye Strain**: Reading assistance for small text or complex interfaces.
- **People with Reading Disabilities**: Text-to-speech makes written content more accessible.
- **Multitaskers**: Read articles aloud while doing other tasks.

💡 Example Use Case: Imagine you're **cooking dinner** and need to check a recipe—VoiceOver can read the steps aloud while your hands remain free!

### Best Practices for Using VoiceOver Effectively

- **Practice gestures**: Use the **VoiceOver Practice** menu to get comfortable.
- **Adjust settings gradually**: Start with **basic features**, then fine-tune as needed.
- **Use Siri to toggle VoiceOver** quickly.
- **Try Speak Screen for a simpler experience** before enabling full VoiceOver.
- **Keep the screen curtain in mind**: It enhances privacy by turning off the display while using VoiceOver.

💡 Tip: If you ever feel stuck, **ask Siri to turn off VoiceOver** or use **the Accessibility Shortcut** (triple-click the Side button).

By mastering VoiceOver and other screen-reading features, you can fully navigate your iPhone with ease, improve accessibility, and ensure that text-based content is always within reach.

# Customizing Buttons and Touch Gestures for Your Comfort

Your iPhone is designed to be intuitive and adaptable, but sometimes the default settings don't fit your needs perfectly. Maybe you find certain gestures tricky to perform, or maybe you wish the buttons were easier to press. The good news? You can customize your iPhone's buttons and touch gestures to make navigation smoother, easier, and more tailored to you.

This section will walk you through modifying physical button actions, customizing touch gestures, and using Apple's built-in accessibility tools to create a seamless iPhone experience that works for you—not the other way around.

## Why Customize Buttons and Gestures?

Not everyone interacts with their iPhone in the same way. Some users prefer quick, one-handed gestures, while others might need more deliberate movements. Accessibility features allow you to:

- **Change the way buttons respond** to prevent accidental presses.
- **Modify gestures** for easier swiping and tapping.
- **Enable assistive tools** that make navigation more effortless.
- **Create shortcuts** for frequently used actions.

Customizing these settings doesn't just help with accessibility—it can also make your iPhone feel more natural and efficient for daily use.

## Customizing the Side and Home Button Actions

Apple allows you to change the way your iPhone's phys- ical buttons respond. Whether it's adjusting the click speed of the Side Button or modifying the Home Button functions, here's how to personalize them:

1.  Adjusting the Side Button Click Speed

The Side Button (formerly known as the Sleep/Wake button) is used for actions like activating Siri, turning off your phone, or using Apple Pay. If you find that pressing it feels too fast or too slow, you can adjust the click speed:

1.  **Go to Settings → Accessibility → Side Button**.
2.  Under **Click Speed**, choose **Default, Slow, or Slowest**.
3.  Try each setting to see which one feels most comfortable.

> 💡 **Tip:** If you **accidentally activate Siri too often**, setting it to **Slowest** can help prevent this.

2.  Modifying Home Button Behavior (For iPhones with a Home Button)

If you're using an iPhone SE or an older model with a Home Button, you can adjust how it responds:

1.  **Go to Settings → Accessibility → Home Button**.
2.  Adjust the **Click Speed** (Default, Slow, or Slowest).
3.  Toggle **Rest Finger to Open** ON to unlock your phone without pressing.

> 💡 **Tip:** If you **struggle with pressing the Home Button**, enabling **Rest Finger to Open** lets you unlock your phone **just by resting your finger on Touch ID**—no pressing needed!

## Customizing Touch Gestures for Easier Navigation

Gestures are a big part of using an iPhone, but not all gestures are equally comfortable for everyone. Apple's AssistiveTouch and Touch Accommodations let you customize taps, swipes, and multi-finger gestures to fit your needs.

1.  Enabling AssistiveTouch for One-Tap Controls

If swiping or pressing buttons is inconvenient, you can use AssistiveTouch, a floating on-screen menu that lets you control your iPhone with a single tap:

1.  **Go to Settings → Accessibility → Touch → AssistiveTouch**.
2.  Toggle **AssistiveTouch** ON.
3.  Tap **Customize Top Level Menu** to add **Shortcuts** like Home, Volume, Screenshot, or Siri.

> 💡 Tip: You can even set a **custom gesture** like a **double-tap to open the camera**!

2.  Using Touch Accommodations to Modify Tap Sensitivity

If you find that taps register too quickly or don't always register at all, Touch Accommodations can help:

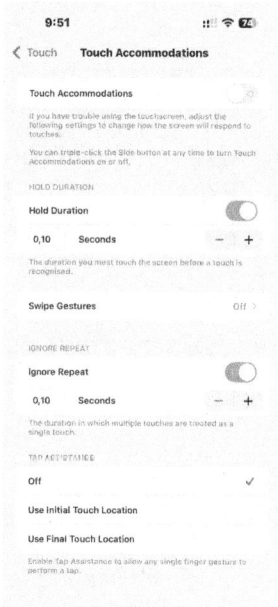

1.  **Go to Settings → Accessibility → Touch → Touch Accommodations**.
2.  Toggle **Touch Accommodations** ON.
3.  Adjust **Hold Duration** (how long you must touch before the iPhone registers the tap).
4.  Enable **Ignore Repeat** to prevent accidental double taps.

> 💡 Tip: This setting is useful for **tremors or accidental touches** that make tapping difficult.

## Creating Custom Gestures for Faster Actions

If standard gestures don't feel natural, you can create your own custom gestures for actions like scrolling, zooming, or opening the app switcher.

1.  **Go to Settings → Accessibility → Touch → AssistiveTouch**.
2.  Scroll down and tap **Create New Gesture**.
3.  **Perform the gesture** (e.g., swipe up for the App Switcher).

4. Tap **Save**, then name the gesture.
5. Assign it to **AssistiveTouch or Back Tap**.

> 💡 Tip: If you **struggle with swiping**, creating a **one-finger shortcut** to swipe up can make switching apps easier.

## Using Back Tap for Quick Actions

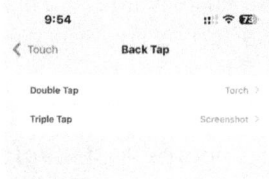

Apple's Back Tap feature lets you double-tap or tri-ple-tap the back of your iPhone to perform actions like taking a screenshot, opening Control Center, or launch-ing an app.

1. **Go to Settings → Accessibility → Touch → Back Tap**.
2. Choose **Double Tap or Triple Tap**.
3. Assign it to **an action**, such as Screenshot, Home, or Magnifier.

> 💡 Tip: You can even **assign a custom shortcut**, like opening your favorite app with a double tap!

## Best Practices for Customizing Buttons and Gestures

- **Start small**: Try one or two changes first, then adjust as needed.
- **Use AssistiveTouch if physical buttons are hard to press**.
- **Experiment with Back Tap for easy shortcuts**.
- **Fine-tune Touch Accommodations** for better touch sensitivity.
- **Practice new gestures in the VoiceOver or Touch settings menu** to get comfortable.

By customizing buttons and gestures, you can create an iPhone experience tai-lored to your comfort, making navigation smoother, quicker, and perfectly suited to your needs.

## Using Guided Access for Simplified Device Use

If you've ever wished for a way to temporarily lock your iPhone into a single app, prevent accidental taps, or control how much someone else can interact with your phone, Guided Access is the perfect tool. Whether you're handing your phone to a child, assisting someone with cognitive challenges, or simply want to stay focused without distractions, Guided Access ensures that the device stays on track with minimal interruptions.

This feature is a game-changer for parents, caregivers, educators, and anyone who needs a more controlled iPhone experience. In this section, we'll explore what Guided Access does, how to set it up, and creative ways to use it in daily life.

## What is Guided Access and Who is it For?

Guided Access is an iOS accessibility feature that limits your iPhone to a single app session and disables specific features, such as the Home Button, gestures, or parts of the screen.

Who can benefit from Guided Access?

- **Parents**: Keep kids inside one app (like a learning app or a movie) without allowing them to access anything else.
- **Educators**: Lock students into an educational app during a lesson to prevent distractions.
- **Individuals with disabilities**: Prevent accidental taps and limit distractions for users who may have cognitive or motor impairments.
- **Self-discipline users**: Stay focused on a single task by locking yourself into an app (e.g., a study timer).

> 💡 Tip: If you're using your iPhone for **kiosk mode** (e.g., displaying a menu in a store or restaurant), Guided Access ensures that customers can't exit the display.

## How to Enable and Start Guided Access

Setting up Guided Access is quick and easy. Here's how to enable it and start a session:

1. Turn On Guided Access in Settings
1. **Go to** Settings → **Accessibility** → **Guided Access**.
2. Toggle **Guided Access ON**.
3. Tap **Passcode Settings** → **Set Guided Access Passcode** to create a passcode.
4. (Optional) Enable **Face ID or Touch ID** to end sessions more easily.

> 💡 Tip: Using Face ID instead of a passcode makes exiting Guided Access much quicker—especially useful if you're setting it up for a child.

2. Start a Guided Access Session

Once Guided Access is enabled, you can start a session inside any app:

1. **Open the app** you want to restrict.
2. **Triple-click** the Side Button (or Home Button on older iPhones).

3. The **Guided Access menu** will appear, allowing you to adjust settings.
4. Tap **Start** to begin.

Now, the iPhone is locked into the chosen app—the user cannot exit or switch apps until Guided Access is turned off.

## Customizing Your Guided Access Session

Before starting a session, you can customize what's restricted:

1. Disable Certain Parts of the Screen

If you're worried about accidental taps, you can disable parts of the screen:

1. On the **Guided Access screen**, tap **Options**.
2. Use your finger to **draw a circle over areas** of the screen you want to disable.
3. Tap **Done** to confirm.

> 💡 Example: If you're playing a video for a child, you can disable the **Pause** and **Skip** buttons to keep them from stopping playback.

2. Turn Off Hardware Buttons

You can disable the volume buttons, Side Button, and motion detection to prevent unintended interactions:

1. Tap **Options** in the Guided Access menu.
2. Toggle **off** any of the following:
   » **Sleep/Wake Button (**prevents turning off the screen).
   » **Volume Buttons (**prevents volume adjustments).
   » **Motion (**stops screen rotation and shake-to-undo).
3. Tap **Done** to save settings.

> 💡 Example: If you're using an **iPhone for digital signage**, you can disable the **Sleep/Wake button** to keep the screen always on.

## How to End a Guided Access Session

To exit Guided Access:

1. **Triple-click** the Side Button (or Home Button on older models).
2. Enter your **passcode** or use **Face ID/Touch ID**.
3. Tap **End**.

> 💡 Tip: If you've **forgotten your passcode**, restart the iPhone to disable Guided Access.

## Creative Uses for Guided Access

Guided Access is incredibly versatile. Here are some real-life ways to use it:

1.  Keeping Kids Focused on Learning Apps

If you hand an iPhone to a child for educational purposes, Guided Access ensures they stay in the app rather than switching to YouTube or a game.

Example: A parent sets up Guided Access for a phonics learning app, preventing their child from closing the app or adjusting settings.

2.  Running a Kiosk or Display Mode

Retail stores, museums, and event venues often use Guided Access to lock iPads and iPhones into kiosk mode.

Example: A coffee shop uses an iPad to display its digital menu, ensuring customers can't exit the menu screen.

3.  Using Guided Access for Focus and Productivity

If you struggle with distractions, lock yourself into a productivity app to stay focused.

Example: A college student using a Pomodoro timer app activates Guided Access to prevent distractions during study sessions.

4.  Assisting Individuals with Cognitive Disabilities

For people with Alzheimer's, autism, or other cognitive conditions, Guided Access provides a controlled digital environment.

Example: A caregiver sets up a simple communication app for a loved one, ensuring they can interact with only that app.

## Guided Access vs. Screen Time: What's the Difference?

Both Guided Access and Screen Time restrictions help control access, but they serve different purposes:

| FEATURE | GUIDED ACCESS | SCREEN TIME |
|---|---|---|
| Limits to one app? | ■ Yes | ✘ No |
| Prevents app switching? | ■ Yes | ✘ No |
| Time limits for app usage? | ✘ No | ■ Yes |
| Can disable screen areas? | ■ Yes | ✘ No |
| Requires passcode to exit? | ■ Yes | ■ Yes |

*Use both together:* Guided Access is great for temporary, on-the-spot restrictions, while Screen Time works well for setting long-term app limits.

### Best Practices for Using Guided Access

- **Set up your passcode and Face ID first** to prevent accidental exits.
- **Use the disable screen feature** to block distracting parts of apps.
- **Turn off volume and sleep buttons** to prevent accidental taps.
- **Use Guided Access with Screen Time** for full control over usage.
- **Restart your iPhone if you forget your passcode.**

By using Guided Access, you can create a distraction-free, controlled iPhone experience—whether for focus, learning, accessibility, or security.

CHAPTER 14

# Growing Confidence Through Practice

## Interactive Exercises for Mastering the Basics

Mastering the basics of your iPhone doesn't have to feel like studying for an exam. In fact, the best way to get comfortable with a new device is through hands-on practice. Think of it like learning how to cook a new recipe—reading about it is useful, but actually chopping the vegetables, stirring the pot, and tasting the dish makes the process truly stick. This chapter provides interactive exercises designed to help you build confidence in using your iPhone's essential features, from navigation to communication, so that everyday tasks feel effortless.

### Getting Comfortable with Touch and Gestures

Many iPhone users, especially those transitioning from older models with physical buttons, find it challenging to adjust to gesture-based navigation. If you're new to the world of swipes and taps, start by familiarizing yourself with these core movements:

1. **Swipe up from the bottom** – This takes you back to the Home Screen from any app. Try opening Safari, then swiping up to exit.
2. **Swipe down from the top-right corner** – This reveals the Control Center, where you can adjust brightness, enable Airplane Mode, or control music. Swipe down and explore each option.
3. **Swipe down from the middle of the Home Screen** – This opens Spotlight Search, a quick way to find apps, contacts, or information. Try searching for "Settings" and tapping on it.
4. **Pinch to zoom** – Open Photos and use two fingers to zoom in and out of an image.
5. **Long press (Haptic Touch)** – Hold down an app icon to see quick actions. Try this on the Camera app and select "Take Selfie."

Spending just five minutes practicing these gestures daily will make navigating your iPhone second nature. If you ever feel stuck, remember that a simple swipe up always brings you back to square one—your Home Screen.

## Practicing Typing and Dictation

Typing on a touchscreen keyboard can feel awkward at first, especially if you're used to physical keys. The best way to improve your speed and accuracy is through practice. Start with this exercise:

1. Open the Notes app and create a new note.
2. Type the sentence: *"The quick brown fox jumps over the lazy dog."* This sentence contains every letter of the alphabet, helping you practice each key.
3. Now, turn on dictation by tapping the microphone icon on the keyboard. Say the sentence out loud and check how well your iPhone transcribes it.

Dictation is a fantastic tool when typing feels slow or cumbersome, especially for longer messages or notes. If Siri struggles to understand certain words, speak clearly and try again. Over time, you'll notice that the iPhone adapts to your voice, improving its accuracy.

## Sending and Receiving Messages

Texting is one of the most common tasks on an iPhone, and mastering it means you can easily stay connected with friends and family. If you're new to Messages, follow this exercise:

1. Open the Messages app and tap the compose button.
2. Type a message to a trusted contact, such as *"Hi, I'm testing my new iPhone! Can you reply when you get this?"*
3. Wait for their reply, then practice using different message features:

   » Double-tap their message and select a reaction (heart, thumbs up, etc.).
   » Hold down their message and select "Reply" to respond in a thread.
   » Tap the camera icon and send a quick photo.

If you have an iPhone that supports iMessage, you'll notice that messages between Apple users appear in blue bubbles, while SMS messages to non-iPhone users appear in green. Understanding this distinction helps when troubleshooting why certain features (like read receipts or reactions) may not work in some conversations.

## Managing Apps and Organizing Your Home Screen

A cluttered iPhone can make it difficult to find the apps you need. Fortunately, organizing your Home Screen is simple:

1. Long-press any app icon until they start wiggling.

2. Drag an app onto another to create a folder. Try grouping similar apps, like social media or shopping apps.
3. Move less frequently used apps to the App Library by swiping left past your last Home Screen.
4. Try using widgets: Long-press an empty area on your Home Screen, tap the "+" in the top-left corner, and add a widget like Weather or Calendar.

Rearranging your apps can make a huge difference in efficiency. If you ever need to reset your layout, you can go to *Settings > General > Reset > Reset Home Screen Layout* to restore the default organization.

## Taking and Sharing Photos

Your iPhone's camera is one of its most powerful features, but snapping a photo is just the beginning. Try this simple exercise to improve your photography skills:

1. Open the Camera app and take a photo of something in your room.
2. Swipe up on the photo to reveal quick editing tools.
3. Adjust brightness, contrast, and color to enhance the image.
4. Tap the share button and send the edited photo to a contact or upload it to your favorite social media platform.

Playing around with the camera settings helps you understand how to capture better photos in different lighting conditions. Don't be afraid to experiment—after all, digital photos don't cost a thing!

## Exploring Siri for Everyday Tasks

If you haven't used Siri much, it's time to start integrating it into your routine. Siri can help with hands-free commands, saving time and making tasks more efficient. Here's a challenge:

1. Activate Siri by saying *"Hey Siri"* or holding the side button.
2. Ask Siri to set a timer for three minutes.
3. While the timer runs, ask Siri to check the weather.
4. When the timer ends, ask Siri to create a new reminder: *"Call [friend's name] tomorrow at 10 AM."*

Using Siri for simple, repetitive tasks can help reduce screen time and improve accessibility, especially when you're on the go.

These exercises are designed to help you feel more comfortable using your iPhone's most essential features. The more you practice, the more confident you'll become, making everyday interactions with your device smooth and stress-free.

# Weekly Challenges to Build Confidence with Your iPhone

Gaining confidence with your iPhone isn't just about reading instructions—it's about putting them into practice in a way that feels natural and fun. The best way to do this? Weekly challenges that gradually introduce new skills, encourage experimentation, and reinforce what you've already learned. These challenges are designed to help you integrate your iPhone into your daily life, making it a tool that works for you rather than something you struggle to keep up with.

## Why Weekly Challenges Matter

Many new iPhone users, especially those transitioning from older models or other smartphone brands, feel overwhelmed by the sheer number of features at their fingertips. It's easy to stick to the basics—calling, texting, and maybe taking a photo or two—but this can limit the true potential of your device. Weekly challenges create a structured yet flexible approach to mastering key iPhone functions at your own pace.

By focusing on one new skill each week, you can:

- Avoid information overload by learning in small, manageable steps.
- Reinforce new skills through repetition and daily practice.
- Discover features that make your life easier or more enjoyable.
- Gain confidence in navigating and customizing your iPhone to fit your needs.

Each challenge is designed to be engaging, with real-world applications that help you see immediate benefits.

### Week 1: Mastering iPhone Navigation

Your first challenge is all about feeling at home with your iPhone's interface. If you've recently upgraded or switched from an Android device, navigation might feel unfamiliar at first. This week, focus on:

- Using gestures to switch between apps, return to the Home Screen, and access the App Switcher.
- Exploring the Control Center and adding useful shortcuts like flashlight, screen recording, or magnifier.
- Customizing the Home Screen by rearranging apps, creating folders, and adding widgets.

By the end of the week, you should be able to move around your iPhone fluidly, knowing exactly where to find what you need.

### Week 2: Improving Communication Skills

Your iPhone is a powerful communication tool, but are you using it to its full potential? This week's challenge is to explore different messaging and calling features:

- Send a voice message in iMessage instead of typing out a text.
- Try FaceTime video and audio calls with a friend or family member.
- Set up and use group messages to stay connected with multiple people at once.
- Experiment with Live Text by copying or translating text from a photo.

These small changes can make staying in touch more convenient and even more enjoyable.

## Week 3: Boosting Productivity with Notes and Reminders

Your iPhone isn't just for entertainment—it can also help you stay organized. This week, challenge yourself to:

- Use the Notes app to create a grocery list, jot down ideas, or store important information.
- Try the scanning feature in Notes to digitize a document.
- Set up daily reminders for tasks, appointments, or habits you want to develop.
- Create a location-based reminder (e.g., "Remind me to buy milk when I arrive at the store").

By incorporating Notes and Reminders into your routine, you'll find it easier to keep track of tasks and important details.

## Week 4: Exploring Siri for Hands-Free Assistance

Many users overlook Siri, but Apple's virtual assistant can save you time and effort once you get used to it. This week, try using Siri in different situations:

- Set alarms, timers, and calendar events using only your voice.
- Ask Siri to send a text or make a call.
- Use Siri for calculations, conversions, or looking up information.
- Create a custom shortcut with Siri to automate a frequent task.

The more you interact with Siri, the more natural and helpful it will become.

## Week 5: Enhancing Your Photos and Videos

Your iPhone's camera is one of its standout features, and this week is all about making the most of it. Try:

- Taking Live Photos and experimenting with the different effects (Loop, Bounce, Long Exposure).
- Capturing high-quality portrait mode shots.
- Recording a slow-motion or time-lapse video.
- Editing a photo using the built-in tools (crop, brightness, contrast, etc.).

By the end of this challenge, you'll not only capture better photos but also feel more comfortable managing and editing them.

A cluttered iPhone can make it harder to find what you need, so this week's goal is to streamline your device:

- Delete unused apps and organize the ones you use most.
- Customize your notifications to minimize distractions.
- Set up Focus Modes to help you stay productive or unwind.
- Try using the Files app to organize documents and downloads.

A well-organized iPhone improves both efficiency and ease of use.

Each of these weekly challenges is designed to build upon the previous one, helping you gain confidence with your iPhone step by step. The key is consistency—small daily interactions with these features will soon make them second nature. The more you practice, the more you'll appreciate how much your iPhone can simplify and enhance your daily life.

## Scenarios to Practice Troubleshooting Common Issues

Learning how to troubleshoot common iPhone issues is a crucial part of gaining confidence with your device. Even the most well-designed technology can occasionally present problems, and knowing how to resolve them quickly can save you frustration and time. By practicing different troubleshooting scenarios, you'll build a skill set that allows you to handle issues independently rather than relying on others for help.

Let's walk through some real-world scenarios where troubleshooting comes in handy. These practical exercises will help you develop a step-by-step approach to identifying and fixing common iPhone problems.

### Scenario 1: Your iPhone Won't Turn On

Imagine this: You wake up, grab your iPhone, and press the power button, but nothing happens. The screen stays black. Panic starts to set in—has your iPhone stopped working completely? Before jumping to conclusions, follow these troubleshooting steps:

1. **Check the Battery** – The most common reason an iPhone won't turn on is that the battery has drained completely. Connect it to a charger and wait a few minutes. If the screen remains black, try a different charging cable and adapter.
2. **Perform a Force Restart** – If your iPhone is unresponsive, force restarting it might help. Depending on your model, the method varies:

- iPhone 8 or later: Press and release the Volume Up button, press and release the Volume Down button, then hold the Side button until you see the Apple logo.

- iPhone 7: Hold the Volume Down and Sleep/Wake buttons together until the Apple logo appears.
- iPhone 6s and earlier: Hold the Home and Sleep/Wake buttons simultaneously until the Apple logo appears.

3. **Check for Hardware Damage** – If the iPhone has been dropped or exposed to water, internal damage could be preventing it from turning on. Look for cracks, dents, or moisture indicators inside the SIM tray.
4. **Restore Using a Computer** – If nothing else works, connect the iPhone to a computer, open Finder (Mac) or iTunes (PC), and try restoring the device.

Practicing these steps on a working iPhone before you ever encounter this issue in real life can help you react calmly and confidently if it ever happens.

## Scenario 2: Your iPhone Is Frozen and Unresponsive

You're using your iPhone as usual when suddenly, the screen stops responding. You swipe, tap, press buttons—nothing works. Instead of panicking, try these steps:

1. **Force Quit the Problematic App** – If an app is frozen, it might be causing the issue. Swipe up from the bottom (or double-press the Home button on older models) to access the App Switcher. Close the unresponsive app by swiping it up.
2. **Restart Your iPhone** – If your entire device is frozen, perform a force restart using the steps outlined in Scenario 1.
3. **Check for Updates** – Sometimes, outdated software can cause system instability. Go to *Settings > General > Software Update* and check if a new iOS version is available.
4. **Free Up Storage Space** – A full storage drive can lead to sluggish performance. Delete unnecessary apps, photos, and files to improve responsiveness.

Testing these solutions when your iPhone is working normally can help you build muscle memory so that when a freeze happens, you can fix it swiftly.

## Scenario 3: No Sound During Calls

You answer a phone call, but you can't hear the other person—or they can't hear you. If this happens, follow these steps:

1. **Check Volume and Mute Settings** – Make sure your iPhone isn't muted. Use the volume buttons to turn up the sound, and ensure Silent Mode is off.
2. **Clean the Speaker and Microphone** – Dirt or lint can block the speaker or microphone. Use a soft-bristled brush to clean them.
3. **Turn Off Bluetooth** – If your iPhone is connected to a Bluetooth device, the audio might be routed there instead. Go to *Settings > Bluetooth* and disconnect any paired devices.

4. **Test with Other Apps** – Try playing a song or making a FaceTime call to determine whether the issue is with the iPhone itself or just the Phone app.
5. **Reset Network Settings** – If the issue persists, go to *Settings > General > Transfer or Reset iPhone > Reset > Reset Network Settings*. This won't delete your data but will reset Wi-Fi and Bluetooth connections.

Going through these steps on a working iPhone allows you to practice before you find yourself in a real-world situation where you need to troubleshoot sound issues quickly.

## Scenario 4: Your iPhone Won't Connect to Wi-Fi

You try to connect to a Wi-Fi network, but it won't work. Instead, your iPhone keeps displaying a loading icon or an error message. Here's what to do:

1. **Toggle Wi-Fi Off and On** – Go to *Settings > Wi-Fi* and turn it off for a few seconds, then turn it back on.
2. **Forget and Reconnect to the Network** – Tap the Wi-Fi network name, select "Forget This Network," then reconnect by entering the password again.
3. **Restart Your iPhone and Router** – Restarting both devices can clear temporary connection issues.
4. **Check for Network Issues** – If other devices also struggle to connect, the issue may be with the router. Try moving closer to the router or checking with your internet provider.
5. **Reset Network Settings** – If nothing else works, reset your network settings as mentioned in Scenario 3.

Trying this process with a known Wi-Fi network can give you confidence in handling Wi-Fi problems when they arise unexpectedly.

## Scenario 5: Your iPhone Battery Drains Too Quickly

If your battery doesn't seem to last as long as it should, try these troubleshooting steps:

1. **Check Battery Usage** – Go to *Settings > Battery* to see which apps are using the most power.
2. **Enable Low Power Mode** – This can be turned on from *Settings > Battery* or Control Center to extend battery life.
3. **Close Background Apps** – Some apps continue running in the background, draining power. Close apps you're not actively using.
4. **Update to the Latest iOS Version** – Apple frequently releases battery optimizations in updates.
5. **Disable Background App Refresh** – This can be found in *Settings > General > Background App Refresh*. Turning it off for non-essential apps can improve battery life.

These battery-saving techniques are useful even if your iPhone isn't currently experiencing issues. Practicing them regularly can help you maximize your device's efficiency.

Practicing these troubleshooting scenarios in a low-pressure environment will help you feel more prepared when something unexpected happens. The more you familiarize yourself with these techniques, the more confident you'll become in handling common iPhone issues on your own.

# Connecting with Community Support for Encouragement

Mastering an iPhone, especially if you're not naturally tech-savvy, can feel like a journey filled with small victories and occasional frustrations. You might have moments when everything clicks, and then suddenly, you run into a feature or problem that seems impossible to figure out. This is where having a supportive community comes in. Learning doesn't have to be a solitary experience—connecting with others who are on a similar path can provide encouragement, new insights, and even fun along the way.

Whether you prefer one-on-one guidance, online groups, or in-person workshops, community support is a powerful tool for building confidence in your iPhone skills.

## Why Community Support Matters

One of the biggest hurdles for new iPhone users is feeling isolated when struggling with a feature or setting. It's easy to assume that everyone else just "gets it" while you're left fumbling through menus. But in reality, many users face the same challenges, and connecting with a community can help normalize the learning process.

A strong support system offers:

- **Encouragement** – When you see others overcoming similar obstacles, it motivates you to push forward.
- **Shared Knowledge** – Someone else's solution to a problem might be exactly what you need.
- **A Safe Space for Questions** – There's no such thing as a silly question in a supportive environment.
- **Accountability** – Engaging with a group can keep you motivated to continue learning.

## Finding the Right Type of Community Support

Not all learning styles are the same, so it's important to find a type of community that fits your preferences and comfort level.

1. Online Forums and Social Media Groups

If you enjoy learning at your own pace but still want access to a group of like-minded individuals, online communities can be a great resource.

- **Apple Support Community** – Apple's official discussion forums allow users to ask questions and get answers from both fellow users and Apple experts.
- **Facebook Groups** – There are several groups dedicated to helping iPhone beginners, where members share tips, troubleshooting steps, and tutorials.
- **Reddit Communities** – Subreddits like r/iphone and r/applehelp provide a space for users to ask questions and read about common issues.
- **Nextdoor or Local Groups** – Some local community groups have tech-help sections where neighbors share advice.

These online spaces are excellent for both quick answers and long-term learning. You can search past discussions, ask new questions, and learn from others' experiences without feeling pressured.

2. Apple's In-Person and Virtual Support

For those who prefer a hands-on approach, Apple offers direct support options that can help you get personalized guidance.

- **Today at Apple Sessions** – These free workshops, hosted in Apple Stores, cover various iPhone features and are a great way to learn in an interactive setting.
- **Apple Support App and Website** – If you prefer a more structured approach, Apple's official support tools include step-by-step guides and live chat options.
- **AppleCare Support Calls** – Speaking directly with an Apple specialist can be useful for troubleshooting specific issues.

Attending a Today at Apple session or calling Apple Support can provide reassurance that you're learning from trusted experts who understand your concerns.

3. Local Tech Support Groups

Many libraries, senior centers, and community colleges offer free or low-cost classes for mastering digital devices. These sessions often cater to beginners and create a comfortable environment where you can ask questions without feeling rushed.

If you learn best in person and appreciate having a structured class, checking out a local tech workshop might be a great option.

## How to Get the Most Out of Community Support

Once you've found a group or resource that works for you, there are ways to make sure you're getting the most out of the experience.

1. **Engage Regularly** – Don't just read posts or attend a session once and disappear. Stay involved, even if just by reading discussions.
2. **Ask Specific Questions** – Instead of asking, "How do I use my iPhone bet-

ter?" try "How can I organize my home screen to find apps faster?" Specific questions lead to more useful answers.

3. **Share Your Own Experiences** – If you've learned something new, post about it! Teaching others reinforces your own knowledge.

4. **Practice What You Learn** – After attending a workshop or reading a forum discussion, immediately try the feature on your iPhone to solidify what you've learned.

5. **Be Patient with Yourself** – Learning takes time. Seeing others succeed should be inspiring, not discouraging. Everyone started somewhere.

## When to Reach Out for Help

Some users hesitate to ask for help, feeling they should "just figure it out." However, struggling alone can lead to frustration and make the learning process more difficult than it needs to be.

Consider reaching out when:

- You've tried searching for a solution but can't find a clear answer.
- A feature isn't working as expected, and you're unsure if it's a setting or a bug.
- You feel stuck and need a fresh perspective.
- You're making progress but need motivation to keep going.

A simple question in a friendly community can often save you hours of trial and error.

Connecting with a supportive community can turn learning into a shared experience rather than a solo struggle. Whether through online groups, Apple's resources, or in-person workshops, the encouragement and advice of others can help you grow your confidence with your iPhone.

# Celebrating Milestones: Tracking Your Progress

Learning how to use an iPhone effectively isn't just about mastering settings or memorizing features—it's about growing in confidence, becoming more independent with technology, and, most importantly, recognizing your progress along the way. It's easy to get caught up in what you *don't* know yet, but taking time to reflect on what you've already accomplished can be incredibly motivating.

Tracking your progress and celebrating small wins can make learning feel rewarding rather than overwhelming. Whether you're a complete beginner or someone refining your skills, acknowledging milestones builds confidence and keeps you engaged in your learning journey.

## Why Tracking Your Progress Matters

Think back to when you first picked up your iPhone. Maybe you hesitated before opening the Settings app or felt nervous about downloading an app on your own. Now, you're navigating menus with more ease, adjusting settings to fit your needs, and perhaps even teaching a friend or family member something new. That's progress!

Celebrating milestones isn't just about recognizing achievements—it's about reinforcing your learning. Each small victory builds on the last, making more advanced tasks feel achievable. Tracking progress can:

- **Boost confidence** – Seeing how far you've come encourages you to keep going.
- **Reduce frustration** – It's easier to stay motivated when you can measure success.
- **Turn learning into a habit** – Small wins make you more likely to keep practicing.
- **Encourage exploration** – Mastering one feature often leads to curiosity about others.

A common challenge for beginners is the feeling of *not knowing enough*. But growth happens in layers. What seemed intimidating a few weeks ago might now feel effortless. Recognizing that shift in perspective is crucial.

## Ways to Track Your Progress

Everyone learns differently, and tracking progress doesn't have to be rigid. Some people enjoy keeping journals, while others prefer visual reminders. Here are a few ways to make sure you recognize and celebrate your milestones:

### KEEP A SIMPLE LOG OF ACHIEVEMENTS

Maintaining a small notebook or using the Notes app to record what you've learned each week can be a great motivator. Entries can be as simple as:

- *Learned how to use FaceTime today!*
- *Organized my Home Screen—finally found a layout I like!*
- *Figured out how to scan documents with the Notes app—game-changer!*

Over time, looking back on these small victories provides a powerful reminder of how much you've grown.

### SET PERSONAL LEARNING GOALS

Instead of just learning randomly, setting small, achievable goals can create a sense of purpose. These don't have to be technical—think about what you actually *want* to accomplish with your iPhone. Examples might include:

- Send a text with an emoji or GIF
- Set a reminder using Siri
- Make a video call to a family member
- Edit a photo using the built-in tools
- Try a new app for something fun (e.g., a game, podcast, or wellness tracker)

Breaking learning into bite-sized goals makes progress feel manageable rather than overwhelming.

### TAKE SCREENSHOTS OF YOUR IMPROVEMENTS

A fun way to track progress is by taking screenshots of your iPhone as your skills improve. For example:

- Before and after organizing your Home Screen
- A message you sent using voice dictation for the first time
- A beautifully edited photo you're proud of
- A completed checklist in the Reminders app

Visual progress can be just as rewarding as written notes, giving you a concrete way to see how much you've advanced.

### REFLECT ON YOUR COMFORT LEVEL OVER TIME

One of the biggest signs of progress isn't just *what* you can do, but *how* you feel about it. Think about moments that used to make you nervous—maybe using Apple Pay at a store or setting up a new device. Over time, these things start to feel natural.

Checking in with yourself regularly and asking, *Do I feel more comfortable with my iPhone than I did last month?* can be a great way to measure growth.

## Rewarding Yourself for Progress

Celebrating milestones doesn't mean you need to throw a party every time you master a new feature (unless you *want* to—go for it!). But rewarding yourself in small ways can make learning feel enjoyable rather than like a chore.

A few simple ways to celebrate your achievements:

- **Share what you've learned** – Teaching someone else is a great way to rein-force knowledge. Show a friend or family member a new trick you picked up.
- **Treat yourself** – Finished a big learning goal? Reward yourself with a coffee break, a fun app download, or even a relaxing evening off from learning.
- **Create a "tech success" folder** – Save screenshots or notes of your favorite discoveries to look back on.
- **Join a discussion group** – Engaging with others who are also learning can boost confidence and make the journey more fun.

Small rewards reinforce positive learning habits, making it easier to stay engaged.

## What to Do When Progress Feels Slow

No learning journey is completely smooth. There might be days when a setting won't cooperate, Face ID refuses to recognize you in the morning, or an update changes things just as you were getting comfortable. That's normal!

If progress feels slow:

- **Take a break** – Stepping away for a bit can help reset frustration levels.
- **Revisit what you** *have* **learned** – Reminding yourself of past successes can be motivating.
- **Ask for help** – Whether through a friend, an online group, or Apple Support, there's always someone willing to help.
- **Reframe mistakes as learning opportunities** – Every misstep teaches you something new.

Patience is key. The more you practice, the more second nature things will become.

Recognizing your progress isn't just about celebrating the end result—it's about appreciating the small steps along the way. By tracking achievements, setting goals, and rewarding yourself, you can make learning your iPhone an enjoyable and empowering experience.

# CHAPTER 15

# Looking Ahead: Staying Updated and Excited

## Preparing for iOS Updates and Understanding New Features

Keeping your iPhone up to date ensures you have access to the latest features, security improvements, and performance enhancements. But let's be honest—updates can sometimes feel like a double-edged sword. On one hand, they bring exciting new tools and optimizations, but on the other, they might introduce changes that disrupt familiar routines. The good news? By understanding how iOS updates work and preparing for them, you can embrace each update with confidence rather than hesitation.

### Why iOS Updates Matter

Apple consistently releases iOS updates to improve the iPhone experience. These updates do more than just add new features; they also:

- **Enhance security** – Each update patches vulnerabilities to protect your data.
- **Improve performance** – Older devices often benefit from optimizations that make them run smoother.
- **Introduce new features** – Updates bring exciting additions like redesigned apps, enhanced privacy controls, or new ways to interact with your device.
- **Ensure compatibility** – Apps and services evolve alongside iOS, so staying updated helps prevent compatibility issues.

If you've ever wondered whether an update is *really* necessary, consider this: skipping updates for too long can eventually lead to apps not working correctly or missing out on essential security fixes.

### How to Prepare for an iOS Update

Before diving into an update, it's helpful to take a few precautionary steps to ensure the process goes smoothly.

## CHECK COMPATIBILITY

Apple typically supports iPhones for several years, but some older models may not be eligible for the latest iOS version. To check if your device is compatible:

1. Open **Settings** and go to **General**.
2. Tap **About** and find your iPhone model.
3. Cross-check it with Apple's official iOS update compatibility list (available on Apple's website).

If your iPhone is nearing the end of its support cycle, it's worth considering whether future updates might affect performance. Older devices sometimes experience slower speeds with major updates, though Apple optimizes newer iOS versions to minimize this impact.

## BACK UP YOUR IPHONE

While iOS updates are designed to install smoothly, it's always a good idea to back up your data in case anything goes wrong. There are two primary ways to do this:

1. **iCloud Backup** – Automatically saves your photos, settings, and app data to the cloud.
2. **Computer Backup** – Uses Finder (on macOS) or iTunes (on Windows) for a full backup.

Backing up ensures that if anything unexpected happens during the update, you can restore your iPhone without losing valuable information.

## FREE UP STORAGE SPACE

Major iOS updates can require a significant amount of storage space to install. If you receive a notification that your iPhone doesn't have enough storage:

- Delete unused apps.
- Transfer large videos or photos to iCloud or an external drive.
- Clear Safari's cache and old downloads.

This quick cleanup not only helps with updates but also improves your iPhone's overall performance.

## Understanding the Update Process

When Apple releases a new iOS version, you'll typically receive a notification prompting you to install it. You can also check manually by going to Settings > General > Software Update.

1. **Over-the-Air (OTA) Update** – The easiest method, done directly from your iPhone. Simply tap **Download and Install** and follow the prompts.
2. **Using a Computer** – If you're experiencing issues updating, connecting your iPhone to a computer via Finder (Mac) or iTunes (Windows) can sometimes be more reliable.

Most users opt for the OTA method because it's straightforward and doesn't require additional steps.

## What to Expect After Updating

Once the update is installed, your iPhone will restart, and you might notice subtle changes immediately—perhaps a new lock screen design, an updated Messages app, or improvements in battery performance.

### Navigating Changes Smoothly

If an update introduces changes to settings or app layouts, don't panic! Adjusting to new features can take time, but Apple usually provides helpful tooltips or guides after major updates.

- Take a few minutes to explore the updated features.
- If something feels unfamiliar, Apple's Support website and user communities can provide quick answers.
- Keep an eye on battery life—after major updates, the system often runs background processes that temporarily drain more power.

## Exciting Features in iOS Updates

Each iOS release brings a mix of usability improvements and exciting new features. While specific changes depend on the version, here are a few examples of what Apple has introduced in past updates:

- **Widgets and Home Screen Customization** – Allows users to personalize their iPhones like never before.
- **Live Text** – Lets you copy and interact with text directly from images.
- **Focus Modes** – Helps filter notifications based on what you're doing.
- **Privacy Enhancements** – Adds more control over data sharing with apps.
- **Siri Improvements** – Expands Siri's offline capabilities and responsiveness.

Before each major update, Apple hosts an event showcasing upcoming features, which can be a great way to get excited about what's next.

## Should You Update Right Away?

While Apple thoroughly tests iOS updates, some users prefer to wait a few days before installing a major release. This allows time for early adopters to report any unexpected bugs or performance issues.

If you rely on your iPhone for work or daily tasks and can't afford interruptions, consider waiting a week before updating. Apple typically releases small follow-up updates (like iOS 18.0.1) to address initial bugs.

For security updates, however, installing them promptly is crucial since they protect against vulnerabilities.

## Making Updates a Habit

Updating your iPhone doesn't have to be a stressful experience. By staying informed and preparing in advance, you can ensure each update feels like an upgrade rather than an inconvenience.

- Set a reminder to check for updates every few months.
- Stay informed about Apple's announcements regarding upcoming features.
- Approach updates with curiosity—new features are designed to enhance your iPhone experience!

Staying up to date means your iPhone will continue to serve you well, keeping you connected, secure, and ready to enjoy the latest innovations Apple has to offer.

# Exploring Apple's Ecosystem: Devices and Services You May Love

Apple's ecosystem is more than just a collection of devices—it's an interconnected experience designed to make your life easier, more efficient, and even more enjoyable. Whether you're using an iPhone, an iPad, or a Mac, Apple's ecosystem ensures that everything works together seamlessly. But what does this mean for you, and how can you take full advantage of it? Let's explore the world of Apple devices and services that you may love, especially if you're looking to enhance your digital experience without unnecessary complexity.

## What is the Apple Ecosystem?

If you've ever experienced the frustration of transferring files between different brands of devices, you'll appreciate why Apple's ecosystem is so popular. Everything is designed to communicate effortlessly, removing barriers that often make technology feel intimidating.

Apple's ecosystem includes:

- **Devices**: iPhone, iPad, Mac, Apple Watch, Apple TV, and HomePod.
- **Software & Services**: iCloud, Apple Music, Apple Pay, Apple Fitness+, and more.
- **Continuity Features**: Handoff, Universal Clipboard, AirDrop, and Sidecar for seamless device interactions.

For someone who may have only used an iPhone in the past, discovering how these devices and services work together can be eye-opening.

## Seamless Connection Between Apple Devices

One of the greatest advantages of Apple's ecosystem is the seamless transition between devices. You can start a task on one device and finish it on another without interruption.

### HANDOFF: START ON ONE DEVICE, CONTINUE ON ANOTHER

Imagine you start writing an email on your iPhone but realize it would be easier to finish on a larger screen. With Handoff, you can pick up exactly where you left off on your iPad or Mac. This works across apps like Mail, Safari, Notes, and Messages.

For example:

- If you're browsing a recipe on Safari on your iPhone, you can open your Mac and continue reading without needing to search for it again.
- If you start a message on your iPad but realize you need to attach a file from your Mac, just switch over and keep typing where you left off.

### UNIVERSAL CLIPBOARD: COPY AND PASTE BETWEEN DEVICES

Copying and pasting between Apple devices is as simple as it gets. If you copy text, an image, or even a file on one device, you can paste it on another without any extra steps.

For example:

- Copy a quote from an article on your iPhone and paste it directly into a document on your Mac.
- Take a screenshot on your iPad and paste it into a text message on your iPhone.

### AIRDROP: THE EASIEST WAY TO SHARE FILES

Gone are the days of emailing yourself photos just to transfer them between devices. AirDrop allows you to send files, photos, and even website links instantly between Apple devices.

For example:

- If your friend has an iPhone and you want to share a picture, just use AirDrop to send it instantly.
- Need to transfer a PDF from your iPhone to your Mac? No cables, no wait-ing—just AirDrop it.

## Apple Services That Enhance Your Experience

Beyond devices, Apple offers a suite of services designed to make life easier and more enjoyable.

### iCloud: Your Digital Storage Solution

iCloud is the backbone of Apple's ecosystem, allowing you to access your data from anywhere. It automatically syncs:

- Photos and videos across all your devices.
- Notes, reminders, and contacts so they're always up to date.
- Documents stored in iCloud Drive, accessible from your iPhone, iPad, or Mac.

If you ever lose your iPhone, Find My iPhone (part of iCloud) helps you locate it or remotely wipe it for security.

### Apple Music: A Personalized Listening Experience

If you enjoy music, Apple Music offers millions of songs, playlists, and curated recommendations. The beauty of it? Your music library syncs across all your Apple devices.

For example:

- Start playing a song on your iPhone and switch to your Mac without missing a beat.
- Download songs for offline listening when traveling with just your iPhone.

### Apple Pay: A Safer Way to Pay

Carrying a wallet everywhere isn't necessary when you have Apple Pay. It allows you to make secure payments with your iPhone, Apple Watch, or even your Mac.

- Pay for groceries with a tap of your iPhone.
- Use Apple Pay for online purchases without typing in your card details.
- Send money to friends using Apple Cash within Messages.

Security is built in, ensuring that your transactions remain private.

## Wearable and Home Devices That Complement Your iPhone

Apple's ecosystem extends beyond phones and computers—there are devices designed to enhance your health, entertainment, and daily convenience.

### Apple Watch: The Perfect iPhone Companion

If you're considering a smartwatch, Apple Watch is the best fit for iPhone users. It allows you to:

- Receive notifications and reply to messages without picking up your phone.
- Track your steps, heart rate, and even detect falls in emergencies.
- Pay with Apple Pay right from your wrist.

It's especially useful for anyone who wants hands-free convenience, whether at home or on the go.

### Apple TV: Elevating Home Entertainment

Apple TV provides a seamless way to stream content, and it integrates with your other Apple devices.

- Use **AirPlay** to cast videos from your iPhone to your TV.
- Enjoy Apple Fitness+ workouts on a larger screen with live tracking from your Apple Watch.
- Access Apple TV+ original shows and movies.

### HomePod: Smart Audio for Your Home

Apple's HomePod isn't just a speaker—it's a voice assistant that connects with your Apple devices.

- Ask Siri to play music, set reminders, or control smart home accessories.
- Use **Intercom** to send messages between HomePods in different rooms.
- Sync HomePod with Apple Music for a high-quality audio experience.

## Making the Most of the Apple Ecosystem

If you already own an iPhone, integrating more Apple products can provide convenience that non-Apple alternatives struggle to match.

- Want seamless messaging? **iMessage syncs across all devices.**
- Need a secure way to store documents? **iCloud keeps everything backed up.**
- Looking for a stress-free way to pay? **Apple Pay handles purchases with ease.**

For those who may feel hesitant about adding more Apple products to their setup, remember that each device is designed to simplify your digital life. Rather than creating complexity, they remove friction—so you can focus more on what matters and less on troubleshooting tech issues.

With Apple's ecosystem, your devices aren't just standalone tools; they work together to create an effortless experience that feels intuitive and natural. If you've ever felt frustrated by technology that doesn't "just work," this ecosystem might be exactly what you've been looking for.

## Using Technology to Stay Connected with Future Generations

Technology has transformed the way families stay in touch, and for many, it has become a bridge between generations. Whether it's a grandparent video calling a grandchild, a family group chat filled with daily updates, or shared photo albums preserving special moments, technology helps maintain relationships despite physical distance. If you're looking for ways to stay engaged with younger generations—whether it's your children, grandchildren, or even great-grandchildren—there are countless tools available to make communication fun, meaningful, and effortless.

### Why Staying Connected Matters

For many older adults, staying connected with family is a top priority, but traditional means of communication, like phone calls or letters, may not be enough to keep up with fast-paced, digital-native younger generations. Today, children and teenagers are growing up in a world where FaceTime, social media, and instant messaging are their primary forms of interaction. Adapting to this new landscape doesn't mean abandoning traditional values—it means embracing new ways to engage with loved ones.

Some benefits of staying connected through technology include:

- **Strengthening Relationships**: Regular interactions through digital tools help maintain a close bond, even if family members live far apart.
- **Reducing Loneliness**: Studies show that social interaction—whether in person or virtual—can improve mental well-being and reduce feelings of isolation.
- **Being Part of Important Moments**: Whether it's a child's first steps, a graduation, or a simple everyday conversation, technology allows you to share in life's special moments.
- **Bridging the Generational Gap**: Learning to use the same platforms as younger generations makes it easier to communicate in ways they find familiar and engaging.

### Easy-to-Use Tools for Staying in Touch

#### FaceTime: Video Calls That Feel Like Real Conversations

FaceTime is one of the easiest ways to have face-to-face conversations with family members, no matter where they are. If you're not already using FaceTime, it's a simple way to stay in touch with grandkids, especially younger ones who may not yet be comfortable with texting.

With FaceTime, you can:

- Call anyone with an Apple device using their phone number or Apple ID.
- Add multiple people to a call for a **virtual family reunion**.
- Use fun **effects like Memoji and filters** to make calls more entertaining for younger kids.
- Turn on **Live Captions** to read along with what's being said if you have hearing difficulties.

A fun way to use FaceTime with younger generations is reading bedtime stories to grandkids or playing games like "I Spy" over video.

## MESSAGING APPS: MORE THAN JUST TEXT

Texting might feel impersonal, but Apple's iMessage offers many ways to make conversations more engaging. Unlike traditional SMS, iMessage allows you to:

- Send photos, voice messages, and stickers to add personality to your conversations.
- Share your location so family members know you're safe when traveling.
- Use **Tapback reactions** (thumbs-up, heart, etc.) to respond quickly to messages without typing.

If you have family members who use Android, apps like WhatsApp or Facebook Messenger are also great for text-based communication and video calls.

## SHARED PHOTO ALBUMS: A WINDOW INTO DAILY LIFE

Apple's Shared Albums in the Photos app is a wonderful way to exchange pictures and videos with family members. Instead of waiting for someone to send you pictures from a recent vacation or a child's first day of school, you can have access to a constantly updated family album.

How to use Shared Albums effectively:

- Family members can **add, comment, and like** photos, creating a digital scrapbook.
- Photos are **stored in iCloud**, so they don't take up space on your phone.
- It's a private and **safe way to share photos**, unlike social media.

For those who enjoy reminiscing, scrolling through a shared album can be a great way to feel close to family even when they're far away.

## Fun Ways to Engage with Younger Generations

Once you've mastered the basics of communication, there are plenty of creative ways to use technology to deepen connections with younger family members.

## PLAYING GAMES TOGETHER

Many children and teenagers love gaming, and Apple makes it easy to join in the fun. With Game Center, you can challenge family members to games like:

- **Words With Friends** – A Scrabble-style game that's great for bonding.
- **Chess.com** – A classic game that can be played across generations.
- **Heads Up!** – A fun guessing game that's perfect for video calls.

Even if you're not an experienced gamer, participating in a game with grandkids can be a fun way to connect while also challenging your mind.

## WATCHING MOVIES AND SHOWS TOGETHER

Apple's SharePlay feature lets you watch movies or listen to music with family members during a FaceTime call. If your grandchild is away at college, you can still watch a TV show together in real time, reacting and commenting as if you were in the same room.

Some great ways to use SharePlay:

- Watch a Disney movie with a young grandchild and discuss their favorite scenes.
- Listen to music together and talk about favorite songs from different generations.
- Follow a cooking tutorial at the same time and **make the same recipe** from different locations.

## VOICE ASSISTANTS: ANOTHER WAY TO INTERACT

Apple's Siri can be a great tool to interact with kids in a playful way. Try asking Siri questions together like:

- "Siri, tell us a joke."
- "Siri, what's the weather like where [grandchild's name] is?"
- "Siri, sing a song."

For younger children, this can feel like a game, while also helping you become more comfortable with voice assistants.

## Overcoming Common Concerns About Technology

It's understandable to have some hesitations about embracing new technology, but many of these concerns can be addressed with simple solutions:

- **Worried about privacy?** Use **Screen Time and Family Sharing** to set limits on shared content and communication preferences.
- **Not sure how to use certain features?** Apple offers **free workshops and support** at their stores and online.

- **Feel like you'll never catch up with younger generations?** The key is not to become an expert overnight but to **adopt one new tool at a time**.

## Embracing Technology as a Tool for Connection

Technology isn't just about convenience—it's about staying involved in the lives of your loved ones. Whether it's sending a quick text, sharing a laugh over FaceTime, or playing a game together, these small moments add up to stronger relationships.

By integrating even a few of these tools into your routine, you're not only making life easier for yourself but also creating meaningful, lasting connections with younger generations.

# Setting Goals for Continuous Learning and Exploration

Technology is constantly evolving, and staying up to date with new features, apps, and digital tools can feel overwhelming at times. But instead of looking at it as a challenge, consider it an opportunity—an exciting journey of discovery that keeps your mind active, enhances your daily life, and strengthens your connection with loved ones. Learning about technology isn't about mastering every single feature; it's about gradually becoming more comfortable, confident, and curious. Setting personal goals for continuous learning can help you stay engaged, explore new possibilities, and enjoy your iPhone to the fullest.

## Why Continuous Learning Matters

Learning doesn't stop at a certain age or stage in life. In fact, studies have shown that staying mentally active through continuous learning can improve cognitive function and overall well-being. Technology, in particular, offers an excellent avenue for growth—it allows you to stay connected, entertained, and informed, all while keeping your brain engaged.

Setting learning goals with your iPhone has several benefits:

- **Increased Confidence**: The more familiar you become with your device, the less intimidating it will feel.
- **More Meaningful Connections**: Learning to use new apps or communication tools can enhance relationships with friends and family.
- **Better Efficiency**: Knowing how to use features like Siri, Notes, or Calendar effectively can help organize your daily life.
- **Greater Independence**: Being comfortable with technology means relying less on others for help.
- **Personal Enjoyment**: Discovering new ways to use your iPhone—whether it's for photography, journaling, or entertainment—can add joy to your routine.

## Creating a Personal Learning Plan

One of the best ways to ensure steady progress is to create a simple and achievable learning plan. The key is to focus on small, specific goals rather than trying to absorb everything at once.

### STEP 1: IDENTIFY AREAS OF INTEREST

What do you want to get better at? Maybe you want to learn how to take professional-looking photos, or perhaps you're interested in using Apple's Health app to track wellness goals. Identifying areas that excite you will make the learning process more enjoyable.

Here are a few ideas:

- **Improving Texting Skills**: Learning to use voice dictation, emojis, or GIFs to make conversations more engaging.
- **Exploring Photography**: Mastering the different camera modes, editing photos, and organizing albums.
- **Learning to Use Apps Efficiently**: Discovering time-saving features in Notes, Reminders, or Apple Maps.
- **Voice Control & Accessibility**: Using Siri and accessibility features to make navigation easier.
- **Apple Pay & Digital Wallets**: Getting comfortable with making secure payments and storing important cards.

### STEP 2: SET SMALL, ACHIEVABLE GOALS

Instead of overwhelming yourself with everything at once, break it down into manageable weekly or monthly goals. For example, if you want to improve your texting skills, a goal for the week might be:

*"Send at least one text message per day using voice dictation."*

Or if you're learning how to use the camera, a goal could be:

*"Take five photos using Portrait Mode and experiment with different lighting conditions."*

By setting small, realistic goals, you create a sense of accomplishment, which encourages you to keep going.

## Exploring Learning Resources

There are countless ways to learn new things about your iPhone—some are built right into the device, while others involve engaging with external resources.

## APPLE'S BUILT-IN LEARNING TOOLS

Apple provides helpful tools to guide you as you explore new features:

- **Apple Support App**: Offers step-by-step tutorials on different features.
- **Settings App Tips**: Apple periodically suggests useful features within your settings.
- **Safari Search**: Typing a question about your iPhone into Safari often leads to Apple's official support pages.

## ONLINE COMMUNITIES & CLASSES

If you prefer a more interactive learning experience, consider:

- **Apple's Free Classes at Apple Stores**: Apple regularly offers in-person and virtual workshops on various iPhone topics.
- **YouTube Tutorials**: Many tech experts provide free, easy-to-follow video guides.
- **Online Forums**: Websites like Apple Support Community or Reddit have discussions where users share tips and solutions.

## Tracking Your Progress

Just like any other learning journey, keeping track of what you've learned can be motivating. Consider using an app like Notes or Reminders to log new skills or features you've mastered.

Some fun ways to track progress:

- **Create a "Tech Journal"** in the Notes app, where you jot down what you've learned each week.
- **Set a weekly reminder** to review new skills and explore a new feature.
- **Take screenshots of your progress**, such as your first successfully edited photo or your first FaceTime call with a grandchild.

Over time, you'll be surprised by how much more confident you've become with your iPhone.

## Learning at Your Own Pace

It's important to remember that technology is meant to serve you—not the other way around. There's no rush to learn everything overnight. Some days, you might feel excited to explore a new app; other days, you might simply want to stick with what you already know. Both are perfectly okay.

By setting small learning goals, staying curious, and using the tools available to you, you'll not only expand your tech skills but also open doors to new experiences, conversations, and connections. The joy of learning never stops—especially when it enhances your everyday life.

# Final Thoughts: Unlocking Joy and Connection Every Day

Technology is more than just a tool—it's a bridge that connects us to the people we love, the knowledge we seek, and the moments that bring us joy. As you've explored different aspects of your iPhone, you've likely realized that learning how to use technology isn't about mastering every single feature—it's about using what matters most to you in a way that enhances your life. Whether it's making video calls to loved ones, capturing special memories, or simply making daily tasks easier, your iPhone is there to serve you, not the other way around.

## Embracing the Joy of Learning

One of the most rewarding aspects of using an iPhone—or any piece of technology—is the continuous journey of discovery. Unlike the days when you had to rely on printed manuals or lengthy tech support calls, you now have access to a wealth of knowledge at your fingertips.

Think about how far you've come:

- You've learned to navigate your iPhone with confidence, customizing it to fit your needs.
- You've discovered how to stay connected with family and friends, whether through FaceTime, messages, or shared albums.
- You've explored how to capture, organize, and preserve your memories in ways that were once impossible.
- You've set goals, tackled challenges, and built new habits that make technology feel less intimidating and more enjoyable.

Each small step you've taken has contributed to a larger sense of confidence and independence. The key takeaway? You're capable of learning, adapting, and growing—at your own pace, in your own way.

## Technology as a Tool for Connection

At its core, technology is about connection—not just to devices, but to the world around you. It allows you to:

- **Stay in touch with loved ones** through calls, messages, and shared content.
- **Preserve and share family stories**, passing down knowledge and memories to future generations.
- **Engage in lifelong learning**, from exploring new hobbies to staying informed on current events.
- **Enhance your everyday life** with tools that simplify tasks, improve accessibility, and bring entertainment and joy.

When used intentionally, your iPhone becomes an extension of your relationships, your creativity, and your personal growth. It's not about using every feature—it's about using the right features in a way that feels meaningful to you.

## Overcoming Challenges with a Positive Mindset

If there's one thing to keep in mind as you continue using your iPhone, it's this: frustration is a normal part of learning, but it doesn't have to stop you from moving forward.

There may be moments when:

- An update changes the way something works, and it feels unfamiliar.
- You try a new feature but struggle to remember how to use it.
- You make a mistake and worry about "breaking" something.

These are all completely normal experiences, even for the most tech-savvy users. The best way to handle these moments is with patience and curiosity. Instead of feeling discouraged, remind yourself that every challenge is an opportunity to learn something new.

A helpful strategy? Practice asking for help without hesitation—whether it's from a family member, an online tutorial, or a tech support community. You're never alone in your learning journey, and there are always resources available to guide you.

## Making Technology Work for You

As you continue using your iPhone in your daily life, ask yourself: What brings me the most joy? What makes my life easier? What do I want to explore next?

Perhaps you want to:

- Start using **Apple's Health app** to track fitness or mindfulness habits.
- Explore **creative apps like digital sketching or music-making tools**.
- Improve your use of **voice commands to make navigation even easier**.
- Learn how to **integrate smart home features** for convenience.

Whatever excites you, let that be your guide. Technology is most rewarding when it's aligned with your interests and needs, rather than feeling like an obligation.

## Looking Ahead with Confidence

As new updates, features, and apps emerge, it's natural to feel a mix of excitement and hesitation. But remember—you've already proven that you can adapt, learn, and grow. You don't have to rush to keep up with every change; instead, you can choose what's relevant to you and embrace the learning process on your own terms.

Your iPhone is a tool for empowerment. It enables you to connect, create, and discover in ways that weren't possible before. And as you continue to explore its possibilities, you'll find that the real magic isn't just in the technology itself—it's in the ways it helps you experience and share the moments that matter most.

# Get Your Exclusive iPhone 16 Bonus Pack – Free!

Congratulations on taking the first step toward mastering your iPhone 16! But why stop here when you can **unlock even more power, convenience, and confidence**—all for FREE?

We've put together the **ultimate bonus package** to help you get the most out of your iPhone 16, whether you're a total beginner or looking to sharpen your skills.

## Here's What You Get – Absolutely Free!

### 52 Video Tutorials on iPhone 16 Shortcuts to Automate Your Life

Turn your iPhone 16 into your **personal assistant**. Learn **shortcut secrets** that eliminate repetitive tasks and **save you hours** every week—effortlessly.

### 20+ Hours of iPhone 16, 16 Plus, Pro & Pro Max Fast-Track Mastery

Why spend months figuring it out on your own? This **comprehensive training** takes you from basic user to **power user**, unlocking **hidden features and pro tricks** that will **transform** how you use your iPhone.

### The Family Connection Planner

Stay **closer than ever** to your loved ones with this simple guide to **scheduling FaceTimes, sharing photos, and making tech bring your family together**.

### The Ultimate iPhone Camera Guide

Want to **take photos like a pro**—without buying an expensive camera? Discover **insider tips** to capture **stunning** photos and videos with ease.

### Photo Album Wizard

Cherish your memories forever with **step-by-step instructions** for creating **beautiful digital albums** that you and your family will love.

### The Simplified Siri Handbook

Master **powerful voice commands** that will turn Siri into your **most helpful assistant**—so you can get things done faster than ever before.

### Quick Fix Toolkit

Become your **own tech support**! Solve **common iPhone issues in minutes** with this easy-to-follow troubleshooting guide.

### Hidden Gems Cheat Sheet

Your iPhone 16 has **secret features** that most users never discover. With this cheat sheet, you'll unlock **exciting tricks and time-saving shortcuts** that will amaze you.

### Grandparent's Tech Guide

Stay **connected with your grandkids** like never before! Learn fun and practical ways to **play games, send creative messages, and make technology bring your family closer together**.

## Claim Your Free Bonuses Now!

Getting your **exclusive bonus package** is easy. Simply **scan the QR-CODE below** and download everything in seconds!

This is our way of saying **THANK YOU** for choosing this guide. **Don't miss out—get your free bonuses today!**

Printed in Dunstable, United Kingdom

66169120R00147